LITERARY AND PHILOSOPHICAL ESSAYS

JEAN-PAUL SARTRE

Literary and Philosophical Essays

TRANSLATED FROM THE FRENCH BY ANNETTE MICHELSON

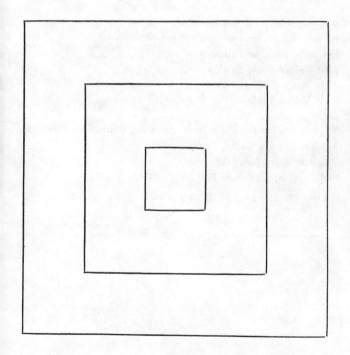

COLLIER BOOKS *New York, N.Y.*

10377

Contents

* Note: Camus' *The Outsider* was published in the U.S. under the
title of *The Stranger*.

Chapter 1

Francois Mauriac and Freedom

THE NOVEL DOES NOT present things, but rather their signs.[1] How, with these mere signs, these words that are *indications* in a vacuum, are we to build a world that holds together? How does Stavrogin come alive? It would be an error to think that he draws his life from my imagination. When we muse over words, they beget images, but when I read, I am not musing; I am deciphering. I do not imagine Stavrogin; I wait for him; I wait expectantly for his acts, for the end of his adventure.

The thick substance I brew as I read *The Possessed* is my own expectancy, my own time. For a book is either a mere stack of dry leaves or else a great form in motion, in other words, the act of reading. The novelist takes hold of this movement, guides and inflects it, makes of it the stuff of his characters. A novel is a series of readings, of little parasitic lives, none of them longer than a dance. It swells and feeds on the reader's time. But in order for the duration of my impatience and ignorance to be caught and then moulded and finally presented to me as the flesh of these creatures of invention, the novelist must know how to draw it into the trap, how to hollow out in his book, by means of the signs at his disposal, a time resembling my own, one in which the future does not exist. If I suspect that the hero's future actions are determined in advance by heredity, social influence or some other mechanism, my own time ebbs back into me; there remains only myself, reading and persisting, confronted by a static book. Do you want your characters to live? See to it that they are free.

---

[1] The observations in the present essay might also have been based on M. Mauriac's more recent works, such as *Maimona* or *Plongées*. But his particular purpose in writing *La Fin de la Nuit* was to treat the problem of freedom. That is why I prefer to draw my examples from this book.

It is not a matter of defining passions and unpredictable acts, still less of explaining them (in novels, even the best psychological analyses have a mouldy smell), but rather of *presenting* them. Neither you nor I know what Rogogine is going to do. I know that he is going to see his guilty mistress again, but I cannot tell whether he will control himself or whether his anger will drive him to murder; he is free. I slip into his skin, and there he is, awaiting himself with my waiting. He is afraid of himself, *inside me; he is alive.

It occurred to me, as I was about to begin *La Fin de la Nuit,* that Christian writers, by the very nature of their belief, have the kind of mentality best suited to the writing of novels. The religious man is free. The supreme forbearance of the Catholic may irritate us, because it is an acquired thing. If he is a novelist, it is a great advantage. The fictional and the Christian man, who are both centres of indeterminacy, do have characters, but only in order to escape from them. They are free, above and beyond their natures, and if they succumb to their natures, here again, they do so freely. They may get caught up in psychological machinery, but they themselves are never mechanical.

Even the Christian conception of sin corresponds to one of the principles of the writing of fiction. The Christian sins, and the hero of the novel must err. If the existence of the error—which cannot be effaced and which must be redeemed —does not reveal to the reader the irreversibility of time, the substantial duration of the work of art lacks the urgency that gives it its necessity and cruelty. Thus, Dostoevsky was a Christian novelist. Not a novelist and a Christian, as Pasteur was a Christian *and* a scientist, but a novelist in the service of Christ.

M. Mauriac is also a Christian novelist, and his book, *La Fin de la Nuit,* tries to penetrate to the inmost depths of a woman's freedom. He tells us in his preface that he is trying to depict "the power accorded to creatures who have all the odds against them, the power to say *no* to the law that beats them down." Here we touch the heart of the art of fiction and the heart of faith. Nevertheless, I must admit that the book has disappointed me. Not for a moment was I taken in, never did I forget *my* time; I went on existing, I felt myself living. Occasionally I yawned. Now and then I said to myself, "Well done." I thought more often of M. Mauriac than of Thérèse Desqueyroux—of M. Mauriac, subtle, sensitive and narrow, with his immodest discretion, his intermittent good will, his nervous pathos, his bitter and fumbling poetry, his pinched style, his sudden vulgarity. Why was I unable to forget him or myself? And what had become of this Christian predisposition for the novel? We must go back to the question of freedom. What are the processes by which M. Mauriac reveals to us the freedom he has conferred upon his heroine?

Thérèse Desqueyroux struggles against her destiny. Well and good. There are thus two elements in her make-up. One part of her is entirely an element of Nature; we can say this of her as we would of a stone or log. But another whole side of her defies description or definition. because it is simply an absence. If freedom accepts Nature, the reign of fatality begins. If it rejects and resists it, Thérèse Desqueyroux is free, free to say no, or free, at least, not to say yes. ("All that is asked of them is that they not resign themselves to darkness.") This is Cartesian freedom, infinite, formless, nameless and without destiny, "forever starting anew," whose only power is that of sanction, but which is sovereign because it can refuse sanction. There it is—at least as we see it in the preface. Do we find it in the novel?

The first thing to be said is that this suspensive will seems more tragic than novelistic. Thérèse's oscillations between the impulses of her nature and the action of her will are reminiscent of Rotrou's stanzas. The real conflict in a novel is rather between freedom and itself. In Dostoevsky, freedom is poisoned at its very source. It gets tangled up in the very time it wants to untangle. Dmitri Karamazov's pride and irascibility are as free as Aliosha's profound peace. The nature that stifles him and against which he struggles is not God-made but self-made; it is what he has sworn to be and what remains fixed because of the irreversibility of time. Alain says, in this connection, that a character is an oath. While reading M. Mauriac—and this may be to his credit—we dream of another Thérèse who might have been abler and greater. But

it is the venerable antiquity and orthodoxy of this conflict between freedom and nature which finally commend it to us.
It is the struggle of reason against the passions; the rebellion
of the Christian soul, linked by the imagination to the body,
against the body's appetites. Let us accept this theme pro-
visionally, even though it may not seem true; it is enough that
it be beautiful.

But is this "fatality" against which Thérèse must struggle
merely the determinism of her inclinations? M. Mauriac calls
it destiny. Let us not confuse destiny and character. Character is still ourselves; it is the combination of mild forces
which insinuate themselves into our intentions and imperceptibly deflect our efforts, always in the same direction.

When Thérèse gets furious with Mondoux, who has humiliated her, M. Mauriac writes, "This time it was really she
speaking, the Thérèse who was ready to tear things apart."
Here it is really a question of Thérèse's character. But a little
later, as she is leaving, after managing to make a wounding
reply,[2] I read, "This sure-handed blow helped her to gauge
her power, to become aware of her mission." What mission?
Then I remember the following words from the preface: "the
power given her to poison and corrupt." And there we have
the destiny which envelops and prevails over the character
and which represents, within Nature itself and in M. Mauriac's
work, basely psychological as it sometimes is, the power of
the Supernatural.

It is a fixed law, independent of Thérèse's will, that governs
her acts as soon as they escape from her, and that leads them
all, even the best-intentioned of them, to unhappy consequences. It reminds one of the fairy's punishment: "Every
time you open your mouth, frogs will jump out." If you do
not believe, this spell will have no meaning for you. But the
believer understands it very well. What is it, after all, but
the expression of that other spell, Original Sin? I therefore
grant that M. Mauriac is in earnest when he speaks of destiny
as a Christian. But when he speaks as a novelist, I can no

[2] I know of few scenes more vulgar than this one, and the curious
thing is that this vulgarity must evidently be attributed to
M. Mauriac himself.

longer follow him. Thérèse Desqueyroux's destiny is composed, on the one hand, of a flaw in her character and, on the other, of a curse that hangs over her acts. But these two factors are incompatible. One of them is visible from the inside, to the heroine herself; the other would require an infinite number of observations made from the outside by an observer intent on following Thérèse's acts to their ultimate consequences.

M. Mauriac is so keenly aware of this that, when he wishes to show Thérèse as a predestined character, he resorts to an artifice; he shows her to us as she appears *to others.* "It was not surprising that people turned to look back as she passed; an evil-smelling animal betrays itself at once." Here, then, is the great hybrid presence we are made to see throughout the novel: Thérèse—though not limited to her pure freedom—Thérèse as she escapes from herself, to lose herself in a world of baleful fog. But how, then, can Thérèse know she has a destiny, if not because she already consents to it? And how does M. Mauriac know it? The idea of destiny is poetic and contemplative. But the novel is an action, and the novelist does not have the right to abandon the battlefield and settle himself comfortably on a hill as a spectator musing on The Fortunes of War.

But we must not think that M. Mauriac has accidentally surrendered for once to poetic temptation. This way of first identifying himself with his character and then abandoning her suddenly to consider her from the outside, like a judge, is characteristic of his art. He has, from the first, given us to understand that he was going to adopt Thérèse's point of view to tell the story, but, as a matter of fact, we immediately feel the translucent density of another consciousness between our eyes and Thérèse's room, her servant and the noises that rise from the street. But when, a few pages further on, we think we are still inside her, we have already left her; we are outside, with M. Mauriac, and we are looking at her.

The reason is that M. Mauriac makes use, for purposes of illusion, of the ambiguity of the "third person." In a novel, the pronoun "she" can designate *another,* that is, an opaque object, someone whose exterior is all we ever see—as when

I write, for example, "I saw *that she* was trembling." But it also happens that this pronoun leads us into an intimacy which ought logically to express itself in the third person. "She was astounded to hear the echo of her own words." There is really no way of my knowing this unless I am in a position to say that I have heard the echo of my own words. In actual fact, novelists use this quite conventional mode of expression out of a kind of discretion, so as not to demand of the reader an unreserved complicity, so as to screen the dizzying intimacy of the *I*. The heroine's mind represents the opera-glass through which the reader can look into the fictional world, and the word "she" gives the illusion of the perspective of the opera-glass. It reminds us that this revealing consciousness is also a fictional creation; it represents a viewpoint on the privileged point of view and fulfills for the reader the fond desire of the lover to be both himself and someone else.

The same word has thus two opposing functions: "she-subject" and "she-object." M. Mauriac takes advantage of this indefiniteness in order to shift us imperceptibly from one aspect of Thérèse to another. "Thérèse was ashamed of her feelings." Very well. This Thérèse is a subject, that is, a *me*, kept at a certain distance from myself, and I experience this shame *inside Thérèse* because Thérèse herself knows that she feels it. But, in that case, since I read into her with her eyes, all I can ever know of her is what she knows—everything she knows, but nothing more.

In order to understand who Thérèse really *is*, I would have to break this complicity and close the book. All that would remain with me would be a memory of this consciousness, a consciousness still clear, but now hermetically closed, like all things of the past, and I would try to interpret it as though it were a fragment of my own earlier life. Now, at this point, while I am still in this absolute proximity with his characters, their dupe when they dupe themselves, their accomplice when they lie to themselves, M. Mauriac, suddenly and unbeknown to them, sends streaks of lightning through them, illuminating for me alone the essence of their beings, of which they are unaware and on which their characters have been struck as

on a medal. "Never had the slightest relationship been established in Thérèse's mind between her unknown adventure and
a criminal affair . . . *at least, in her conscious* mind," etc. . . .
I find myself in a strange situation; I *am* Thérèse, and, at a
certain aesthetic distance, she is myself. Her thoughts are my
thoughts; as hers take shape, so do mine.

And yet I have insights into her which she does not have.
Or else, seated in the centre of her consciousness, I help her
lie to herself, and, at the same time, I judge and condemn
her, I put myself inside her, as *another person*. "She could
not help but be aware of her lie; she settled down into it,
made her peace with it." This sentence gives a fair idea of
the constant duplicity M. Mauriac requires of me. Thérèse
lies to herself, reveals her lies and, nevertheless, tries to hide
them from herself. This behaviour is something I have no
way of knowing except through Thérèse herself. But the very
way in which this attitude is revealed to me involves a pitiless
judgment from without.

Besides, this uneasiness does not last long. Suddenly, by
means of that "third person" whose ambiguity I have noted,
M. Mauriac slips out, taking me along with him. " 'Make-up
does wonders for you, my dear . . .' This was Thérèse's first
remark, the remark of one woman to another." The flame of
Thérèse's consciousness has gone out; this face, no longer
lighted from within, has reassumed its compact opacity. But
neither the name nor the pronoun which designates her, nor
even the character of the narrative, has changed.

M. Mauriac finds this see-sawing so natural that he moves
from Thérèse-subject to Thérèse-object within a single sentence. "She heard the clock strike nine. She had some time to
kill, because it was still too early to take the pill which
would assure her of a few hours' sleep; *not that such was the
habit of this cautious and desperate woman,* but tonight she
could not do without this aid." Who is judging Thérèse to be
a "cautious and desperate woman"? It cannot be Thérèse herself. No, it is M. Mauriac, it is myself; we have the Desqueyroux record before us and we are pronouncing judgment.

But M. Mauriac plays other tricks as well. Like Asmodeus,
that nosey and mischievous devil so dear to his heart, he likes

to pry off the corners of roofs. When it suits his purpose, he leaves Thérèse and suddenly installs himself inside another character, whether it be Georges or Marie or Bernard Desqueyroux, or Anne the servant. He takes a look about and then trundles off, like a marionette. "Thérèse was unable to understand the meaning of that troubled look on the girl's face and *did not know* that the other was thinking, 'In all my life, I'll never live through half of what that old woman has been through in a few days.' " Didn't she know? It doesn't matter. M. Mauriac suddenly abandons her, leaves her to her ignorance, drops in on Marie and brings back a little snapshot for us.

On the other hand, at times he generously permits one of his creatures to share in the novelist's divine lucidity. "She stretched out her arms to draw him to her, but he drew violently away, and she *realized* that she had lost him." The indications are uncertain, and besides, they involve only the present. But what does it matter? M. Mauriac has decided that Georges is lost to Thérèse. He has decided, just as the ancient Gods decreed Oedipus' parricide and incest. Then, in order to inform us of his decree, he lends his creature, for a few moments, some of Tiresias' power of divination; have no fear; she will soon relapse into darkness. Besides, here is the curfew. The minds of all the characters go out. Tired, M. Mauriac suddenly withdraws from all of them. There remains only the façade of a world, a few puppets in a cardboard set:

The child spread the fingers that covered her eyes.

"I thought you were sleeping."

The voice begged her again, "Swear to me that you're happy."

There are gestures and sounds in the shadows. M. Mauriac is seated nearby, thinking, " 'How you must have suffered, Mummy!' 'Oh no, I didn't feel a thing . . .' What? Could it be that the rattling in her throat and her purple face had not been signs of suffering? Can a person go through a hell of pain and then forget about it completely?"

It is obvious to anyone familiar with Marie's character that the girl wastes no time in such reflections. No, what we have here is rather M. Mauriac resting from his labours on the seventh day and thrilled with his creation.

And now here is the real reason for his failure. He once wrote that the novelist is to his own creatures what God is to His. And that explains all the oddities of his technique. He takes God's standpoint on his characters. God sees the inside and outside, the depths of body and soul, the whole universe at once. In like manner, M. Mauriac is omniscient about everything relating to his little world. What he says about his characters is Gospel. He explains them, categorizes them and condemns them without appeal. If anyone were to ask him how he knows that Thérèse is a cautious and desperate woman he would probably reply, with great surprise, "Didn't I create her?"

No, he didn't! The time has come to say that the novelist is not God. We would do well to recall the caution with which Conrad suggests to us that Lord Jim may be "romantic." He takes great care not to state this himself; he puts the word into the mouth of one of his characters, a fallible being, who utters it hesitantly. The word "romantic," clear as it is, thereby acquires depth and pathos and a certain indefinable mystery. Not so with M. Mauriac. "A cautious and desperate woman" is no hypothesis; it is an illumination which comes to us from above. The author, impatient to have us grasp the character of his heroine, suddenly gives us the key. But what I maintain is precisely the fact that he has no right to make these absolute judgments. A novel is an action related from various points of view. And M. Mauriac is well aware of this, having written, in *La Fin de la Nuit,* that ". . . the most conflicting judgments about a single person can be correct; it is a question of lighting, and no one light reveals more than another." But each of these interpretations must be in motion, drawn along, so to speak, by the very action it interprets.

It is, in short, the testimony of a participant and should reveal the man who testifies as well as the event to which he testifies. It should arouse our impatience (will it be confirmed or denied by events?), and thus give us a feeling of the dragging of time. Thus, each point of view is relative, and the best one will be that which makes the reader feel most acutely the dragging of time. The participants' interpretations and explanations will all be hypothetical. The reader may have an inkling, beyond these conjectures, of the event's absolute reality, but it is for him alone to re-establish it. Should he care to try this sort of exercise, he will never get beyond the realm of likelihood and probability.

In any case, the introduction of absolute truth or of God's standpoint constitutes a twofold error of technique. To begin with, it presupposes a purely contemplative narrator, withdrawn from the action. This inevitably conflicts with Valéry's law of aesthetics, according to which any given element of a work of art ought always to maintain a plurality of relationships with the other elements. And besides, the absolute is non-temporal. If you pitch the narrative in the absolute, the string of duration snaps, and the novel disappears before your eyes. All that remains is a dull truth, *sub specie aeternitatis*.

But there is something even more serious. The definitive judgments with which M. Mauriac is always ready to intersperse the narrative prove that he does not conceive his characters as he ought. He fabricates their natures before setting them down, he decrees that they *will be* this or that. The essence of Thérèse, the evil-smelling animal, the desperate and cautious woman, is, I admit, complex, and not to be expressed in a single sentence. But what exactly is this essence? Her inmost depths? Let us look at it more closely. Conrad saw clearly that the word "romantic" had meaning when it expressed an aspect of character *for other people*. Such words as "desperate and cautious" and "evil-smelling animal" and "castaway" and other such neat phrases are of the same sort as the word that Conrad puts into the mouth of the merchant of the islands. When Thérèse resumes her story,

> For years she had been unaware that the pattern of her destiny had been a series of attempts to get out of a rut, each ending in failure. But now that she had emerged from the darkness, she saw clearly . . .

she is able to judge her past so easily only because she cannot return to it. Thus, when he thinks he is probing the hearts of his characters, M. Mauriac remains outside, at the door.

This would be quite all right if M. Mauriac were aware of it and wrote novels like Hemingway's, in which we hardly know the heroes except through their gestures and words, and the vague judgments they pass on each other. But when M. Mauriac, making full use of his creative authority, forces us to accept these exterior views as the inner stuff of his creatures, he is transforming his characters into *things*. Only things can simply *be*; they have only exteriors. Minds cannot simply be; they become. Thus, in shaping his Thérèse *sub specie aeternitatis*, M. Mauriac first makes of her a thing, after which he adds, on the sly, a whole mental thickness. But in vain. Fictional beings have their laws, the most rigorous of which is the following: the novelist may be either their witness or their accomplice, but never both at the same time. The novelist must be either inside or out. Because M. Mauriac does not observe these laws, he does away with his characters' minds.

We are now back at freedom, Thérèse's other dimension. What becomes of her in this darkened world? Until now, Thérèse has been a *thing*, an ordered succession of motives and patterns, of passions, habits and interests, a *story* one could sum up in a few maxims—a *fatality*. This witch, this possessed creature, is now presented to us as free. M. Mauriac takes pains to tell us what we are to understand by this freedom.

But yesterday, in particular, when I decided to give up my fortune, I felt deep delight. I floated a thousand cubits *above my real self*. I climb, climb, climb . . . and then suddenly I slide back and find myself in that evil, cold, wilfulness, which is what I am when I make no effort, *which is what I fall back on when I fall back on myself*.[3]

Thus, freedom is not Thérèse's "real self" any more than consciousness is. This self, "what I fall back on when I fall

[3] The italics are mine.

back on myself," is a piece of data, a *thing*. Consciousness and freedom come later, consciousness as power to have illusions about oneself, and freedom as power to escape from oneself.

We must understand that for M. Mauriac, freedom cannot *construct*. A man, using his freedom, cannot create himself or forge his own history. Free will is merely a discontinuous force which allows for brief escapes, but which produces nothing, except a few short-lived events. Thus, *La Fin de la Nuit,* which, according to M. Mauriac, is the novel of someone's freedom, appears to be, above all, the story of an enslavement. So much so that the author, who, at first, wanted to show us "the stages of a spiritual ascension," confesses in his preface that Thérèse has led him, in spite of himself, into hell. "The finished work," he observes, not without regret, "disappoints in part the hopes contained in the title." But how could it have been otherwise?

Freedom, by the very fact of its having been thus tacked on to Thérèse's dense and fixed nature, loses its omnipotence and indeterminacy. Freedom itself is defined and characterized, since we know *in opposition to what* it is freedom. M. Mauriac goes even further and imposes a law upon it. "I climb, climb, climb . . . and then suddenly I slide back . . ." Thus, it is decreed in advance that Thérèse will sink back again each time. We are even informed in the preface that it would be indiscreet to ask more of her. "She belongs to that race of beings who emerge from darkness only when they depart from life. All that is asked of them is that they not resign themselves to darkness." It is Thérèse herself who speaks of the "pattern of her destiny." Freedom is a phase of this pattern. Even in her freedom, Thérèse is predictable. M. Mauriac has measured out with the precision of a doctor's prescription or of a cooking recipe the little freedom he allows her. I expect nothing from her: I know everything. Her ups and downs affect me little more than those of a cockroach climbing a wall with stupid obstinacy.

The reason is that no allowance has been made for freedom. Because Thérèse's freedom has been doled out with a dropper, it no more resembles real freedom than her mind resembles a real mind. And when M. Mauriac, absorbed in describing Thérèse's psychological mechanisms, wants us to feel that she is no longer a mechanism, he suddenly finds that he lacks the necessary devices. Of course he shows us Thérèse struggling against her evil inclinations. "Thérèse tightened her jaw. 'I won't talk about Garcin to him,' she said to herself." But what proof have I that a closer analysis would not reveal the deterministic links and reasons behind this sudden revolt? M. Mauriac feels this so acutely that occasionally, in desperation, he tugs at our sleeve and whispers, "Look! This time it's the real thing! She's free!" As in the following passage: "She interrupted herself in the middle of a sentence (for she was being entirely honest)." I know of no clumsier device than this parenthetical admonition, but the author is obviously obliged to use it.

On the basis of this hybrid creature of M. Mauriac's begetting which he calls Thérèse's nature, *there is no way of distinguishing between a free action and a passion.* But perhaps there is: through a sort of evanescent grace that plays over the features or the soul of a character fresh from a victory over himself:

> The expression on her face was as beautiful as he had ever seen it.
> She did not feel herself suffering, she felt relieved, delivered of some nameless burden, as if she were no longer going round in circles, as if she were suddenly going forward.

But these moral recompenses are not enough to convince us. On the contrary, they show us that, for M. Mauriac, freedom differs from slavery in *value,* and not in nature. Any intention directed upwards, toward Good, is free, and any will to Evil is fettered. It is needless for us to discuss the intrinsic worth of this distinguishing principle. In any case, it stifles freedom in fiction and, with it, the immediate duration which is the substance of the novel.

How *could* Thérèse's story have duration? It involves the old theological conflict between divine omniscience and human freedom. Thérèse's "pattern of destiny," the graph of her ups and downs, resembles a fever curve; it is dead time, since the future is spread out like the past and simply repeats it. The reader of a novel does not want to be God. In order for my duration to be transfused into the veins of Thérèse and Marie Desqueyroux, I must, at least once, be unaware of their fate and impatient to know it. But M. Mauriac does not bother to play upon my impatience. His sole aim is to make me as knowing as himself. He showers me with information. No sooner do I feel my curiosity begin to stir than it is satisfied beyond measure. Dostoevsky would have surrounded Thérèse with dense and mysterious figures whose meaning would have been at the brink of surrender on every page, only to elude my grasp. But M. Mauriac places me straight away in the very depths of his characters' hearts. No one has any secrets; he spreads an even light over everyone.

Thus, even if I were ever curious about the development of events, I could not identify my own impatience with that of Thérèse, since we are not waiting for the same things and what she would like to know, I have known for a long time. To me, she is like one of those abstract partners in the explanation of a bridge game who are kept in hypothetical ignorance of the opposing hands and who plan in terms of that very ignorance, whereas I can see all the cards already and know the errors in their hopes and calculations.

It is plain to see, moreover, that M. Mauriac has no liking for time, no fondness for the Bergsonian necessity of waiting "for the sugar to melt." To him, his creature's time is a dream, an all-too-human illusion; he gets rid of it and resolutely sets himself up within the eternal. But this alone, to my way of thinking, should have deterred him from writing novels. The real novelist is stirred by things that offer resistance; he is excited by doors because they must be opened, by envelopes because they must be unsealed.

In Hemingway's admirable *A Farewell to Arms*, objects are time-traps; they fill the narrative with innumerable tiny, obstinate resistances which the hero must break down one after the other. But M. Mauriac detests these lowly barriers that deter him from his purpose; he speaks of them as little as possible. He even wants to economize on the time of his characters' conversations; he suddenly speaks up for them and summarizes, in a few words, what they are going to say.

"Love," said Thérèse, "isn't everything in life—especially for men . . ." She went off on this theme. She could have talked till dawn; the sensible remarks she was making out of duty and with an effort were not the kind . . . etc.

There is, perhaps, no graver error in all the book than this stinginess. By cutting short the dialogue of his characters just when they begin to interest me, M. Mauriac projects me suddenly (and how can he fail to see this?) out of their time and out of their story. For these dialogues do not stop; I know they go on somewhere, but my right to sit in on them has been withdrawn. He would probably regard these sudden stops and sudden beginnings as "foreshortenings." I, for my part, prefer to regard them as breakdowns. Of course a novelist has to "foreshorten" now and then, but that does not in the least mean that he suddenly drains off the duration. In a novel, you must tell all or keep quiet; above all, you must not omit or skip anything. A foreshortening is simply a change of speed in the narration. M. Mauriac is in a hurry; he has probably sworn that no work of his will ever exceed the dimensions of a long short story.

I look in vain through *La Fin de la Nuit* for the long, stammering conversations, so frequent in English novels, in which the heroes are forever going over their stories, without managing to make them advance. I look in vain for the respites that suspend the action only to increase its urgency, the "between-times" in which, beneath a dark and cloudy sky, the characters busily absorb themselves in their familiar occupations. M. Mauriac treats only the essential passages, which he then joins together with brief summaries.

It is because of this taste for concision that his creatures talk as though they were in the theatre. M. Mauriac is interested only in getting them to say what they have to say as quickly and clearly as possible. Rejecting the superfluity, repetition and fumbling of actual speech, he gives to his heroes' remarks their naked power of significance. And since we must, nevertheless, be able to sense a difference between what he himself writes and what he makes them say, he imparts to these overclear speeches a sort of torrential speed which is that of the theatre. Listen, for example, to Thérèse:

"What? How dare you? Do you mean to say I didn't commit the act? But I did. Though it is nothing compared to my other more cowardly, more secret crimes—crimes that involved no risk."

This passage should be spoken aloud rather than read. Notice the oratorical movement of the beginning, and the question which swells with repetition. Doesn't it recall Hermione's jealous rages in *Andromaque*? I catch myself whispering the words aloud, struck by that rhetorical beginning typical of all good tragic dialogue. Now read this:

"However rash your friend may be, he cannot be so rash as to think you attractive. Had I meant to make him jealous, I should have taken more care to make the matter seem credible."

Doesn't the reader recognize the turn of phrase dear to the comic writers of the eighteenth century? The novel is not at all suited to graces of this kind, not because people ought to talk in the novel as they do in life, but because the novel has its own kind of stylization. The transition to dialogue ought to be marked by a kind of flickering of the lights. It is dark, the hero struggles to express himself; his words are not pictures of his soul, but rather free and clumsy acts, which say too much and too little. The reader gets impatient; he tries to see beyond these involved and fumbling statements. Dostoevsky, Conrad and Faulkner have known how to use this resistance of words, which is a source of endless misunderstandings and involuntary revelations, and thereby to make of dialogue "the fictional moment," the time when the sense of duration is richest. M. Mauriac's classicism is probably repelled by such woolly conversation. But everyone knows that French classicism is rhetorical and theatrical.

Nor is this all. M. Mauriac also insists that each of these conversations be effective and, consequently, he complies with another theatrical law—for it is only in the theatre that the dialogue must keep the action going forward. He therefore builds up "scenes." The entire novel is made up of four scenes each of which ends in a "catastrophe." Each scene is prepared exactly as in a tragedy.

Take, for example, the following: At Saint-Clair, Marie receives a letter from Georges, her fiancé, who backs out of his engagement. Convinced, through a misunderstanding, that her mother is responsible for the break, she leaves immediately for Paris. We know all about this turbulent, selfish, passionate, rather silly girl, who is also capable of good impulses. She is shown during this journey as being mad with rage, her claws bared, determined to fight, to wound, to pay back with interest the blows she has received. Thérèse's state is described with no less precision. We know that she has been consumed by suffering, that she is half out of her mind. Is it not obvious that the meeting of these two women is brought about as in a play? We know the forces present. The situation is rigorously defined; it is a confrontation. Marie does not know that her mother is mad. What will she do when she realizes it? The problem is clearly formulated.

We have only to leave everything to determinism, with its movements and counter-movements, its dramatic and anticipated reversals. It will lead us inevitably to the final catastrophe, with Marie playing the nurse and prevailing upon her mother to come back to the Desqueyroux home. Doesn't this recall Sardou or the great scene in Bernstein's *The Spy,* or the second act of *The Thief?* I quite understand M. Mauriac's being tempted by the theatre. While reading *La Fin de la Nuit,* I felt, time and again, as if I were reading the argument and chief passages of a four-act play.

Let us look at the passage in *Beauchamp's Career* where

Meredith shows us the last meeting of Beauchamp and Renée. They are still in love and are within an ace of confessing their feelings, but they part. When they meet, *anything* is possible between them. The future does not yet exist. Gradually their little weaknesses and mistakes and resentments begin to get the better of their good will. They cease to see straight. Nevertheless, up to the very end, even when I begin to fear that they may break up, I still feel that *it may all still work out*. The reason is that they are free. Their final separation will be of their own making. *Beauchamp's Career* is a novel!

La Fin de la Nuit is not a novel. How can anyone call this angular, glacial book, with its analyses, theatrical passages and poetic meditations, a "novel"? How can anyone confuse these bursts of speed and violent jamming of the brakes, these abrupt starts and breakdowns, with the majestic flow of fictional time? How can anyone be taken in by this motionless narrative, which betrays its intellectual framework from the very start, in which the mute faces of the heroes are inscribed like angles in a circle? If it is true that a novel is a *thing*, like a painting or architectural structure, if it is true that a novel is made with time and free minds, as a picture is painted with oil and pigments, then *La Fin de la Nuit* is not a novel. It is, at most, a collection of signs and intentions. M. Mauriac is not a novelist.

Why? Why hasn't this serious and earnest writer achieved his purpose? Because, I think, of the sin of pride. Like most of our writers, he has tried to ignore the fact that the theory of relativity applies in full to the universe of fiction, that there is no more place for a privileged observer in a real novel than in the world of Einstein, and that it is no more possible to conduct an experiment in a fictional system[4] in order to determine whether the system is in motion or at rest than it is in a physical system. M. Mauriac has put himself first. He has chosen divine omniscience and omnipotence.

[4] By fictional system, I mean the novel as a whole, as well as the partial systems that make it up (the minds of the characters, their combined psychological and moral judgments).

But novels are written *by* men and *for* men. In the eyes of God, Who cuts through appearances and goes beyond them, there is no novel, no art, for art thrives on appearances. God is not an artist. Neither is M. Mauriac.

(*February* 1939)

Chapter 2

Camus' *The Outsider*

M. CAMUS' *The Outsider* was barely off the press when it began to arouse the widest interest. People told each other that it was 'the best book since the end of the war." Amidst the literary productions of its time, this novel was, itself, an outsider. It came to us from the other side of the Equator, from across the sea. In that bitter spring of the coal shortage, it spoke to us of the sun, not as of an exotic marvel, but with the weary familiarity of those who have had too much of it. It was not concerned with re-burying the old regime with its own hands, nor with filling us with a sense of our own unworthiness.

We remembered, while reading this novel, that there had once been works which had not tried to prove anything, but had been content to stand on their own merits. But hand in hand with its gratuitousness went a certain ambiguity. How were we to interpret this character who, the day after his mother's death, "went swimming, started a liaison with a girl and went to see a comic film," who killed an Arab "because of the sun," who claimed, on the eve of his execution, that he "had been happy and still was," and hoped there would be a lot of spectators at the scaffold "to welcome him with cries of hate." "He's a poor fool, an idiot," some people said; others, with greater insight, said, "He's innocent." The meaning of this innocence still remained to be understood.

In *The Myth of Sisyphus,* which appeared a few months later, M. Camus provided us with a precise commentary upon his work. His hero was neither good nor bad, neither moral nor immoral. These categories do not apply to him. He belongs to a very particular species for which the author reserves the word "absurd." But in M. Camus' work this word takes on two very different meanings. The absurd is both a state of fact and the lucid awareness which certain people acquire of this state of fact. The "absurd" man is the man who does not hesitate to draw the inevitable conclusions from a fundamental absurdity.

There is the same displacement of meaning as when we give the name "swing" to the youthful generation that dances to "swing" music. What is meant by the absurd as a state of fact, as primary situation? It means nothing less than man's relation to the world. Primary absurdity manifests a cleavage, the cleavage between man's aspirations to unity and the insurmountable dualism of mind and nature, between man's drive toward the eternal and the *finite* character of his existence, between the "concern" which constitutes his very essence and the vanity of his efforts. Chance, death, the irreducible pluralism of life and of truth, the unintelligibility of the real— all these are extremes of the absurd.

These are not really very new themes, and M. Camus does not present them as such. They had been sounded as early as the seventeenth century by a certain kind of dry, plain, contemplative rationalism, which is typically French and they served as the commonplaces of classical pessimism.

Was it not Pascal who emphasized "the natural misfortune of our mortal and feeble condition, so wretched that when we consider it closely, nothing can console us"? Was it not he who put reason in its place? Would he not have wholeheartedly approved the following remark of M. Camus: "The world is neither (completely) rational, nor quite irrational either"? Does he not show us that "custom" and "diversion" conceal man's "nothingness, his forlornness, his inadequacy, his impotence and his emptiness" from himself? By virtue of the cool style of *The Myth of Sisyphus* and the subject of his essays, M. Camus takes his place in the great tradition of those French moralists whom Andler has rightly termed the precursors of Nietzsche.

As to the doubts raised by M. Camus about the scope of our reasoning powers, these are in the most recent tradition of French epistemology. If we think of scientific nominalism, of Poincaré, Duhem and Meyerson, we are better able to understand the reproach our author addresses to modern science. "You tell me of an invisible planetary system in which electrons revolve about a nucleus. You explain the world to me by means of an image. I then realize that you have ended in poetry . . ." [1] This idea was likewise expressed, and at just about the same time, by another writer, who draws on the same material when he says, "Physics uses mechanical, dynamic and even psychological models without any preference, as if, freed of ontological aspirations, it were becoming indifferent to the classical antinomies of the mechanism or dynamism which presupposes a nature-in-itself." [2] M. Camus shows off a bit by quoting passages from Jaspers, Heidegger and Kierkegaard, whom, by the way, he does not always seem to have quite understood. But his real masters are to be found elsewhere.

The turn of his reasoning, the clarity of his ideas, the cut of his expository style and a certain kind of solar, ceremonious and sad sombreness, all indicate a classic temperament, a man of the Mediterranean. His very method ("only through a balance of evidence and lyricism shall we attain a combination of emotion and lucidity.") [3] recalls the old "passionate geometries" of Pascal and Rousseau and relate him, for example, not to a German phenomenologist or a Danish existentialist, but rather to Maurras, that other Mediterranean from whom, however, he differs in many respects.

But M. Camus would probably be willing to grant all this. To him, originality means pursuing one's ideas to the limit; it certainly does not mean making a collection of pessimistic maxims. The absurd, to be sure, resides neither in man nor in the world, if you consider each separately. But since man's dominant characteristic is "being-in-the-world," the absurd is, in the end, an inseparable part of the human condition. Thus, the absurd is not, to begin with, *the object of a mere idea; it is revealed to us in a doleful illumination.* "Getting up, tram, four hours of work, meal, sleep, and Monday, Tuesday, Wednesday, Thursday, Friday, Saturday, in the same routine . . .", [4] and then, suddenly, "the setting col-

[1] *The Myth of Sisyphus.*
[2] M. Merleau Ponty, *La Structure du Comportement.*
[3] *The Myth of Sisyphus.*
[4] *Ibid.*

lapses," and we find ourselves in a state of hopeless lucidity.

If we are able to refuse the misleading aid of religion or of existential philosophies, we then possess certain basic, obvious facts: the world is chaos, a "divine equivalence born of anarchy"; tomorrow does not exist, since we all die. "In a universe suddenly deprived of light and illusions, man feels himself an outsider. This exile is irrevocable, since he has no memories of a lost homeland and no hope of a promised land." [5] The reason is that man *is not* the world. "If I were a tree among other trees . . . this life would have a meaning, or rather this problem would have none, for I would be part of this world. I *would be* this world against which I set myself with my entire mind . . . It is preposterous reason which sets me against all creation." [6] This explains, in part, the title of our novel; the outsider is man confronting the world. M. Camus might as well have chosen the title of one of George Gissing's works, *Born in Exile*. The outsider is also man among men. "There are days when . . . you find that the person you've loved has become a stranger." [7] The stranger is, finally, myself in relation to myself, that is, natural man in relation to mind: "The stranger who, at certain moments, confronts us in a mirror." [8]

But that is not all; there is a *passion* of the absurd. The absurd man will not commit suicide; he wants to live, without relinquishing any of his certainty, without a future, without hope, without illusion and without resignation either. He stares at death with passionate attention and this fascination liberates him. He experiences the "divine irresponsibility" of the condemned man.

Since God does not exist and man dies, everything is permissible. One experience is as good as another; the important thing is simply to acquire as many as possible. "The ideal of the absurd man is the present and the succession of present moments before an ever-conscious spirit." [9] Confronted with

[5] *The Myth of Sisyphus.*
[6] *Ibid.*
[7] *Ibid.*
[8] *Ibid.*
[9] *Ibid.*

this "quantitative ethic" all values collapse; thrown into this world, the absurd man, rebellious and irresponsible, has "nothing to justify." He is *innocent,* innocent as Somerset Maugham's savages before the arrival of the clergyman who teaches them Good and Evil, what is lawful and what is forbidden. For this man, *everything* is lawful. He is as innocent as Prince Mishkin, who "lives in an everlasting present, lightly tinged with smiles and indifference." Innocent in every sense of the word, he too is, if you like, an "Idiot."

And now we fully understand the title of Camus' novel. The outsider he wants to portray is precisely one of those terrible innocents who shock society by not accepting the rules of its game. He lives among outsiders, but to them, too, he is an outsider. That is why some people like him—for example, his mistress, Marie, who is fond of him "because he's odd." Others, like the courtroom crowd whose hatred he suddenly feels mounting towards him, hate him for the same reason. And we ourselves, who, on opening the book are not yet familiar with the feeling of the absurd, vainly try to judge him according to our usual standards. For us, too, he is an outsider.

Thus, the shock you felt when you opened the book and read, "I thought that here was another Sunday over with, that Mama was buried now, that I would go back to work again and that, on the whole, nothing had changed," was deliberate. It was the result of your first encounter with the absurd. But you probably hoped that as you progressed your uneasiness would fade, that everything would be slowly clarified, would be given a reasonable justification and explained. Your hopes were disappointed. *The Outsider* is not an explanatory book. The absurd man does not explain; he describes. Nor is it a book which proves anything.

M. Camus is simply presenting something and is not concerned with a justification of what is fundamentally unjustifiable. *The Myth of Sisyphus* teaches us how to accept our author's novel. In it, we find the theory of the novel of absurdity. Although the absurdity of the human condition is its sole theme, it is not a novel with a message; it does not come out of a "satisfied" kind of thinking, intent on furnishing formal proofs. It is rather the product of a thinking which is "limited, rebellious and mortal." It is a proof in itself of the futility of abstract reasoning. "The fact that certain great novelists have chosen to write in terms of images rather than of arguments reveals a great deal about a certain kind of thinking common to them all, a conviction of the futility of all explanatory principles, and of the instructive message of sensory impressions." [10]

Thus, the very fact that M. Camus delivers his message in the form of a novel reveals a proud humility. This is not resignation, but the rebellious recognition of the limitations of human thought. It is true that he felt obliged to make a philosophical translation of his fictional message. *The Myth of Sisyphus* is just that, and we shall see later on how we are to interpret this parallel commentary. But the existence of the translation does not, in any case, alter the gratuitousness of the novel.

The man who creates an absurdity has lost even the illusion of his work's necessity. He wants us, on the contrary, to be constantly aware of its contingent nature. He would like to see, inscribed below it, "might never have been," as Gide wanted "could be continued" written at the end of *The Coiners*. This novel might not have been, like some stone or stream or face. It is a thing in the present that happens, quite simply, like all other happenings in the present. It has not even the subjective necessity that artists pretend to when, speaking of their works, they say, "I had to write it, I had to get it off my chest." In it we find one of the themes of surrealist terrorism sifted through the classic sun. The work of art is only a leaf torn from a life. It does, of course, express this life. But it need not express it. And besides, everything has the same value, whether it be writing *The Possessed* or drinking a cup of coffee.

M. Camus does not require that attentive solicitude that writers who "have sacrificed their lives to art" demand of the reader. *The Outsider* is a leaf from his life. And since the most absurd life is that which is most sterile, his novel aims

[10] *The Myth of Sisyphus.*

at being magnificently sterile. Art is an act of unnecessary
generosity. We need not be over-disturbed by this; I find,
hidden beneath M. Camus' paradoxes, some of Kant's wise
observations on the "endless end" of the beautiful. Such, in
any case, is *The Outsider,* a work detached from a life, un-
justified and unjustifiable, sterile, momentary, already for-
saken by its author, abandoned for other present things.
And that is how we must accept it, as a brief communion
between two men, the author and the reader, beyond reason,
in the realm of the absurd.

This will give us some idea as to how we are to regard the
hero of *The Outsider.* If M. Camus had wanted to write a
novel with a purpose, he would have had no difficulty in
showing a civil servant lording it over his family, and then
suddenly struck with the intuition of the absurd, struggling
against it for a while and finally resolving to live out the
fundamental absurdity of his condition. The reader would
have been convinced along with the character, and for the
same reasons.

Or else, he might have related the life of one of those
saints of the Absurd, so dear to his heart, of whom he speaks
in *The Myth of Sisyphus:* Don Juan, the Actor, the Con-
queror, the Creator. But he has not done so, and Meursault,
the hero of *The Outsider,* remains ambiguous, even to the
reader who is familiar with theories of the absurd. We are,
of course, assured that he is absurd, and his dominant characteristic is a pitiless clarity. Besides, he is, in more ways
than one, constructed so as to furnish a concerted illustration
of the theories expounded in *The Myth of Sisyphus.* For
example, in the latter work, M. Camus writes, "A man's
virility lies more in what he keeps to himself than in what he
says." And Meursault is an example of this virile silence, of
this refusal to indulge in words: "[He was asked] if he had
noticed that I was withdrawn, and he admitted only that I
didn't waste words." [11] And two lines before this, the same
witness has just declared that Meursault "was a man." "[He
was asked] what he meant by that, and he said that everyone
knew what he meant."

[11] *The Outsider.*

In like manner M. Camus expatiates on love in *The Myth of Sisyphus.* "It is only on the basis of a collective way of seeing, for which books and legends are responsible, that we give the name *love* to what binds us to certain human beings." [12] And similarly, we read in *The Outsider:* "So she wanted to know whether I loved her. I answered . . . that it didn't mean anything, but that I probably didn't love her." [13] From this point of view, the debate in the courtroom and in the reader's mind as to whether or not Meursault loved his mother is doubly absurd.

First of all, as the lawyer asks, "Is he accused of having buried his mother or of having killed a man?" But above all, the words "to love" are meaningless. Meursault probably put his mother into an old people's home because he hadn't enough money and because "they had nothing more to say to one another." And he probably did not go to see her often, "because it wasted [his] Sunday—not to speak of the effort involved in getting to the bus, buying tickets and taking a two-hour trip." [14] But what does this mean? Isn't he living completely in the present, according to his present fancies? What we call a feeling is merely the abstract unity and the meaning of discontinuous impressions.

I am not constantly thinking about the people I love, but I claim to love them even when I am not thinking about them —and I am capable of compromising my well-being in the name of an abstract feeling, in the absence of any real and immediate emotion. Meursault thinks and acts in a different way; he has no desire to know these noble, continuous, completely identical feelings. For him, neither love nor individual loves exist. All that counts is the present and the concrete. He goes to see his mother when he feels like it, and that's that.

If the desire is there, it will be strong enough to make this sluggard run at full speed to jump into a moving truck. But he still calls his mother by the tender, childish name of "Mama," and he never misses a chance to understand her and identify himself with her. "All I know of love is that

[12] *The Myth of Sisyphus.*
[13] *The Outsider.*
[14] *The Outsider.*

mixture of desire, tenderness and intelligence that binds me to someone." [15] Thus we see that the *theoretical* side of Meursault's character is not to be overlooked. In the same way, many of his adventures are intended chiefly to bring out some aspect or other of the basic absurdity of things. *The Myth of Sisyphus,* for example, extols, as we have seen, the "perfect freedom of the condemned prisoner to whom, some particular daybreak, the prison doors swing open," [16] and it is in order to make us taste this daybreak and freedom that M. Camus has condemned his hero to capital punishment. "How could I have failed to see," says Meursault, "that nothing was more important than an execution . . . and that it was even, in a way, the only really interesting thing for a man!" One could multiply the examples and quotations.

Nevertheless, this lucid, indifferent, taciturn man is not entirely constructed to serve a cause. Once the character had been sketched in, he probably completed himself; he certainly had a real weight of his own. Still, his absurdity seems to have been given rather than achieved; that's how he is, and that's that. He does have his revelation on the last page, but he has always lived according to M. Camus' standards. If there were a grace of absurdity, we would have to say that he has grace. He does not seem to pose himself any of the questions explored in *The Myth of Sisyphus;* Meursault is not shown rebelling at his death sentence. He was happy, he has let himself live, and his happiness does not seem to have been marred by that hidden gnawing which M. Camus frequently mentions in his essay and which is due to the blinding presence of death. His very indifference often seems like indolence, as, for instance, that Sunday when he stays at home out of pure laziness, and when he admits to having been "slightly bored." The character thus retains a real opacity, even to the absurd-conscious observer. He is no Don Juan, no Don Quixote of the absurd; he often even seems like its Sancho Panza. He is there before us, he exists, and we can neither understand nor quite judge him. In a word, he is alive, and all that can justify him to us is his fictional density.

[15] *The Myth of Sisyphus.*
[16] *Ibid.*

The Outsider is not, however, to be regarded as a completely gratuitous work. M. Camus distinguishes, as we have mentioned, between the *notion* and the *feeling* of the absurd. He says, in this connection, "Deep feelings, like great works, are always more meaningful than they are aware of being. . . . An intense feeling carries with it its own universe, magnificent or wretched, as the case may be." [17] And he adds, a bit further on, "The feeling of the absurd is not the same as the *idea* of the absurd. The idea is grounded in the feeling, that is all. It does not exhaust it." *The Myth of Sisyphus* might be said to aim at giving us this *idea*, and *The Outsider* at giving us the feeling.

The order in which the two works appeared seems to confirm this hypothesis. *The Outsider,* the first to appear, plunges us without comment into the "climate" of the absurd; the essay then comes and illumines the landscape. Now, absurdity means divorce, discrepancy. *The Outsider* is to be a novel of discrepancy, divorce and disorientation; hence its skilful construction.

We have, on the one hand, the amorphous, everyday flow of reality as it is experienced, and, on the other, the edifying reconstruction of this reality by speech and human reason. The reader, brought face to face with simple reality, must find it again, without being able to recognize it in its rational transposition. This is the source of the feeling of the absurd, that is, of our inability to *think,* with our words and concepts, what happens in the world. Meursault buries his mother, takes a mistress and commits a crime.

These various facts will be related by witnesses at his trial, and they will be put in order and explained by the public prosecutor. Meursault will have the impression that they are talking of someone else. Everything is so arranged as to bring on the sudden outburst of Marie, who, after giving, in the witness-box, an account composed according to human rules, bursts into sobs and says "that that wasn't it, that there was something else, that they were forcing her to say the opposite of what she really thought." These mirror-tricks have been

[17] *The Myth of Sisyphus.*

used frequently since *The Coiners,* and they do not constitute
M. Camus' originality. But the problem to be solved imposes
an original form upon him.

In order to feel the divergence between the prosecutor's
conclusions and the actual circumstances of the murder, in
order, when we have finished the book, to retain the impression of an absurd justice, incapable of ever understanding or
even of making contact with the deeds it intends to punish,
we must first have been placed in contact with reality, or with
one of these circumstances. But in order to establish this
contact, M. Camus, like the prosecutor, has only words and
concepts at his disposal. In assembling thoughts, he is forced
to use words to describe a world that precedes words. The
first part of *The Outsider* could have been given the same
title as a recent book, *Translated from Silence.* Here we
touch upon a disease common to many contemporary writers
and whose first traces I find in Jules Renard. I shall call it
"the obsession with silence." M. Paulhan would certainly
regard it as an effect of literary terrorism.

It has assumed a thousand forms, ranging from the surrealists' automatic writing to Jean-Jacques Bernard's "theatre
of silence." The reason is that silence, as Heidegger says, is
the authentic mode of speech. Only the man who knows how
to talk can be silent. M. Camus talks a great deal; in *The
Myth of Sisyphus* he is even garrulous. And yet, he reveals
his love of silence. He quotes Kierkegaard: "The surest way
of being mute is not to hold your tongue, but to talk." [18] And
he himself adds that "a man is more of a man because of
what he does not say than what he does say." Thus, in *The
Outsider,* he has attempted *to be silent.* But how is one to be
silent with words? How is one to convey through concepts
the unthinkable and disorderly succession of present instants?
This problem involves resorting to a new technique.

What is this new technique? "It's Kafka written by
Hemingway," I was told. I confess that I have found no trace
of Kafka in it. M. Camus' views are entirely of this earth,
and Kafka is the novelist of impossible transcendence; for

[18] Quoted in *The Myth of Sisyphus.* Note also Brice Parain's
theory of language and his conception of silence.

him, the universe is full of signs that we cannot understand; there is a reverse side to the décor. For M. Camus, on the contrary, the tragedy of human existence lies in the absence of any transcendence. "I do not know whether this world has a meaning that is beyond me. But I do know that I am unaware of this meaning and that, for the time being, it is impossible for me to know it. What can a meaning beyond my condition mean to me? I can understand only in human terms. I understand the things I touch, things that offer me resistance."

He is not concerned, then, with so ordering words as to suggest an inhuman, undecipherable order; the inhuman is merely the disorderly, the mechanical. There is nothing ambiguous in his work, nothing disquieting, nothing hinted at. *The Outsider* gives us a succession of luminously clear views. If they bewilder us, it is only because of their number and the absence of any link between them. M. Camus likes bright mornings, clear evenings and relentless afternoons. His favourite season is Algiers' eternal summer. Night has hardly any place in his universe.

When he does talk of it, it is in the following terms: "I awakened with stars about my face. Country noises reached my ears. My temples were soothed by odours of night, earth and salt. The wonderful peace of that sleepy summer invaded me like a tide." [19] The man who wrote these lines is as far removed as possible from the anguish of a Kafka. He is very much at peace within disorder. Nature's obstinate blindness probably irritates him, but it comforts him as well. Its irrationality is only a negative thing. The absurd man is a humanist; he knows only the good things of this world.

The comparison with Hemingway seems more fruitful. The relationship between the two styles is obvious. Both men write in the same short sentences. Each sentence refuses to exploit the momentum accumulated by preceding ones. Each is a new beginning. Each is like a snapshot of a gesture or object. For each new gesture and word there is a new and corresponding sentence. Nevertheless, I am not quite satisfied. The

[19] *The Outsider.*

existence of an "American" narrative technique has certainly been of help to M. Camus. I doubt whether it has, strictly speaking, influenced him.

Even in *Death in the Afternoon,* which is not a novel, Hemingway retains that abrupt style of narration that shoots each separate sentence out of the void with a sort of respiratory spasm. His style is himself. We know that M. Camus has another style, a ceremonious one. But even in *The Outsider* he occasionally heightens the tone. His sentences then take on a larger, more continuous, movement. "The cry of the newsvendors in the relaxed air, the last birds in the square, the calls of the sandwich-vendors, the wail of the trams on the high curves of the city and the distant murmur in the sky before night began to teeter over the port, all set before me a blind man's route with which I was familiar long before entering prison." [20]

Through the transparency of Meursault's breathless account I catch a glimpse of a poetic prose underneath, which is probably M. Camus' personal mode of expression. If *The Outsider* exhibits such visible traces of the American technique, it was deliberate on M. Camus' part. He has chosen from among all the instruments at his disposal the one which seemed to serve his purpose best. I doubt whether he will use it again in future works.

Let us examine the plot a little more closely; we shall get a clearer notion of the author's methods. "Men also secrete the inhuman," writes M. Camus. "Sometimes, in moments of lucidity, the mechanical aspect of their gestures and their senseless pantomime make everything about them seem stupid." [21] This quality must be rendered at once. *The Outsider* must put us right from the start "into a state of uneasiness when confronted with man's inhumanity."

But what are the particular occasions that create this uneasiness in us? *The Myth of Sisyphus* gives us an example. "A man is talking on the telephone. We cannot hear him behind the glass partition, but we can see his senseless mim-

[20] *Ibid.*
[21] *The Myth of Sisyphus.*

icry. We wonder why he is alive?" [22] This answers the question almost too well, for the example reveals a certain bias in the author. The gesturing of a man who is telephoning and whom we cannot hear is really only *relatively* absurd, because it is part of an incomplete circuit. Listen in on an extension, however, and the circuit is completed; human activity recovers its meaning. Therefore, one would have, in all honesty, to admit that there are only relative absurdities and only in relation to "absolute rationalities."

However, we are not concerned with honesty, but with art. M. Camus has a method ready to hand. He is going to insert a glass partition between the reader and his characters. Is there really anything sillier than a man behind a glass window? Glass seems to let everything through. It stops only one thing: the meaning of his gestures. The glass remains to be chosen. It will be the Outsider's mind, which is really transparent, since we see everything it sees. However, it is so constructed as to be transparent to things and opaque to meanings.

"From then on, everything went very quickly. The men went up to the coffin with a sheet. The priest, his followers, the director and I, all went outside. In front of the door was a lady I didn't know. 'Monsieur Meursault,' said the director. I didn't hear the lady's name, and I gathered only that she was a nurse who'd been ordered to be present. Without smiling, she nodded her long, bony face. Then we stood aside to make room for the body to pass." [23]

Some men are dancing behind a glass partition. Between them and the reader has been interposed a consciousness, something very slight, a translucent curtain, a pure passivity that merely records all the facts. But it has done the trick. Just because it is passive, this consciousness records only facts. The reader has not noticed this presence. But what is the assumption implied by this kind of narrative technique? To put it briefly, what had once been melodic structure has been transformed into a sum of invariant elements. This

[22] *Ibid.*
[23] *The Outsider.*

succession of *movements* is supposed to be rigorously identical with the *act* considered as a complete entity. Are we not dealing here with the analytic assumption that any reality is reducible to a sum total of elements? Now, though analysis may be the instrument of science, it is also the instrument of humour. If in describing a rugby match, I write, "I saw adults in shorts fighting and throwing themselves on the ground in order to send a leather ball between a pair of wooden posts," I have summed up what I have *seen,* but I have intentionally missed its meaning. I am merely trying to be humorous. M. Camus' story is analytic and humorous. Like all artists, he *invents,* because he pretends to be reconstituting raw experience and because he slyly eliminates all the significant links which are also part of the experience.

That is what Hume did when he stated that he could find nothing in experience but isolated impressions. That is what the American neo-realists still do when they deny the existence of any but external relations between phenomena. Contemporary philosophy has, however, established the fact that meanings are also part of the immediate data. But this would carry us too far afield. We shall simply indicate that the universe of the absurd man is the analytic world of the neo-realists. In literature, this method has proved its worth. It was Voltaire's method in *L'Ingénu* and *Micromégas,* and Swift's in *Gulliver's Travels.* For the eighteenth century also had its own outsiders, "noble savages," usually, who, transported to a strange civilization, perceived facts before being able to grasp their meaning. The effect of this discrepancy was to arouse in the reader the feeling of the absurd. M. Camus seems to have this in mind on several occasions, particularly when he shows his hero reflecting on the reasons for his imprisonment.

It is this analytic process that explains the use of the American technique in *The Outsider.* The presence of death at the end of our path has made our future go up in smoke; our life has "no future," it is a series of present moments. What does this mean, if not that the absurd man is applying his analytical spirit to Time? Where Bergson saw an indestructible organization, he sees only a series of instants. It is the plurality of incommunicable moments that will finally account for the plurality of beings. What our author borrows from Hemingway is thus the discontinuity between the clipped phrases that imitate the discontinuity of time.

We are now in a better position to understand the form of his narrative. Each sentence is a present instant, but not an indecisive one that spreads like a stain to the following one. The sentence is sharp, distinct and self-contained. It is separated by a void from the following one, just as Descartes' instant is separated from the one that follows it. The world is destroyed and reborn from sentence to sentence. When the word makes it appearance it is a creation *ex nihilo*. The sentences in *The Outsider* are islands. We bounce from sentence to sentence, from void to void. It was in order to emphasize the isolation of each sentence unit that M. Camus chose to tell his story in the present perfect tense.[24] The simple past is the tense of continuity: *"Il se promena longtemps."* These words refer us to a past perfect, to a future. The reality of the sentence is the verb, the act, with its transitive character and its transcendence. *"Il s'est promené longtemps"* conceals the verbality of the verb. The verb is split and broken in two.

On the one hand, we find a past participle which has lost all transcendence and which is as inert as a thing; and on the other, we find only the verb "être," which has merely a copulative sense and which joins the participle to the substantive as the attribute to the subject. The transitive character of the verb has vanished; the sentence has frozen. Its present reality becomes the noun. Instead of acting as a bridge between past and future, it is merely a small, isolated, self-sufficient substance.

If, in addition, you are careful to reduce it as much as possible to the main proposition, its internal structure attains a perfect simplicity. It gains thereby in cohesiveness. It be-

[24] The following passage dealing with M. Camus' use of tenses is not intelligible in translation. The simple past tense in French is almost never used in conversation; it is limited almost exclusively to written narration; the usual French equivalent of the English past is the present perfect. (Translator's note.)

comes truly indivisible, an atom of time. The sentences are not, of course, arranged in relation to each other; they are simply juxtaposed. In particular, all causal links are avoided lest they introduce the germ of an explanation and an order other than that of pure succession. Consider the following passage: "She asked me, a moment later, if I loved her. *I answered that it didn't mean anything, but that I probably didn't love her. She seemed sad.* But while preparing lunch, for no reason at all she suddenly laughed in such a way that I kissed her. Just then, the noise of an argument broke out at Raymond's place." I have cited two sentences which most carefully conceal the causal link under the simple appearance of succession.

When it is absolutely necessary to allude to a preceding sentence, the author uses words like "and," "but," "then" and "just then," which evoke only disjunction, opposition or mere addition. The relations between these temporal units, like those established between objects by the neo-realists, are external. Reality appears on the scene without being introduced and then disappears without being destroyed. The world dissolves and is reborn with each pulsation of time. But we must not think it is self-generated. Any activity on its part would lead to a substitution by dangerous forces for the reassuring disorder of pure chance.

A nineteenth-century naturalist would have written "A bridge spanned the river." M. Camus will have none of this anthropomorphism. He says "Over the river was a bridge." This object thus immediately betrays its passiveness. It *is there* before us, plain and undifferentiated. "There were four negro men in the room . . . in front of the door was a lady I didn't know. . . . Beside her was the director. . . ." People used to say that Jules Renard would end by writing things like "The hen lays." M. Camus and many other contemporary writers would write "There is the hen and she lays." The reason is that they like things for their own sake and do not want to dilute them in the flux of duration. "There is water." Here we have a bit of eternity—passive, impenetrable, incommunicable and gleaming! What sensual delight, if only we could touch it! To the absurd man, this is the one and only good. And that is why the novelist prefers these short-lived little sparkles, each of which gives a bit of pleasure, to an organized narrative.

This is what enables M. Camus to think that in writing *The Outsider* he remains silent. His sentence does not belong to the universe of discourse. It has neither ramifications nor extensions nor internal structure. It might be defined, like Valéry's sylph, as

> Neither seen nor known:
> The time of a bare breast
> Between two shifts.

It is very exactly measured by the time of a silent intuition. If this is so, can we speak of M. Camus' novel as something whole? All the sentences of his book are equal to each other, just as all the absurd man's experiences are equal. Each one sets up for itself and sweeps the others into the void. But, as a result, no single one of them detaches itself from the background of the others, except for the rare moments in which the author, abandoning these principles, becomes poetic.

The very dialogues are integrated into the narrative. Dialogue is the moment of explanation, of meaning, and to give it a place of honour would be to admit that meanings exist. M. Camus irons out the dialogue, summarizes it, renders it frequently as indirect discourse. He denies it any typographic privileges, so that a spoken phrase seems like any other happening. It flashes for an instant and then disappears, like heat lightning. Thus, when you start reading the book you feel as if you were listening to a monotonous, nasal, Arab chant rather than reading a novel. You may think that the novel is going to be like one of those tunes of which Courteline remarked that "they disappear, never to return" and stop all of a sudden. But the work gradually organizes itself before the reader's eyes and reveals its solid substructure.

There is not a single unnecessary detail, not one that is not returned to later on and used in the argument. And when we close the book, we realize that it could not have had any other ending. In this world that has been stripped of its causality and presented as absurd, the smallest incident has weight. There is no single one which does not help to lead the hero to crime and capital punishment. *The Outsider* is a classical work, an orderly work, composed about the absurd and against the absurd. Is this quite what the author was aiming at? I do not know. I am simply presenting the reader's opinion.

How are we to classify this clear, dry work, so carefully composed beneath its seeming disorder, so "human," so open, too, once you have the key? It cannot be called a story, for a story explains and co-ordinates as it narrates. It substitutes the order of causality for chronological sequence. M. Camus calls it a "novel." The novel, however, requires continuous duration, development and the manifest presence of the irreversibility of time. I would hesitate somewhat to use the term "novel" for this succession of inert present moments which allows us to see, from underneath, the mechanical economy of something deliberately staged. Or, if it is a novel, it is so in the sense that *Zadig* and *Candide* are novels. It might be regarded as a moralist's short novel, one with a discreet touch of satire and a series of ironic portraits,[25] a novel that, for all the influence of the German existentialists and the American novelists, remains, at bottom, very close to the tales of Voltaire.

(*February* 1943)

[25] Those of the pimp, the judge, the prosecuting attorney, etc.

Chapter 3

Jean Giraudoux and the Philosophy of Aristotle

EVERYTHING WE KNOW about M. Giraudoux leads us to believe he is "normal," in the most popular as well as in the highest sense of the word. In addition, his critical studies have enabled us to appreciate the subtle delicacy of his intelligence. Nevertheless, immediately upon opening one of his novels, we feel as though we were entering the private universe of one of those waking dreamers known medically as "schizophrenics," who are characterized, as we know, by the inability to adjust to reality.

M. Giradoux assumes and artfully elaborates all the main characteristics of these patients, their rigidity, their attempts to deny the reality of change and to refuse to recognize the present, their geometrical mentality, their fondness for symmetry, generalizations, symbols and magical communication across time and space. These qualities constitute the charm of his books. I have often been intrigued by the contrast between the man and his work. Could it be that M. Giraudoux has been amusing himself by playing the schizophrenic?

Choix des Elues, which appeared in this very review,[1] seemed to me a valuable book because it provided an answer to this question. It is certainly not M. Giradoux's best work. But just because many of his charming devices have developed, in this book, into mechanical tricks, I found it easier to grasp the turn of this curious mind. I realized, first of all, that I had been diverted from the true interpretation of his works by a prejudice which I no doubt shared with many of his readers. Until now, I had always tried to *translate* his books. By this I mean that I proceeded on the assumption that M. Giraudoux had accumulated a great many observations, had extracted a certain wisdom from them, and then,

[1] *Nouvelle Revue Francaise,* March, 1940.

out of a fondness for a certain preciosity, had used a code language to express this experience and wisdom. These attempts at decoding had never been very fruitful. M. Giraudoux's depth is real, but it is valid for his world, not for ours.

And so this time I did not want to translate. I did not look for the metaphor or the symbol or the implication. I took it all at face value, with the aim of acquiring a deeper understanding, not of men, but of M. Giraudoux. In order to enter fully into the universe of *Choix des Elues,* we must first forget the world in which we live. I therefore pretended that I knew nothing at all about this soft, pasty substance traversed by waves whose cause and purpose are exterior to themselves, this world without a future, in which things are always meeting, in which the present creeps up like a thief, in which events have a natural resistance to thought and language, this world in which individuals are accidents, mere pebbles, for which the mind subsequently fabricates general categories.

I was not wrong. In the America of Edmée, Claudie and Pierre, rest and order come first. They are the goal of change and its only justification. These clear little states of rest struck me from the very beginning of the book. The book is composed of rests. A jar of pickles is not the fortuitous aspect assumed by a dance of atoms; it is a state of rest, a form closed in upon itself. A scientist's head, filled with laws and calculations, is another such rest, as is the painter's head which lies lightly on the lap of a beautiful, motionless woman, as is a landscape, a park, and even a fleeting morning light.

These ends, these limits assigned to the evolution of matter, we shall call, in medieval fashion, "substantial forms." M. Giraudoux's mind is such that the first thing he perceives is the species in the individual, and thought in matter: "A truth which was Edmée's face," he writes. That is how things are in his universe; first come truths, first come ideas and meanings that choose their own signs. "Jacques, like an *artless little boy,* with his reticence in joy and sorrow alike, had immediately turned his head aside." This little Jacques is not, to begin with, an accident, a cluster of proliferating cells; he is the embodiment of a truth. The occasion, the hour, the blue of the sky are such that a certain Jacques is meant to represent the truth common to artless little boys in a certain part of America. But this "substantial form" is independent of its embodiments, and many other little boys in many other places look away in order not to see their mothers' tears. We might say, as the Schoolmen did, that in this case matter is the individualizing element. Hence this curious fondness of M. Giraudoux for universal judgments: "All the clocks in the town were ringing ten . . . All the roosters . . . All the villages in France . . ." This is not a matter of schizophrenia. These generalizations, which are tiresome in the evolving world where they would be merely an inventory of chance encounters, correspond here to those exhaustive reviews of all the children meant to embody the "artless little boy" and of all the nickel and enamel cylinders supposed to embody the "clock."

These lists generally end with the mention of an exceptional case, an oddity. "They lunched on the bank . . . feeding the birds with their crumbs, except for one bird, a suspicious fellow who had come to look at them and not to eat, and who flew away during the dessert to deliver a report somewhere." This is what we might term the playfulness of M. Giraudoux. He uses it skilfully; the general survey with the poetic or charming or comic exception is one of his most familiar devices. But this disrespect toward the established order can have significance only in relation to that order. In the work of M. Giraudoux, as in the proverb, the exception exists only in order to prove the rule.

It would be a mistake, however, to regard M. Giraudoux as a Platonist. His forms are not in the heaven of ideas, but among us, inseparable from the matter whose movements they govern. They are stamped on our skin like seals in glass. Nor are they to be confused with simple concepts. A concept contains barely more than a handful of the traits common to all the individuals of a given group. Actually, M. Giraudoux's forms contain no more, but the features that compose them are all perfect. They are norms and canons rather than general ideas. There can be no doubt but that Jacques applies

spontaneously, and without even thinking about them, all the
rules which enable him to make of himself the perfection of
the artless little boy.

The very gesture which created Pierre has made him the
most perfect realization of the scientist-husband. "Edmée's
dogs, so *definitely canine*," writes M. Giraudoux. And further
on: "Jacques, in order to watch over his mother, had assumed Jacques' most touching form." Or again: "The annoy-
ing thing about Pierre was that by dint of wanting to represent humanity, he had actually managed to do so. Each of
his gestures, each of his words, was only the valid sample of
human language and movement." So it is with all of M.
Giraudoux's creatures. His books are samplings. Socrates,
when questioned by Parmenides, hesitated to admit that there
might be an Idea of filth, an Idea of the louse. But M.
Giraudoux would not hesitate. The lice with which he is
concerned are admirable in that each one represents the
perfection of the louse—and each to the same degree, though
in different ways.

That is why these substantial forms deserve to be called
archetypes, a name which the author himself occasionally
employs, rather than concepts. "Pierre looked at Edmée and
drew back so as to see only her archetype." But there are also
individual perfections. Edmée, who, of all mothers is the
most definitely a mother—like all mothers—and of all wives
the most definitely a wife—like all wives—is also the most
definitely and most perfectly Edmée. And even among pickles,
which, for the most part limit themselves resignedly to realizing the perfect type of the pickle, a few rare, privileged
ones are, nevertheless, provided with a special archetype:

She went to get a pickle. Although one does not choose
a pickle, she obeyed and took the one which, by virtue of
its architecture, sculpture and relief, had the best claim to
the title of pickle of the head of a household.

The world of *Choix des Elues* is a botanical atlas in which
all the species are carefully classified, in which the periwinkle
is blue because it is a periwinkle and the oleanders are pink

because they are oleanders. Its only causality is that of the archetype. Determinism, that is, the causative action of the preceding state, is completely foreign to this world. But you will never find an *event* in it either, if by event you mean the irruption of a new phenomenon whose very novelty exceeds all expectation and upsets the conceptual order. There is almost no change, except that of matter as it is acted upon by form. And the action of this form is of two kinds. It can act by *virtue,* like the fire of the Schoolmen which burned because of phlogiston. In this case, it takes root in matter and fashions and directs it at will. The movement is merely the temporal development of the archetype. That is why most of the gestures made in *Choix des Elues* are the gestures of madmen. The characters and objects merely realize their substantial forms in stricter fashion, the former by their acts and the latter by their changes.

No danger floated about these heads, which shone and signalled to happiness like beacons, *each with its own luminous system.* Pierre, the husband, with his two smiles, one big and one little, which followed within a second of each other every minute; Jacques, the son, with his very face, which he raised and lowered; Claudie, the daughter, a more sensitive beacon, with the fluttering of her eyelids.

Thus, the various changes in this universe, which we must reluctantly call events, are always symbols of the forms that produce them. But the form may also operate through elective affinity, whence the title: *Choix des Elues* (*Choice of the Elect*).

There is not one of M. Giraudoux's creatures who is not one of the "elect." A form, lurking in the future, lies in wait for its substance; it has elected it; it draws it unto himself. And that is the second kind of change: a brief transition from one form to another, an evolution narrowly defined by its original and final terms. The bud is a state of rest; its flower is in a state of arrest; and between these two states of rest there is a directed change, the only contingency in this orderly world, a necessary and inexpressible shock. About

this evolution itself there is nothing to say, and M. Giraudoux speaks of it as little as possible. Nevertheless, the subject
of *Choix des Elues* is an evolution, the evolution of Edmée,
the chosen one. But M. Giraudoux presents only its stages.
Each of his chapters is a "stasis": Edmée at her birthday
dinner, Edmée at night, a description of Claudie, Edmée at
Frank's, sitting quietly with the weight of a light head on her
lap; Edmée in the park, "outside time," Edmée at the Leeds',
and so on.

The transitions take place behind the scenes, like the mur-
ders in Corneille. Now we understand that air of schizophrenia
in M. Giraudoux's world which struck us earlier. It is a
world without any present indicative. The noisy and unshapely
present of surprises and catastrophes has shrunk and faded;
it goes by quickly and tactfully, excusing itself as it passes.
There are, to be sure, a few scenes and gestures here and
there that are "performed," a few adventures that "happen."
But these are all more than half generalized away, for they
are primarily descriptions of the symbols of certain archetypes.

While reading, we constantly lose our footing, we glide,
without realizing it, from present individuality into timeless
forms. Not for a moment do we ever *feel* the weight of the
head resting on Edmée's lap, nor do we see this head in its
frivolous and charming individuality, bathed in the light of
an American springtime. But that is unimportant, since we
are concerned only with determining whether it is in the
nature of a scientist's head to weigh more than the wild head
of an artist. The reason is that there are two presents in M.
Giraudoux's work: the ignominious present of the event,
which you hide as best you can, like a family taint—and the
present of the archetypes, which is eternity.

These constant limitations of the developmental process
naturally accentuate the discontinuous character of time.
Since change is a lesser state which exists only in order to
bring about a state of rest, time is no more than a succession
of little jolts, a film that has been stopped. Here is how
Claudie thinks about her past:

There had been a series of a hundred, a thousand little girls, who had succeeded each other day after day in order to result in today's Claudie . . . She assembled the photographs of this multitude of Claudies, Claudettes, Claudines, Clo-Clos—there had been a Clo-Clo, the farm-girl for six months—not as photographs of herself, but as a collection of family portraits.

That is what time is really like in *Choix des Elues;* it is that of a family album. You have to turn the pages, of course, but this is only a trifling disturbance, to be forgotten, between the calm dignity of two portraits.

This explains M. Giraudoux's partiality for first beginnings. "For the first time . . . ," "it was the first time. . . ." Perhaps no other phrase occurs more frequently in his works, and never so frequently, perhaps, as in *Choix des Elues* (see, for example, pp. 16, 32, 58, 59, 66, 68, 69, 83, 86, etc.). The reason is that in M. Giraudoux's world, forces do not involve progression. We, in our world, ponder the past; we vainly seek origins. "When did I begin to love her?" Actually, this love never had a beginning; it came into being gradually, and by the time I finally discovered my feeling, it had already lost its freshness. But in the work of M. Giraudoux, changes are instantaneous because they obey the famous principle of "All or Nothing." When the necessary conditions have been fulfilled, the form suddenly appears and embeds itself in matter. But should it lack one element, one only, the tiniest one—nothing happens.

Thus, as we read, we are led from one beginning to another, through an awakening world. If there is any atmosphere common to *Simon le Pathétique, Eglantine* and *Jerome Bardini,* it is that of morning. Throughout these books, despite ageing and the dying of the day and even massacres, the sun always rises. *Electre* ends in catastrophe and at dawn. But may I venture to say that while reading *Choix des Elues,* I no longer had the impression of those enchanted dawns that Jerome and Bella chose for their meetings? I felt as though I had been condemned to an eternal morning.

The endings, like the beginnings, are absolute. Once the balance has been destroyed, the form goes away just as it came, discreetly and entirely. "Edmée was there in the light of early morning, without a wrinkle or blur on her face, and the long night which had just passed seemed even to have been subtracted from her age." Traces, wrinkles and blemishes will do for our world, but the world of M. Giraudoux is the world of regained virginities. His people share a metaphysical chastity. They make love, of course. But neither love nor maternity leaves any mark on them. The nudity of his women is certainly a nudity that is "most definitely nudity." They are nothing *but* nude, absolutely and perfectly nude, without the desires and swellings and subsidings that are foreign to the archetype of the nude. Like the film stars that Jean Prévost called "glove-skinned women," their bodies are as thoroughly scoured as Dutch kitchens, and their gleaming flesh has the freshness of a tiled floor.

This orderly house is, however, subject to the laws of magic, or rather of alchemy, for in it we find strange trans-mutations—in the medieval sense of the transmutation of metals—strange, remote influences. "The first week of Claudie's life was the first week for Edmée of a world without spiders, without banana peels, without red-hot curling irons." Edmée, who is about to leave her husband, is lying beside him in "a night-gown of an off-cream colour with a yoke and trimming of Valenciennes lace." The objects in the room get angry and insult her. She rushes to the bathroom and puts on a pair of Pierre's pyjamas.

> The bed grew silent . . . And thus the night passed. In these two matching garments, they were like a team. People able to see in the dark might have taken them for twins, for a tandem. Gradually, the objects, beguiled by this un-expected mimicry, calmed down . . .

The following is a description of an exorcism:

> Those that wanted to give Edmée white hair, loose teeth and leathery skin, tried to enter the bed alongside the wall,

disguised as Claudie. She had to accept their convention, take them by Claudie's hand, lead them back to Claudie's bed, and threaten to deprive Claudie of dessert for a week. God knows they didn't care a rap! But they were bound by their disguise and had to obey.

Thus, in order to exorcise the devils who have assumed Claudie's shape, it is enough to treat them *as if* they were Claudie. What does all this mean? M. Giraudoux himself explains it to us:

> With Claudie, *everything that resembled Claudie* in this low world approved of her . . . Her peace with little Claudie meant peace with everything that was not part of the everyday world, with the mineral and vegetable, with all that was great and enduring.

This is what characterises all enchantment and spells, namely, that there is an action that makes for resemblance. We must understand that in the work of M. Giraudoux resemblance is not something perceived by the mind; it is *realized*. The "like" which he uses so frequently is never intended to clarify; it reveals a substantial analogy between acts and between things. But this need not surprise us, since his universe is a Natural History.

For him, objects somehow resemble each other when they somehow share the same form. Edmée, of course, seeks peace with Claudie alone. But Claudie is precisely that which is "not part of the everyday world." Making peace with Claudie means adapting herself more closely to the form she currently embodies, to the form of "what is great," of "what endures." Thus, by drawing closer, through love of Claudie, to the perishable embodiment of an eternal archetype, Edmée thereby finds herself mysteriously in tune with all the embodiments of that archetype, with the desert, the mountains and the virgin forest. But this is *logical,* if you consider that Edmée has come to terms, once and for all, with a universal form. Magic is merely an appearance; it arises from the fact that this form is refracted through innumerable particles of matter. Whence the profound analogies M. Giraudoux likes to reveal between the most varied kinds of objects.

The presence of forms divides the universe into an infinite number of infinite regions, and in each of these regions any object, if properly examined, will inform us about all the others. In each of these regions, loving, hating or insulting any one object means loving, hating or insulting all the others. Analogies, correspondences and symbolisms, those are what constitute the marvellous for M. Giraudoux. But as with medieval magic, all this is nothing more than a strict application of the logic of the concept.

And so we are given a ready-made world, not one which makes itself. It is the world of Linnaeus and not of Lamarck, of Cuvier and not of Geoffroy Saint-Hilaire. Let us ask ourselves what place M. Giraudoux has reserved in it for Man. We can guess that it is cut to size. If we bear in mind that its magic is only an appearance, that it is due only to hyperlogicality, we shall realize that this world is, to its very core, accessible to reason. M. Giraudoux has banished every possible element of surprise or bewilderment, including evolution, development, disorder and novelty. Man, surrounded by ready-made thoughts, the reason of trees and stones, of the moon and water, has only to enumerate and contemplate. As for M. Giraudoux himself, I quite understand his affection for members of the Registry Office.

The writer, as he sees him, is merely a real-estate clerk. Nevertheless, a rational world might be more disturbing. Think of Pascal's infinite spaces or de Vigny's Nature. There is nothing like that here, but rather an inner conformity between Man and Nature. Look at Claudie, who is like the desert, like the virgin forest. Is it not obvious that the toughness, strength and eternity of a forest or desert are also the eternity of an instant, the tender strength and the delicate toughness of a little girl? Man discovers all of Nature's archetypes within himself and, reciprocally, himself in all Nature; he stands at the crossroads of all "regions," he is the world's centre, and its symbol, like the magician's microcosm within the great Cosmos.

Note that this man, who is so comfortably installed everywhere and equally at home in Hollywood, as is Edmée, or on a desert island, as is Suzanne, has not been subjected by M. Giraudoux to any kind of determinism. His character is not the resultant of his personal history, of his stomach trouble, of a thousand and one imponderables; his character is not the product of a gradual process. On the contrary, his personal history and even his stomach trouble result from his character. That is what you call "having a destiny." Observe, for example, the terms in which Edmée tries to warn her young son against love:

"Oh, my little Jacques, haven't you ever seen yourself? Look at yourself in a mirror. It's not that you're homely. But you'll see you're a born victim, ready made. . . . You have just the kind of face made for crying with your head in the pillow, the kind of facial planes made to press against hands trembling with despair, the tall body that waits on street corners in the rain—the breast of a person who sobs without tears . . ."

For Man's character does not really differ in any way from the "essence" of the pickle. It is an archetype realized through human life by human acts and whose perfect symbol is the human body. Thus, the most perfect union of body and spirit is achieved by means of the symbol; the way is paved for characterology and the art of physiognomy. But though we have traded the psychologist's determinism for the logical necessity of essences, we do not seem to have gained much in the exchange. Of course, we no longer have psychology, if by psychology we mean a body of empirically observed laws which govern the course of our moods. But we have not chosen to be what we are; we are "possessed" by a form and can do nothing about it. Nonetheless, this form now protects us against universal determinism. There is no danger of our being diluted in the universe.

Man, as a finite and *definite* reality, is not an effect of the world, not the by-product of any blind causal series; he is "man" or "scientist-husband" or "young boy meant to suffer in love," the way a circle is a circle, and, for this reason, he stands at the zero point of first beginnings; his acts emanate from himself only. Is this freedom? It is, at least, a *certain kind* of freedom. M. Giraudoux seems, moreover, to bestow another kind of freedom on his creatures; man realizes his essence *spontaneously*. For the mineral and the vegetable, obedience is automatic. Man conforms to his archetype of his own free will; he is constantly *choosing himself* as he *is*. This, to be sure, is a one-way freedom, for if the form is not realized *by* him, it will be realized *through* him and without his aid. In order to appreciate the thinness of the line between this freedom and absolute necessity, let us compare the following two passages. Here are freedom and inspiration:

> "Where can we go, Claudie, where we've never been before?"
> "To Washington Park."
> Claudie never hesitated. She had a ready answer to all questions, even the most embarrassing. . . . What a happy inspiration to have chosen to come here just at the very time when parks were of no use to people.

There has obviously been an intuition, a poetic creation of a harmony between the two women and things. But in this very intuition, Claudie has been unable to keep from realizing her essence. She is the "person who never hesitates." It was of her essence to have this intuition. And now here is a case in which the harmony between the world and our archetype manifests itself through us without consulting us:

> Edmée was amazed at the words that came to her own lips, for they were surprising; but she was even more amazed at the phrase's necessity than at its monstrousness.

The difference is not very great. In one case the form is realized through our will, and in the other, it spreads, as if independently, through our body. And yet this is what distinguishes man from the pickle. This fragile and intermittent freedom, which is not an end in itself but only a means, is enough to confer a duty upon us. M. Giraudoux has an ethic. Man must freely realize his finite essence, and in so doing, freely harmonize with the rest of the world. Every man is responsible for the universal harmony and should submit of his own free will to the necessity of the archetypes. When this harmony, this balance between our deepest tendencies, between mind and nature, emerges, when man stands at the centre of an orderly world, when he is "most definitely" a man in a world "most definitely" a world, M. Giraudoux's creature then receives his reward: happiness. We now perceive the character of this author's famous humanism; it is a pagan eudaemonism.

A philosophy of the concept, scholastic problems (which is the individualizing element, matter or form?), a shamefaced evolution defined as the transition from potential to act, a white magic which is simply the superficial appearance of a rigorous logicality, an ethics of balance, happiness and the golden mean—these are the elements revealed by a candid examination of *Choix des Elues*. We are a long way from the waking dreamers. But there is an even stranger surprise in store for us. For it is impossible for the reader not to recognize, from these few characteristic traits, the philosophy of Aristotle.

Was not Aristotle primarily a logician—both a logician of the concept and a magician of logic? Is it not in Aristotle that we find this tidy, finite, classified world, a world rational to the core? Was it not he who regarded knowledge as contemplation and classification? Indeed, for him, as for M. Giraudoux, man's freedom lies less in the contingency of his evolution than in the exact realization of his essence. Both of them accept first beginnings, natural places, discontinuity and the principle of "all or nothing." M. Giraudoux has written the novel of Natural History, and Aristotle its philosophy. However, Aristotle's philosophy was the only one capable of crowning the science of his time. He wanted to systematize the accumulated treasures of observation. Now, we know that observation, by its very nature, ends in classification, and classification, likewise by its very nature, is inspired by the concept. But we are at a loss to understand M. Giraudoux.

For four hundred years philosophers and scientists have been trying to break the rigid bounds of the concept; in every field they have been trying to establish the pre-eminence of free and creative judgment and to substitute continuous evolution for the fixity of species. Today, philosophy is foundering, science is leaking at every seam, ethics is going to seed. Efforts are being made everywhere to make our methods and faculty of judging as supple as possible. No one believes any longer in a pre-established conformity between men and things; no one any longer dares hope that the heart of nature is accessible to us. But suddenly, lo and behold! a fictional world makes its appearance and wins us with its indefinable charm and air of novelty. We draw closer and discover the world of Aristotle, a world that has been buried for four hundred years.

Where does this ghost come from? How could a contemporary writer have chosen, in all simplicity, to illustrate by fictional creations the views of a Greek philosopher who died three centuries before our era? I admit I don't know. No doubt we are all Aristotelians from time to time. One evening, we stroll through the streets of Paris, and suddenly things seem to stand still. This evening of all evenings is a "Paris evening." A certain little street, one of many that lead to the Sacré-Coeur, is a "Montmartre street." Time has stopped. We experience a moment of happiness, an eternity of happiness. Which of us has not had this revelation at least once? I say "revelation," but I am wrong—or rather, it is a revelation that has nothing to teach us.

What I seize on the sidewalks, on the road, on the façades of the houses, is only the concept of street as I have long since possessed it. I have an impression of knowing without knowledge, an intuition of Necessity—without necessity. This human concept, which the street and evening reflect like mirrors, dazzles me and prevents my seeing their non-human aspect, the humble and tenacious smiles of objects. What does it matter? The street is there, it ascends, it is so purely, so magnificently, a street. . . . Whereupon we stop; there is nothing more to say. These unproductive intuitions are akin to what psychologists call the illusion of false recognition rather than to a real act of contemplation.

Is this the necessary explanation of M. Giraudoux's sensibility? It would be quite a presumptuous one, and besides, I do not really know. I suppose, too, that a Marxist would term M. Giraudoux's views an urbane rationalism and that he would explain the rationalism in terms of the triumphant rise of capitalism at the beginning of this century—and the urbanity by M. Giraudoux's very special position within the French bourgeoisie—with his peasant origins, his Hellenic culture and his diplomatic career. I do not know. This discreet and self-effacing writer remains a mystery.

(*March* 1940)

Chapter 4

Aminadab or the Fantastic Considered as a Language

"Thought taken ironically for an object by something other than thought."
—MAURICE BLANCHOT: *Thomas l'Obscur*

THOMAS is walking through a village. Who is Thomas? Where does he come from? Where is he going? We know nothing about him. A woman signals to him from a house. He enters and finds himself suddenly in a strange republic of tenants in which everyone seems both to rule and to be ruled. He is made to undergo incoherent initiation rites; he is chained to an almost mute companion with whom he wanders from room to room and floor to floor, frequently forgetting what he is after but always remembering just in time when someone tries to detain him.

After many adventures, he changes, loses his companion and falls ill. It is then that he receives the final warning. "It's yourself you ought to be questioning," an old clerk tells him. A nurse adds, "You've been the victim of an illusion: You thought you were being called, but there was no one. The call came from yourself." Nevertheless, he perseveres, gets to the upper storeys and finds the woman who had signalled to him, but only to be told, "There was no order summoning you: It was someone else who was expected." Thomas has been growing weaker and weaker.

At nightfall, his former companion-in-chains comes to see him and explains that he had taken the wrong direction. "You failed to recognize your path . . . I was like another self to you. I knew all the ways through the house, and I knew the one you should have followed. You had only to ask me. . . ." Thomas asks one last question, but it is never answered, and the room is invaded by the darkness from outside, "beautiful and soothing . . . an immense dream beyond the reach of the person it envelops."

When summed up in this way, M. Blanchot's intentions seem very clear. Even clearer still is the extraordinary resemblance between his book and the novels of Kafka. There is the same minute and courtly style, the same nightmare politeness, the same preposterous and studied ceremoniousness, the same vain quests that lead nowhere, the same exhaustive and useless discussions, the same sterile initiations that initiate into nothing. M. Blanchot says that at the time he wrote *Aminadab* he had not read anything of Kafka's. This leads us to wonder all the more what strange turn led this young writer, still uncertain of his style, to rediscover, in an effort to express a few banal ideas about human life, the same instrument that once gave forth such extraordinary sounds when played by other hands.

I do not know how this conjunction came about. It interests me only because it allows us to draw up the "present balance sheet" of the literature of the fantastic. For fantasy, like other literary genres, has an essence and history of its own, the latter being only the development of the former. What must the nature of the fantastic be in our time if it leads a French writer, convinced of the necessity of "thinking French," [1] to find himself, upon adopting fantasy as his mode of expression, on the same terrain as a writer of Central Europe?

In order to achieve the fantastic, it is neither necessary nor sufficient to portray extraordinary things. The strangest event will enter into the order of the universe if it is alone in a world governed by laws. If you make a horse talk, I will believe, for a moment, that he is under a spell. But if he goes on talking amidst motionless trees, on solid ground, I will take his talking for granted. I shall cease to see the horse and shall see, in its place, a man disguised as a horse. If, on the other hand, you succeed in convincing me that the horse is a creature of fantasy, then the trees, earth and river are also objects of fantasy, even if you have not said so. You cannot

[1] M. Blanchot was, I believe, a disciple of Charles Maurras.

impose limits on the fantastic; either it does not exist at all, or else it extends throughout the universe. It is an entire world in which things manifest a captive, tormented thought, a thought both whimsical and enchained, that gnaws away from below at the mechanism's links without ever managing to express itself. In this world, matter is never entirely matter, since it offers only a constantly frustrated attempt at determinism, and mind is never completely mind, because it has fallen into slavery and has been impregnated and dulled by matter. All is woe. Things suffer and tend towards inertia, without ever attaining it; the debased, enslaved mind unsuccessfully strives towards consciousness and freedom.

The fantastic presents a reverse image of the union of body and soul. In it, the soul takes the place of the body, and the body that of the soul, and we cannot use clear, distinct ideas in pondering this image. We are forced to resort to blurred thoughts which are in themselves fantastic. In short, we have to indulge, though wide awake and fully mature and in the midst of civilization, in the magical "mentality" of the dreamer, the primitive and the child. Thus, there is no need to resort to fairies. Fairies in themselves are simply pretty girls. The fantastic thing is nature when she obeys the fairies; it is nature within and outside of man, perceived like a man turned inside out.

So long as it was thought possible to escape the conditions of human existence through asceticism, mysticism, metaphysical disciplines or the practice of poetry, fantasy was called upon to fulfil a very definite function. It manifested our human power to transcend the human. Men strove to create a world that was not of this world, whether because, like Poe, one preferred the artificial on principle, or because, like Gazotte or Rimbaud and others who practised "seeing a salon at the bottom of a lake," one believed in the writer's magical mission or because, like Lewis Carroll, one was interested in a systematic application to literature of the mathematician's absolute power to beget a universe on the basis of a few conventions, or whether because, like Nodier, one had recognized that the writer was primarily a liar and so tried to attain the absolute lie.

The object thus created referred only to itself. It did not aim at portraying anything, but only at existing. It compelled recognition only through its own density. Though certain writers did borrow the language of fantasy for the expression of certain philosophical and moral ideas in the guise of entertaining stories, they readily admitted that they had diverted this mode of expression from its usual purposes and that they had only created, so to speak, an illusionist fantasy.

M. Blanchot began to write in an age of disillusion. After the long metaphysical holiday of the post-war period, which ended in disaster, the new generation of artists and writers, out of pride and humility and earnestness, had returned, with much ado, to the human. This tendency had an effect on fantasy itself. For Kafka, who figures in this context as a forerunner, a transcendental reality certainly existed, but it was beyond our reach and served only to give us a sharper feeling of man's abandonment in the realm of the human. M. Blanchot, who does not believe in transcendence, would probably agree with Eddington when he says that we have discovered a strange footprint on the shore of the Unknown and that after having constructed one theory after another to explain its origin we have finally managed to reconstruct the creature who left the footprint, and that this creature happens to be ourselves.

This accounts for the attempt at "a return to the human" in the literature of fantasy. It is certainly not going to be used to prove anything or to instruct. M. Blanchot, in particular, denies that he has written the kind of allegory in which, as he puts it, "the meaning corresponds unequivocally to the story but can also be explained apart from it." However, in order to find a place within the humanism of our time fantasy, like other things, is going to become domesticated, will give up the exploration of transcendental reality and resign itself to transcribing the human condition. Now, at about the same time and as a result of internal factors, this literary genre was pursuing its own evolution and getting rid of fairies, genii and goblins as useless and outworn conventions.

Dali and de Chirico revealed to us a nature that was

haunted and yet had nothing of the supernatural about it. The former depicted a biology of horror, showing us the horrible sprouting of human bodies and of life-contaminated metals; the latter painted the life and sufferings of stones. Through a curious twist, the new humanism gave rise to a new development. After Kafka, M. Blanchot is no longer concerned with spells that have been cast on matter. He probably regards Dali's monstrosities as conventional props, just as Dali regarded haunted castles. For him there is only one fantastic object, man. Not the man of religion and of spiritualism, waist-high only in the things of this world, but man-as-he-is-given, natural man, social man, the man who removes his hat when a hearse goes by, who shaves near a window, who kneels in church, who marches in step behind a flag.

This being is a microcosm; he is the world, he is all of nature. Only in him can the totality of spellbound nature be revealed. In him, not in his body. M. Blanchot is not interested in physiological fantasies; his characters are physically *ordinary*. He characterizes them briefly, in passing, but in their total reality of *homo faber* or *homo sapiens*. Thus, the fantastic, in becoming humanized, approaches the ideal purity of its essence, becomes what it had been. It seems to be stripped of all its artifices; there is nothing in its hands or pockets. We recognize the footprint on the shore as our own. There are no phantoms, no succubi, no weeping fountains. There are only men, and the creator of the fantastic announces that he identifies himself with the fantastic object. For contemporary man, the fantastic is only one of a hundred ways of mirroring his own image.

It is on the basis of these observations that we can try for a better understanding of the extraordinary resemblance between *Aminadab* and *The Castle*. We have seen that it is of the essence of the fantastic to offer the reverse image of the union of body and soul. Now, in Kafka, as in M. Blanchot, the fantastic is limited to expressing the human world. Is it not going to be bound, in both authors, by new conditions? And what will be the significance of the inversion of human relationships?

When I enter a café, the first thing I perceive are implements. Not things, not raw matter, but utensils: tables, seats, mirrors, glasses and saucers. Each of these represents a piece of domesticated matter. Taken as a whole, they belong to an obvious order. The meaning of this ordering is an *end*—an end that is myself, or rather, the man in me, the consumer that I am. Such is the surface appearance of the human world. It would be useless for us to look for "raw material" in this world. Here the means functions as matter, and form—mental order—is represented by the end. Now let us describe the café topsy-turvy.

We will have to show ends crushed by their own means and trying vainly to pierce the enormous layers of matter or, if you prefer, objects that reveal their own instrumentality, but with an indiscipline and disorderly power, a kind of coarse independence that suddenly snatches their end from us just when we think we have it fast. Here, for example, is a door. It is there before us, with its hinges, latch and lock. It is carefully bolted, as if protecting some treasure. I manage, after several attempts, to procure a key; I open it, only to find that behind it is a wall. I sit down and order a cup of coffee. The waiter makes me repeat the order three times and repeats it himself to avoid any possibility of error. He dashes off and repeats my order to a second waiter, who notes it down in a little book and transmits it to a third waiter. Finally, a fourth waiter comes back and, putting an inkwell on my table, says, "There you are." "But," I say, "I ordered a cup of coffee." "That's right," he says, as he walks off.

If the reader, while reading a story of this kind, thinks that the waiters are playing a joke or that they are involved in some collective psychosis, then we have lost the game. But if we have been able to give him the impression that we are talking about a world in which these absurd manifestations appear as normal behaviour, then he will find himself plunged all at once into the heart of the fantastic. The fantastic is the revolt of means against ends; either the object in question noisily asserts itself as a means, concealing its end through the very violence of its assertion, or it refers back to another means, and this one to still another, and so on *ad infinitum*, without our ever being able to discover the ultimate end, or else some interference in means belonging to independent series gives us a glimpse of a composite and blurred image of contradictory ends.

Suppose, on the other hand, I finally manage to perceive an end? All the bridges have been burned; I am unable to discover or invent any method of realizing it. Someone has made an appointment to meet me on the first floor of this café; I absolutely must go upstairs. I see the first floor from below, I see its balcony through a big circular opening, I can even see tables and customers seated at these tables. But though I walk all round the room any number of times, I cannot find the stairs. The means in this case is precise; everything in the situation indicates and requires it; it is latent in the manifest presence of the end.

But it has carried the prank to the point of self-annihilation. Am I to call this world "absurd," as M. Camus does in *The Outsider?* But absurdity means the complete absence of ends. The absurd is the object of clear and distinct thought. It belongs to the right-side-up world, as the actual limit of human powers. In the eccentric and hallucinating world we are trying to describe, the absurd would be an oasis, a respite, and thus there is no place for it. I cannot stop there for an instant; each means refers me constantly to the phantom end by which it is haunted, and each end sends me back to the phantom means through which I might bring about its realization. I am unable to think at all, except in terms of slippery and iridescent notions that disintegrate as I behold them.

It is therefore not surprising to find rigorously identical themes in writers so different from each other as Kafka and Blanchot. They are both trying to depict the same preposterous world. They are primarily concerned with excluding "impassive Nature," and that is why we find the same stifling atmosphere in the novels of both men. The hero of *The Trial* struggles in a great city; he walks through streets and enters houses. Thomas, in *Aminadab*, wanders through the endless corridors of an apartment building. Neither of them ever gets a glimpse of forests, plains and hills. How restful it would be if they could come within sight of a mound of earth or a useless piece of matter! But if they did, the fantastic would immediately vanish; the law of this genre condemns it to encounter instruments only. These instruments are not, as we have seen, meant to serve them, but rather to manifest unremittingly an evasive, preposterous finality. This accounts for the labyrinth of corridors, doors and staircases that lead to nothing, the signposts that point to nothing, the innumerable signs that line the roads and that mean nothing. As a particular instance of the theme of the sign, let us take the motif of the message, which is so important in the work of both M. Blanchot and Kafka. In the "right-side-up" world, a message presupposes a sender, a messenger and a recipient. It has only the value of a means; its end is its contents. In the "topsy-turvy" world, the means is isolated and is posed for its own sake. We are plagued by messages without content, without messenger and without sender. Or the end may even exist, but the means will gradually eat it away.

In one of Kafka's stories, the emperor sends a message to someone who lives in the city, but the messenger has such a long way to go that the message never reaches its destination. M. Blanchot tells us of a message whose contents are progressively changed in the course of the journey. "All these hypotheses," he writes, "make probable the following conclusion: that when the messenger finally gets there, he will, for all his good intentions, have forgotten his message and will be unable to transmit it. Or, granting that he has scrupulously retained the terms of the message, it will be impossible for him to know what it means, for what had meaning here must necessarily have a completely different one or none at all there. . . . I refuse to imagine what will have become of the messenger himself, for I presume that he would seem as different from what I am as the message to be transmitted must be from the one received." It is also possible for a message to reach us and be partly decipherable. But we learn later that it was not meant for us.

In *Aminadab*, M. Blanchot discovers another possibility: a message comes to me which is, of course, incomprehensible; I undertake an investigation and learn, finally, that the sender was myself. Needless to say, these possibilities do not represent a few strokes of bad luck amidst many others. They are part of the *nature* of the message. The sender knows this, the recipient is not unaware of it, and still they continue untiringly, the former to send letters and the latter to receive them, as if the important thing were the message itself and not its content. The means has absorbed the end as the blotter absorbs ink.

The same reasoning which leads our two authors to exclude nature from their stories also leads them to exclude natural man, that is, the isolated person, the individual, the man Celine calls "a fellow," of no collective importance who can be only an absolute end. The fantastic imperative inverts the Kantian imperative. "Always act in such a way," it tells us, "that you treat the human in yourself and in others as a means and never as an end." In order to plunge their heroes into a feverish, harassing, unintelligible activity, M. Blanchot and Kafka have to surround them with men who are instruments. The reader, referred from the implement to the man, as from means to end, discovers that man is, in turn, only a means. This accounts for the civil servants and soldiers and judges who throng Kafka's books, and for the servants, who are also called "employees," who fill *Aminadab.*

As a result, the universe of the fantastic seems like a bureaucracy. Actually, it is the civil service that most resembles a "topsy-turvy" society. Thomas, in *Aminadab,* goes from office to office, from employee to employee, without ever finding either the employer or the director, like the visitors who have requests to make at a government office and who are sent endlessly from one department to another. Besides, the actions of these civil servants remain utterly unintelligible. In the right-side-up world I can distinguish fairly well between the magistrate's sneezing, which is an accident, or his whistling, which is an idiosyncrasy, and his juridical activity, which is the application of the law.

Let us reverse things: the fantastic employees, who are careful and even finical, will seem to me, at first, to be carrying out their functions diligently. But I shall soon learn that this zeal is utterly meaningless, or that it is even wrong; it is a mere caprice. The hasty gesture, on the other hand, which shocks me by its incongruity, proves, upon further examination, to be in perfect conformity with the social dignity of the character; it was performed according to law. Thus, law disintegrates into whim, and whim gives us a sudden insight into law. In vain would I demand codes, rules or decrees; old orders lie about on the desks and the employees conform to them without anyone's being able to know whether these orders have been issued by someone in authority or whether they are the product of an anonymous and time-honoured routine or whether they are not the inventions of the civil servants.

Their very scope is ambiguous, and I shall never be able to decide whether they apply to all members of the community or whether they concern only myself. Nevertheless, this ambiguous law that wavers between rule and caprice, between the universal and the particular, is omnipresent. It hems you in, it overwhelms you. You are violating it when you think you are following it, and when you rebel against it, you find yourself obeying it unknowingly. No one is supposed to be ignorant of it, and yet no one knows what it is. Its aim is not to keep order nor regulate human relationships. It is the Law, purposeless, meaningless and without content, and none can escape it.

But now we must tie things together. No one can penetrate the universe of dreams except in sleep. In like manner, no one can enter the world of the fantastic except by becoming fantastic. We know that the reader begins his reading by identifying himself with the hero of the novel. Thus, the hero, by lending us his point of view, constitutes the sole way of access to the fantastic. The old technique presented him as a man right-side-up, transported miraculously into an upside-down world.

Kafka used this method at least once. Joseph K., in *The Trial,* is a normal man. The advantage of this technique is apparent. It sets off, by contrast, the strange character of the new world; the fantastic novel becomes an "Erziehungs-roman." The reader shares the hero's astonishment and follows him from discovery to discovery. However, he thereby sees the fantastic *from the outside,* as a spectacle, as if waking reason were peacefully contemplating the images of our dreams. In *The Castle* Kafka perfected his technique; the hero himself is fantastic. We know nothing about this surveyor whose adventures and views we share. We know nothing except his incomprehensible obstinacy in remaining in a forbidden village. To attain this end, he sacrifices everything; he treats himself as a means. But we never know the value this end had for him and whether it was worth so much effort.

M. Blanchot has adopted the same method; his Thomas is no less mysterious than the servants in the building. We do not know where he comes from, nor why he persists in reaching the woman who has signalled to him. Like Kafka, like Samsa, like the Surveyor, Thomas is *never surprised;* he becomes outraged, as though the succession of events he witnesses seem to him perfectly natural, but blameworthy, as though he possessed within himself a strange standard of Good and Evil of which M. Blanchot has carefully omitted to inform us.

We are thus forced, by the very laws of the novel, to assume a point of view which is not our own, to condemn without understanding and to contemplate without surprise that which amazes us. In addition, M. Blanchot opens and closes his hero's mind as though it were a box. Sometimes we enter it, and at other times we are left outside at the door. And when we are inside, it is only to find lines of reasoning already begun, that link up like mechanisms and presuppose principles and ends unknown to us. We fall into step; since we *are* the hero, we keep step with his reasoning. But these speeches never lead to anything, as if the important thing were merely to reason. Once again the means has devoured the end. And our reason, which should have set the world to rights, is pulled into this nightmare and itself becomes fantastic. M. Blanchot has gone even further. In an excellent passage in *Aminadab,* his hero suddenly discovers that he is unknowingly employed in the house and that he is fulfilling the functions of executioner.

Thus, we have been patiently questioning the officials, for

they seemed to us to know the law and the secrets of the universe. And now we suddenly learn that we ourselves were civil servants without being aware of it. And now the others look at us imploringly and question us in turn. Perhaps we do know the law, after all. "Knowing," said Alain, "consists in knowing that one knows." But that is a maxim that belongs to the right-side-up world. In the topsy-turvy world, one is unaware of knowing what one knows; and when one knows that one knows, then one does not know. Thus, our last resource, that self-awareness in which stoicism sought refuge, escapes us and disintegrates. Its tranparence is that of the void, and our being is outside, in the hands of others.

Such, in their main features, are the principal themes of *The Castle* and *Aminadab*. I hope I have demonstrated that they were imperative from the moment one chose to paint the world upside-down. But the question may arise as to why it was necessary to paint it upside-down. What a silly thing to do—to describe man by standing him on his head! In actual fact, it is quite true that this world is not fantastic, for the simple reason that everything in it is right-side up. A horror novel can be regarded as a simple transposition of reality because in the course of our lives we do meet with terrible situations. But, as we have seen, there would be no fantastic incidents in it, since the fantastic can exist only as a universe. Let us look into the matter a little more closely. If I am upside-down in a world that is upside-down, then everything seems right-side up to me. If, then, I were fantastic myself and inhabited a fantastic world, I should be unable to regard it as fantastic. This will help us to understand our author's intentions.

Thus, I cannot judge this world, since my judgments are part of it. If I conceive of it as a work of art or as a piece of complicated clockwork, I do so by means of human notions; if, on the other hand, I declare it to be absurd, I do so likewise by means of human concepts. As to the ends pursued by our species, how are they to be described unless in relation to other ends? I can, if need be, hope to know eventually the details of the mechanism that surrounds me, but how is man to judge the entire world, that is, the world with man inside it? Yet I would like to know the underside of the cards, I want to contemplate mankind as it is. The artist persists where the philosopher has given up. He invents convenient fictions to satisfy us: Micromegas, the noble savage, Riquet the dog, or that "Outsider" of whom M. Camus has recently been speaking. These are pure beholders who escape the human condition and can thereby inspect it. In the eyes of these angels, the human world is a *given* reality. They can say that it is this or that and that it could be otherwise. Human ends are contingent; they are simple facts which the angels regard as we regard the ends of bees and ants.

Man's progress is simply a matter of marking time, since he can no more get out of this finite and limitless world than the ant can escape from its ant's universe. However, by forcing the reader to identify himself with an inhuman hero, we make him soar like a bird above the human condition. He escapes, he loses sight of that prime necessity of the universe he is contemplating, that is the fact that man is inside it. How is one to make him see *from the outside* this obligation to be inside? Such is, fundamentally, the problem posed for Blanchot and Kafka. It is an exclusively literary and technical problem and would retain no meaning on the philosophical level.

Here is the solution they have found: they have eliminated the angels' gaze and have plunged the reader into the world with K. and Thomas; but they have left, as it were, a ghost of transcendence, floating about within this immanence. The implements, acts and ends are all familiar to us, and we are on such intimate terms with them that we hardly notice them. But just when we feel shut up with them in a warm atmosphere of organic sympathy, they are presented to us in a cold, strange light. This brush is here in my hand. I have only to take it in order to brush my clothes. But just as I touch it, I stop. It is a brush seen from the outside; it is there, in all its contingency; it refers back to contingent ends, just as the white pebble which the ant stupidly drags towards its hole appears to human eyes. "They brush their clothes every morning," the Angel would say. It would require little more to make this activity seem eccentric and unintelligible.

There is no angel in M. Blanchot's book, but, on the other hand, he tries to make us see *our* ends—those ends which are born of us and which give meaning to our lives—as *ends for other people*. We are shown only the external side of those alienated, petrified ends, the side facing outwards, the side which makes *facts* of them. They are petrified ends, underhand ends, invaded by materiality, ends that are observed before they are wanted. As a result, the means takes on an independent existence. If it is no longer taken for granted that one must brush oneself every morning, the brush seems an undecipherable implement, the wreckage of a civilization that has disappeared. It still has a certain meaning, like the pipe-shaped tools that were found at Pompeii. But we no longer know what they mean. What are those immobilized ends, these monstrous and powerless means, if they are not the universe of the fantastic?

The method is clear: since human activity seems reversed when seen from the outside, Kafka and M. Blanchot, in order to make us see our condition from the outside without resorting to angels, have painted a world that is topsy-turvy. It is a contradictory world in which mind becomes matter, since values look like facts, a world in which matter is eaten away by mind, since everything is both ends and means, a world in which, without ceasing to be within, I see myself from without. Better still, we cannot ponder it at all.

That is the reason why M. Blanchot writes: "The meaning can be grasped only through a fiction and melts away as soon as we try to understand it for itself. . . . The story . . . seems mysterious because it tells everything about something that will not bear telling." There is a sort of marginal existence of the fantastic. Look at it squarely. Try to express its meaning with words. It immediately disappears, for, after all, one must be either inside or out. But if you read the story without trying to translate it, it attacks you by the flank.

The few truths that you will extract from *Aminadab* will lose their colour and their life once they are out of the water.

Yes, of course, man is alone in the world, he alone decides his destiny, he himself invents the law to which he is subject; each of us is a stranger to himself and a victim and executioner for everyone else; we do seek in vain to transcend man's estate, we would do better to acquire a Nietzschean sense of the earth. Yes, to be sure, M. Blanchot's wisdom seems to belong to those "transcendences" of which Jean Wahl has spoken in connection with Heidegger. But after all, none of this sounds very new. Yet, when these truths wove in and out of the narrative, they shone with a strange brilliance. And they did so because we were seeing them wrongside out; they were fantastic truths.

Our authors, who have gone such a long way together, part company here. About Kafka I have nothing more to say, except that he is one of the greatest and most unique writers of our time. And besides, he was the first on the scene; the technique he chose corresponded in him to a need. If he shows us human life everlastingly troubled by an impossible transcendence, it is because he believes in the existence of this transcendence. Only, it is beyond our reach. His universe is both fantastic and rigorously true. M. Blanchot has certainly a considerable talent. But he came afterwards, and the artifices he employs are already too familiar.

In commenting on Jean Paulhan's Les Fleurs de Tarbes he wrote, "Those writers who had, through prodigies of asceticism the illusion of standing apart from all literature, because they wanted to rid themselves of conventions and forms in order to make direct contact with the secret world and the deeper metaphysics that they wished to reveal . . . finally contented themselves with using this world, this secret and this metaphysics as conventions and forms which they revealed with a certain casualness and which constituted both the visible structure and the content of their works. . . . For this sort of writer, metaphysics, religion and feelings take the place of language and technique. They are a system of expression, a literary form, in a word, literature." [2]

I am really afraid that this reproach, if it is a reproach, can be turned against M. Blanchot himself. The system of

[2] Comment la littérature est elle possible? (José Corti), p. 23.

signs which he has chosen does not quite correspond to the thought he is expressing. There was no need to resort to artifices which introduce an external view into consciousness in order to depict "the nature of spirit, its deep split, this struggle of the Same with the Same, which is the means of its power, its torment and its apotheosis." [3] I am inclined to say of M. Blanchot what Lagneau said of Barrès, that he has misused the tool. And this slight discrepancy between the sign and the thing signified turns the deeply experienced themes of Kafka into literary conventions. Thanks to M. Blanchot there is now a "Kafkaesque" stereotype of the fantastic, just as there is a stereotype of haunted castles and stuffed monsters. I am aware that art thrives on conventions, but one must at least know how to choose them. Seen against a transcendence tinged with Maurrassianism, the fantastic gives an effect of having been laid on.

This uneasy feeling on the part of the reader is heightened by the fact that M. Blanchot does not remain faithful to his purpose. He had told us that he hopes that the meaning of *Aminadab* "vanishes as soon as one tries to understand it for itself." Very well, but in that case, why offer us a continual translation, a full commentary on its symbols? In many passages the explanations become so insistent that the story very clearly takes on the aspect of an allegory. Let us choose at random a page from the long account which develops the myth of the servants, for example the following: "I warned you that the staff was invisible most of the time. Such a remark was stupid, a proud temptation to which I yielded and for which I blush. Is the staff invisible? Is it invisible most of the time? But we never see the staff, we never get a glimpse of it, even from afar; we do not even know what the word *see* can mean as regards the staff, nor whether there is a word to express its absence, nor whether the thought of this absence is not an ultimate and disheartening means of making us imagine its arrival.

"The state of negligence in which it keeps us is, in certain ways, unimaginable. Since many people have had their health ruined or have paid with their lives for its inadequate service, we might, then, complain about its apparent indifference to our interests. Still, we should be ready to forgive everything if it gave us some satisfaction now and then. . . ." [4] Replace the word "staff" in the passage by "God" and the word "service" by "Providence," and you will have a perfectly comprehensible statement of a certain aspect of religious feeling. Often, too, the objects in this falsely fantastic world yield their meaning to us "right-side up," without needing any commentary, like the companion-in-chains who is so obviously the body, the humiliated body, mistreated in a society which has declared a divorce between the physical and the spiritual. We then feel as if we were translating a translation, as if we were rendering a text into our native language.

Moreover, I do not pretend to have grasped all the author's intentions and perhaps I have misunderstood a number of them. The fact that these intentions, even when obscure, were obvious, was enough to trouble me. I still think that with more effort or more intelligence I could have cleared them all up. In Kafka, the accidents link up in accordance with the necessities of the plot. In *The Trial,* for example, never for a moment do we lose sight of the fact that K. is struggling to defend his honourable character, his life. But why is Thomas struggling? He has no definite character, he has no purpose, he hardly interests us. And the events accumulate haphazardly. "As they do in life," someone may object. But life is not a novel, and the series of happenings without rhyme or reason that can be drawn from the novel turn our attention, in spite of ourselves, to the secret intentions of the author.

Why does Thomas lose his companion-in-chains and fall ill? Nothing in this upside-down world either prepares for or explains his illness. This means, then, that the reason for it lies outside this world, in the providential intentions of the author. Thus most of the time M. Blanchot is wasting his effort. He does not succeed in ensnaring the reader in the

[4] *Aminadab,* p. 95.

nightmarish world he is portraying. The reader escapes; he is outside—outside with the author himself. He contemplates these dreams as he would a well-assembled machine.

He loses his footing only at rare moments. These moments are, moreover, enough to reveal in M. Blanchot a writer of quality. He is subtle and ingenious, at times profound. He has a love of words; he needs only to find his style. His venture into the fantastic is not without consequence, for it helps us to determine our bearings. Kafka could not be imitated; he remained on the horizon like a perpetual temptation. By having unwittingly imitated him, M. Blanchot delivers us from him. He brings his methods into the open. They are now catalogued, classified, fixed and useless, and no longer frightening or dizzying. Kafka was only a stage on the way. Through him, as through Hoffmann, Poe, Lewis Carroll and the surrealists, the fantastic pursues the continuous progress which should ultimately reunite it with what it has always been.

Chapter 5

William Faulkner's *Sartoris*

WITH A LITTLE PERSPECTIVE, good novels come almost to resemble natural phenomena. We forget that they have authors; we accept them as we do stones or trees, because they are there, because they exist. *Light in August* was just such an hermetic thing, a mineral. We do not accept *Sartoris*, and that is what makes the book so precious. Faulkner betrays himself in it; we catch him red-handed all the way through. This book led me to an understanding of the mainspring of Faulkner's art. This mainspring is illusion. It is true that all art is false. Paintings lie about perspective. There are, however, two kinds of pictures: real pictures and the illusionist kind.

I had accepted the "Man" of *Light in August*. (I thought of him as "Faulknerian Man," the way one thinks of Dostoevskian or Meredithian Man.) I had accepted this big, Godless, divine animal, lost from birth and bent on self-destruction, moral even in murder and redeemed—not by or in death, but in his last moments before death. I had accepted this animal, who is great even in torture and in the most abject humiliation of the flesh. I had accepted him uncritically. I had not forgotten his haughty, threatening, tyrant's visage, nor his sightless eyes. I found him again in *Sartoris*. I recognized Bayard's "gloomy arrogance."

And yet I can no longer accept Faulkner's Man; he is an illusionist creation. It is all done with lighting. There is a trick, and the trick lies in not telling, in keeping secrets—surreptitiously; in telling *just a little*. We are told that old Bayard is upset over the unexpected return of his grandson. We are told surreptitiously, however, in a half-phrase that might almost pass unnoticed, and which Faulkner hopes will pass *almost* unnoticed. Then, when we are expecting stormy outbreaks, we are given a minute and lengthy description of his gestures.

Faulkner is not unaware of our impatience; he counts on it and stops there, to chat innocently of gestures. There have been other chatterers, the realists, for example, Dreiser. But Dreiser's descriptions are informative; they are documentary. Here, the gestures (drawing on boots, climbing a staircase, mounting a horse) have no descriptive purpose, but are intended to conceal things. We watch for something to betray Bayard's agitation, but the Sartorises never get drunk, never betray themselves through gestures. Nevertheless, these idols, whose gestures have something of a ritual-like threat about them, also possess consciousnesses.

They talk, they think to themselves, they become aroused. Faulkner knows this. Now and then he casually reveals a consciousness to us. But it is like a conjurer holding up the box when it is empty. What do we see? Only gestures, no more than we could see from the outside. Or else, we take a relaxed consciousness by surprise as it is falling asleep, and once again we find gestures, tennis, piano, whisky or conversation. And that is what I cannot accept. Everything is aimed at making us believe that these minds are always empty and evasive. Why? Because a consciousness is too human a thing. Aztec Gods do not engage in pleasant little conversations with themselves. But Faulkner knows perfectly well that minds are not and *cannot* be empty. He knows this well enough to write:

. . . she again held her consciousness submerged deliberately deliberately, as you hold a puppy under water until its struggles cease.

But he does not tell us what is *inside* the consciousness he wants to drown. Not exactly that he wants to conceal it. He hopes we will guess it, because whatever is touched by divination becomes magical. And the gestures begin all over again. We feel like complaining of "too many gestures," just as someone told Mozart that his score had "too many notes." There are, also, too many words. Faulkner's volubility, his lofty, abstract, anthropomorphic, preacher's style are still other illusionist devices. The style clogs the everyday gestures, weighs them down, encumbers them with an epic magnificence and makes them sink, like clay pigeons. This is done intentionally. Faulkner is actually aiming at just this pompous, sickening monotony, this ritual of everyday life.

The gestures imply a world of boredom. These rich people, decent and uncultivated, who have neither work nor leisure, prisoners on their own land, masters enslaved to their own negroes, try to fill in the time with gestures. But this boredom (has Faulkner always managed to distinguish between his heroes' boredom and that of his readers?) is only an appearance; it is Faulkner's defence against us, and the Sartorises' defence against themselves. The boredom is in the social order, the monotonous languor of everything they can see, hear or touch. Faulkner's landscapes are as bored as his characters.

The real drama is *behind,* behind the boredom, behind the gestures, behind the characters' consciousness. Suddenly, from the depths of this drama, like a bolt from the blue, appears the Act. At last, an act! something *happening,* a message! But Faulkner disappoints us again; he rarely describes acts, because he encounters and by-passes an old problem of fictional technique. Acts are of the essence of the novel. They are carefully prepared, and then, by the time they happen, they are utterly simple, as smooth and polished as bronze. They slip between our fingers. There is nothing more to say about them; the mere mention of them suffices. Faulkner does not speak of acts, never mentions them, and thus suggests that there is no naming them, that they are beyond language. He shows only their results: an old man, dead in his seat, a car turned over in the river and two feet sticking out of the water. These brutal and static consequences, as solid and compact as the Act is fleeting, appear amidst the fine, close rain of everyday gestures to flaunt themselves in their inexplicable finality.

These undecipherable acts of violence will later change into "stories"; they will be given names, will be analysed and recounted. All these men, all these families, have their stories. The Sartoris family carries the heavy burden of two wars and of two series of stories, the Civil War, in which Bayard, the ancestor, died, and the World War, in which John Sartoris died. The stories appear and disappear, passing from mouth to mouth, dragging on along with the gestures of everyday life. They do not belong completely to the past; they are, rather, a super-present.

> As usual, old man Falls had brought John Sartoris into the room with him . . . Freed as he was of time and flesh, he was a far more palpable presence than either of the other two old men who sat shouting periodically into one another's deafness . . .

They constitute the poetry and fatality of the present: "fatal immortality and immortal fatality." It is with these stories that Faulkner's heroes forge their destinies. A nameless act, buried for years, beckons, through tales that have been embellished by generations, to other Acts, charming and attracting them, as a rod attracts lightning. Such is the subtle power of stories and words. Yet, Faulkner does not believe in these incantations:

> What had been a hare-brained prank of two heedless and reckless boys wild with their own youth had become a gallant and finely tragical focal point to which the history of the race had been raised . . . by two angels valiantly fallen and strayed, altering the course of human events . . .

He never allows himself to be entirely taken in. He knows these tales for what they are worth, since it is he who is telling them, since he, like Sherwood Anderson, is "a story-teller, an inventor." But he dreams of a world in which the stories would be believed, in which they would really affect men, and his novels depict the world of his dreams. We are familiar with the "technique of disorder" of *The Sound and the Fury* and of *Light in August,* those inextricable mixtures of past and present. I thought I had found their twofold origin in *Sartoris.* On the one hand, there is the irresistible need to interrupt the action in order to relate a story. This seems to me characteristic of many lyrical novelists. And, on the other hand, there is that half-sincere, half-imaginary faith in the magical power of stories. But when Faulkner wrote *Sartoris*, he had not yet perfected his technique; the transitions from present to past and from gesture to story are very clumsily managed.

This, then, is man as Faulkner asks us to accept him. Faulkner's man is *undiscoverable*. He is to be understood neither in terms of his gestures, which are a façade, nor through his tales, which are imaginary, nor yet by his acts, for they are lightning flashes that defy description. And yet, beyond behaviour and beyond words, beyond empty consciousness, Man exists. We have an inkling of a genuine drama, a kind of intelligible nature that might explain everything. But just what is this nature? Is it a racial or family taint, an Adlerian inferiority complex, a repressed libido? Sometimes it is one, sometimes the other, depending on the story and the character. Faulkner often does not tell us. And, furthermore, this does not particularly interest him.

What matters to him is rather the *nature* of this new creature, a nature that is *poetic* and magical, full of manifold, but veiled, contradictions. This "nature"—what else can we call it?—which we grasp in terms of its psychological manifestations, does have a psychological existence. It is not even completely subconscious, since it often seems as if the men impelled by it can look back and contemplate it. But, on the other hand, it is fixed and immutable, like an evil spell. Faulkner's heroes bear it within them from the day of their birth.

It is as obstinate as stone or rock; it is *a thing,* a *spirit-thing,* an opaque, solidified spirit behind consciousness. It is a shadow, but a shadow whose essence is clarity—the magical object par excellence. Faulkner's creatures are bewitched, enveloped in a stifling atmosphere of witchcraft. That is what I meant by illusion. These spells are impossible. They are not even conceivable. And Faulkner takes care not to let us conceive them. His entire method aims at suggesting them.

Is he nothing more than an illusionist? I believe he is. Or, if not, he is tricking himself. There is a curious passage in *Sartoris* that provides us with the key to his deviousness and sincerity alike.

"Your Arlens and Sabatinis talk a lot, and nobody ever had more to say and more trouble saying it than old Dreiser."

"But they have secrets," she explained. "Shakespeare doesn't have any secrets. He tells everything."

"I see. Shakespeare had no sense of discrimination and no instinct for reticence. In other words, he wasn't a gentleman," he suggested.

"Yes . . . That's what I mean."

"And so, to be a gentleman, you must have secrets."

"Oh, you make me tired."

This dialogue is ambiguous and probably ironical. Narcissa is not very intelligent, and besides, Sabatini and Michael Arlen are bad writers. Yet, it seems to me that in this passage Faulkner reveals a good deal of himself. Though Narcissa may be somewhat lacking in literary taste, her instinct is sound in making her choose Bayard, a man who has secrets. Horace may be right in liking Shakespeare, but he is talkative and weak; he tells all, he is not a man. The men Faulkner likes—the negro in *Light in August*, the father in *Absalom*, Bayard Sartoris—are men who have secrets and keep quiet. Faulkner's humanism is probably the only acceptable kind. He hates our prattling, well-adjusted minds, our engineering mentality. But doesn't he realize that his great, dark figures are only façades? Is he taken in by his own art? He would probably not be satisfied by the repression of our secrets into the unconscious. He dreams of total darkness within consciousness itself, a total darkness that we ourselves make, within our very selves. This dream of silence, a silence outside us and a silence within us, is the futile dream of a puritan ultra-stoicism. Is he shamming? What does he do when he is alone? Does he put up with the endless prattle of his all too human consciousness? To know this, we would have to know Faulkner himself.

(*February* 1938)

Chapter 6

On *The Sound and the Fury:*
Time in the Work of Faulkner

THE FIRST THING that strikes one in reading *The Sound and the Fury* is its technical oddity. Why has Faulkner broken up the time of his story and scrambled the pieces? Why is the first window that opens out on this fictional world the consciousness of an idiot? The reader is tempted to look for guidemarks and to re-establish the chronology for himself:

> Jason and Caroline Compson have had three sons and a daughter. The daughter, Caddy, has given herself to Dalton Ames and become pregnant by him. Forced to get hold of a husband quickly . . .

Here the reader stops, for he realizes he is telling another story. Faulkner did not first conceive this orderly plot so as to shuffle it afterwards like a pack of cards; he could not tell it in any other way. In the classical novel, action involves a central complication; for example, the murder of old Karamazov or the meeting of Edouard and Bernard in *The Coiners*. But we look in vain for such a complication in *The Sound and the Fury*. Is it the castration of Benjy or Caddy's wretched amorous adventure or Quentin's suicide or Jason's hatred of his niece? As soon as we begin to look at any episode, it opens up to reveal behind it other episodes, all the other episodes. Nothing happens; the story does not unfold; we discover it under each word, like an obscene and obstructing presence, more or less condensed, depending upon the particular case. It would be a mistake to regard these irregularities as gratuitous exercises in virtuosity. A fictional technique always relates back to the novelist's metaphysics. The critic's task is to define the latter before evaluating the former. Now, it is immediately obvious that Faulkner's metaphysics is a metaphysics of time.

Man's misfortune lies in his being time-bound.

. . . a man is the sum of his misfortunes. One day you'd think misfortune would get tired, but then time is your misfortune . . .

Such is the real subject of the book. And if the technique Faulkner has adopted seems at first a negation of temporality, the reason is that we confuse temporality with chronology. It was man who invented dates and clocks.

Constant speculation regarding the position of mechanical hands on an arbitrary dial which is a symptom of mind-function. Excrement Father said like sweating.

In order to arrive at real time, we must abandon this invented measure which is not a measure of anything.

. . . time is dead as long as it is being clicked off by little wheels; only when the clock stops does time come to life.

Thus, Quentin's gesture of breaking his watch has a symbolic value; it gives us access to a time without clocks. The time of Benjy, the idiot, who does not know how to tell time, is also clockless.

What is thereupon revealed to us is the present, and not the ideal limit whose place is neatly marked out between past and future. Faulkner's present is essentially catastrophic. It is the event which creeps upon us like a thief, huge, unthinkable—which creeps up on us and then disappears. Beyond this present time there is nothing, since the future does not exist. The present rises up from sources unknown to us and drives away another present; it is forever beginning anew. "And . . . and . . . and then." Like Dos Passos, but much more discreetly, Faulkner makes an accretion of his narrative. The actions themselves, even when seen by those who perform them, burst and scatter on entering the present.

I went to the dresser and took up the watch with the face still down. I tapped the crystal on the dresser and caught the fragments of glass in my hand and put them into the ashtray and twisted the hands off and put them in the tray. The watch ticked on.

The other aspect of this present is what I shall call a sinking in. I use this expression, for want of a better one, to indicate a kind of motionless movement of this formless monster. In Faulkner's work, there is never any progression, never anything which comes from the future. The present has not first been a future possibility, as when my friend, after having been *he for whom I am waiting,* finally appears. No, to be present means to appear without any reason and to sink in. This sinking in is not an abstract view. It is within things themselves that Faulkner perceives it and tries to make it felt.

The train swung around the curve, the engine puffing with short, heavy blasts, and they passed smoothly from sight that way, with that quality of shabby and timeless patience, of static serenity . . .

And again,

Beneath the sag of the buggy the hooves neatly rapid like motions of a lady doing embroidery, *diminishing without progress*[1] like a figure on a treadmill being drawn rapidly off-stage.

It seems as though Faulkner has laid hold of a frozen speed at the very heart of things; he is grazed by congealed spurts that wane and dwindle without moving.

This fleeting and unimaginable immobility can, however, be arrested and pondered. Quentin can say, "I broke my watch," but when he says it, his gesture is *past.* The past is named and related; it can, to a certain extent, be fixed by con-

[1] The author's italics.

cepts or recognized by the heart. We pointed out earlier, in connection with *Sartoris,* that Faulkner always showed events when they were already over. In *The Sound and the Fury* everything has already happened. It is this that enables us to understand that strange remark by one of the heroes, *"Fui. Non sum."* In this sense, too, Faulkner is able to make man a sum total without a future: "The sum of his climactic experiences," "The sum of his misfortunes," "The sum of what have you." At every moment, one draws a line, since the present is nothing but a chaotic din, a future that is past. Faulkner's vision of the world can be compared to that of a man sitting in an open car and looking backwards. At every moment, formless shadows, flickerings, faint tremblings and patches of light rise up on either side of him, and only afterwards, when he has a little perspective, do they become trees and men and cars.

The past takes on a sort of super-reality; its contours are hard and clear, unchangeable. The present, nameless and fleeting, is helpless before it. It is full of gaps, and, through these gaps, things of the past, fixed, motionless and silent as judges or glances, come to invade it. Faulkner's monologues remind one of aeroplane trips full of air-pockets. At each pocket, the hero's consciousness "sinks back into the past" and rises only to sink back again. The present is not; it becomes. Everything *was*. In *Sartoris,* the past was called "the stories" because it was a matter of family memories that had been constructed, because Faulkner had not yet found his technique.

In *The Sound and the Fury* he is more individual and more undecided. But it is so strong an obsession that he is sometimes apt to disguise the present, and the present moves along in the shadow, like an underground river, and reappears only when it itself is past. When Quentin insults Blaid,[2] he is not even aware of doing so; he is reliving his dispute with Dalton Ames. And when Blaid punches his nose, this brawl is covered over and hidden by Quentin's past brawl with Ames.

[2] Compare the dialogue with Blaid inserted into the middle of the dialogue with Ames: "Did you ever have a sister?" etc., and the inextricable confusion of the two fights.

Later on, Shreve relates how Blaid hit Quentin; he relates this scene because it has become a story, but while it was unfolding in the present, it was only a furtive movement, covered over by veils. Someone once told me about an old monitor who had grown senile. His memory had stopped like a broken watch; it had been arrested at his fortieth year. He was sixty, but didn't know it. His last memory was that of a schoolyard and his daily walk around it. Thus, he interpreted his present in terms of his past and walked about his table, convinced that he was watching students during recreation.

Faulkner's characters are like that, only worse, for their past, which is in order, does not assume chronological order. It is, in actual fact, a matter of emotional constellations. Around a few central themes (Caddy's pregnancy, Benjy's castration, Quentin's suicide) gravitate innumerable silent masses. Whence the absurdity of the chronology of "the assertive and contradictory assurance" of the clock. The order of the past is the order of the heart. It would be wrong to think that when the present is past it becomes our closest memory. Its metamorphosis can cause it to sink to the bottom of our memory, just as it can leave it floating on the surface. Only its own density and the dramatic meaning of our life can determine at what level it will remain.

Such is the nature of Faulkner's time. Isn't there something familiar about it? This unspeakable present, leaking at every seam, these sudden invasions of the past, this emotional order, the opposite of the voluntary and intellectual order that is chronological but lacking in reality, these memories, these monstrous and discontinuous obsessions, these intermittences of the heart—are not these reminiscent of the lost and recaptured time of Marcel Proust? I am not unaware of the differences between the two; I know, for instance, that for Proust salvation lies in time itself, in the full reappearance of the past. For Faulkner, on the contrary, the past is never lost, unfortunately; it is always there, it is an obsession. One escapes from the temporal world only through mystic ecstasies. A mystic is always a man who wishes to forget something, his self or, more often, language or objective representations. For Faulkner, time must be forgotten.

> "Quentin, I give you the mausoleum of all hope and desire; it's rather excruciatingly apt that you will use it to gain the reductio ad absurdum of all human experience which can fit your individual needs no better than it fitted his or his father's. I give it to you not that you may remember time, *but that you might forget it now and then for a moment* and not spend all your breath trying to conquer it. Because no battle is ever won he said. They are not even fought. The field only reveals to man his own folly and despair, and victory is an illusion of philosophers and fools."

It is because he has forgotten time that the hunted negro in *Light in August* suddenly achieves his strange and horrible happiness.

> It's not when you realize that nothing can help you—religion, pride, anything—it's when you realize that you don't need any aid.

But for Faulkner, as for Proust, time is, above all, *that which separates*. One recalls the astonishment of the Proustian heroes who can no longer enter into their past loves, of those lovers depicted in *Les Plaisirs et Les Jours,* clutching their passions, afraid they will pass and knowing they will. We find the same anguish in Faulkner.

> . . . people cannot do anything very dreadful at all, they cannot even remember tomorrow what seemed dreadful today . . .

and

> . . . a love or a sorrow is a bond purchased without design and which matures willynilly and is recalled without warn-

ing to be replaced by whatever issue the gods happen to be floating at the time . . .

To tell the truth, Proust's fictional technique *should have been* Faulkner's. It was the logical conclusion of his metaphysics. But Faulkner is a lost man, and it is because he feels lost that he takes risks and pursues his thought to its uttermost consequences. Proust is a Frenchman and a classicist. The French lose themselves only a little at a time and always manage to find themselves again. Eloquence, intellectuality and a liking for clear ideas were responsible for Proust's retaining at least the semblance of chronology.

The basic reason for this relationship is to be found in a very general literary phenomenon. Most of the great contemporary authors, Proust, Joyce, Dos Passos, Faulkner, Gide and Virginia Woolf have tried, each in his own way, to distort time. Some of them have deprived it of its past and future in order to reduce it to the pure intuition of the instant; others, like Dos Passos, have made of it a dead and closed memory. Proust and Faulkner have simply decapitated it. They have deprived it of its future, that is, its dimension of deeds and freedom. Proust's heroes never undertake anything. They do, of course, make plans, but their plans remain stuck to them and cannot be projected like a bridge beyond the present. They are day-dreams that are put to flight by reality. The Albertine who appears is not the one we were expecting, and the expectation was merely a slight, inconsequential hesitation, limited to the moment only. As to Faulkner's heroes, they never look ahead. They face backwards as the car carries them along. The coming suicide which casts its shadow over Quentin's last day is not a human possibility; not for a second does Quentin envisage the possibility of *not* killing himself. This suicide is an immobile wall, a *thing* which he approaches backwards, and which he neither wants to nor can conceive.

. . . you seem to regard it merely as an experience that will whiten your hair overnight so to speak without altering your appearance at all . . .

It is not an *undertaking,* but a fatality. In losing its element of possibilty it ceases to exist in the future. It is already present, and Faulkner's entire art aims at suggesting to us that Quentin's monologues and his last walk *are already* his suicide. This, I think, explains the following curious paradox: Quentin thinks of his last day in the past, like someone who is remembering. But in that case, since the hero's last thoughts coincide approximately with the bursting of his memory and its annihilation, who is remembering? The inevitable reply is that the novelist's skill consists in the choice of the present moment from which he narrates the past. And Faulkner, like Salacrou in *L'Inconnu d'Arras,* has chosen the infinitesimal instant of death. Thus, when Quentin's memory begins to unravel its recollections ("Through the wall I heard Shreve's bed-springs and then his slippers on the floor hishing. I got up . . .") *he is already dead.* All this artistry and, to speak frankly, all this illusion are meant, then, merely as substitutions for the intuition of the future lacking in the author himself. This explains everything, particularly the irrationality of time; since the present is the unexpected, the formless can be determined only by an excess of memories. We now also understand why duration is "man's characteristic misfortune." If the future has reality, time withdraws us from the past and brings us nearer to the future; but if you do away with the future, time is no longer that which separates, that which cuts the present off from itself. "You cannot bear to think that someday it will no longer hurt you like this." Man spends his life struggling against time, and time, like an acid, eats away at man, eats him away from himself and prevents him from fulfilling his human character. Everything is absurd. "Life is a tale told by an idiot, full of sound and fury, signifying nothing."

But is man's time without a future? I can understand that the nail's time, or the clod's or the atom's is a perpetual present. But is man a thinking nail? If you begin by plunging him into universal time, the time of planets and nebulae, of tertiary flexures and animal species, as into a bath of sulphuric acid, then the question is settled. However, a consciousness buffeted so from one instant to another ought, *first of all,* to be a consciousness and then, *afterwards,* to be temporal; does anyone believe that time can come to it from the outside? Consciousness can "exist within time" only on condition that it become time as a result of the very movement by which it becomes consciousness. It must become "temporalized," as Heidegger says. We can no longer arrest man at each present and define him as "the sum of what he has." The nature of consciousness implies, on the contrary, that it project itself into the future. We can understand what it is only through what it will be. It is determined in its present being by its own possibilities. This is what Heidegger calls "the silent force of the possible." You will not recognize within yourself Faulkner's man, a creature bereft of possibilities and explicable only in terms of what he has been. Try to pin down your consciousness and probe it. You will see that it is hollow. In it you will find only the future.

I do not even speak of your plans and expectations. But the very gesture that you catch in passing has meaning for you only if you project its fulfillment out of it, out of yourself, into the not-yet. This very cup, with its bottom that you do not see—that you might see, that is, at the end of a movement you have not yet made—this white sheet of paper, whose underside is hidden (but you could turn over the sheet) and all the stable and bulky objects that surround us display their most immediate and densest qualities in the future. Man is not the sum of what he has, but the totality of what he does not yet have, of what he might have. And if we steep ourselves thus in the future, is not the formless brutality of the present thereby attenuated? The single event does not spring on us like a thief, since it is, by nature, a Having-been-future. And if a historian wishes to explain the past, must he not first seek out its future? I am afraid that the absurdity that Faulkner finds in a human life is one that he himself has put there. Not that life is not absurd, but there is another kind of absurdity.

Why have Faulkner and so many other writers chosen this particular absurdity which is so un-novelistic and so untrue? I think we should have to look for the reason in the social conditions of our present life. Faulkner's despair seems to me to precede his metaphysics. For him, as for all of us, the future is closed. Everything we see and experience impels us to say, "This can't last." And yet change is not even conceivable, except in the form of a cataclysm. We are living in a time of impossible revolutions, and Faulkner uses his extraordinary art to describe our suffocation and a world dying of old age. I like his art, but I do not believe in his metaphysics. A closed future is still a future. "Even if human reality has nothing more 'before' it, even if 'its account is closed,' its being is still determined by this 'self-anticipation.' The loss of all hope, for example, does not deprive human reality of its possibilities; it is simply a way of *being* toward these same possibilities." [3]

(July 1939)

[3] Heidegger, *Zein und Zeit.*

Chapter 7

John Dos Passos and *1919*

A NOVEL IS A MIRROR. So everyone says. But what is meant by *reading* a novel? It means, I think, jumping into the mirror. You suddenly find yourself on the other side of the glass, among people and objects that have a familiar look. But they merely look familiar. We have never really seen them. The things of our world have, in turn, become outside reflections. You close the book, step over the edge of the mirror and return to this honest-to-goodness world, and you find furniture, gardens and people who have nothing to say to you. The mirror that closed behind you reflects them peacefully, and now you would swear that art is a reflection. There are clever people who go so far as to talk of distorting mirrors.

Dos Passos very consciously uses this absurd and insistent illusion to impel us to revolt. He has done everything possible to make his novel seem a mere reflection. He has even donned the garb of populism. The reason is that his art is not gratuitous; he wants to prove something. But observe what a curious aim he has. He wants to show us this world, our own—to *show* it only, without explanations or comment. There are no revelations about the machinations of the police, the imperialism of the oil kings or the Ku-Klux-Klan, no cruel pictures of poverty. We have already seen everything he wants to show us, and, so it seems at first glance, seen it exactly as he wants us to see it. We recognize immediately the sad abundance of these untragic lives. They are our own lives, these innumerable, planned, botched, immediately forgotten and constantly renewed adventures that slip by without leaving a trace, without involving anyone, until the time when one of them, no different from any of the others, suddenly, as if through some clumsy trickery, sickens a man for good and throws a mechanism out of gear.

Now, it is by depicting, as we ourselves might depict, these too familiar appearances with which we all put up that Dos Passos makes them unbearable. He arouses indignation in people who never get indignant, he frightens people who fear nothing. But hasn't there been some sleight-of-hand? I look about me and see people, cities, boats, the war. But they aren't the real thing; they are discreetly queer and sinister, as in a nightmare. My indignation against this world also seems dubious to me; it only faintly resembles the other indignation, the kind that a mere news item can arouse. I am on the other side of the mirror.

Dos Passos' hate, despair and lofty contempt are real. But that is precisely why his world is not real; it is a created object. I know of none—not even Faulkner's or Kafka's—in which the art is greater or better hidden. I know of none that is more precious, more touching or closer to us. This is because he takes his material from our world. And yet, there is no stranger or more distant world. Dos Passos has invented only one thing, an art of story-telling. But that is enough to create a universe.

We live in time, we calculate in time. The novel, like life, unfolds in the present. The perfect tense exists on the surface only; it must be interpreted as a present *with aesthetic distance,* as a stage device. In the novel the dice are not loaded, for fictional man is free. He develops before our eyes; our impatience, our ignorance, our expectancy are the same as the hero's. The tale, on the other hand, as Fernandez has shown, develops in the past. But the tale explains. Chronological order, life's order, barely conceals the causal order, which is an order for the understanding. The event does not touch us; it stands half-way between fact and law. Dos Passos' time is his own creation; it is neither fictional nor narrative. It is rather, if you like, historical time. The perfect and imperfect tenses are not used simply to observe the rules; the reality of Joe's or of Eveline's adventures lies in the fact they are now part of the past. Everything is told as if by someone who is remembering.

"The years Dick was little he never heard anything

about his Dad . . ." "All Eveline thought about *that winter* was going to the Art Institute . . ." "They waited two weeks in Vigo while the officials quarrelled about their status and they got pretty fed up with it."

The fictional event is a nameless presence; there is nothing one can say about it, for it develops. We may be shown two men combing a city for their mistresses, but we are not told that they "do not find them," for this is not true. So long as there remains one street, one café, one house to explore, it is not yet true. In Dos Passos, the things that happen are named first, and then the dice are cast, as they are in our memories.

Glen and Joe only got ashore for a few hours and couldn't find Marcelline and Loulou.

The facts are clearly outlined; they are ready for *thinking about*. But Dos Passos never thinks them. Not for an instant does the order of causality betray itself in chronological order. There is no narrative, but rather the jerky unreeling of a rough and uneven memory, which sums up a period of several years in a few words only to dwell languidly over a minute fact. Like our real memories, it is a jumble of miniatures and frescoes. There is relief enough, but it is cunningly scattered at random. One step further would give us the famous idiot's monologue in *The Sound and the Fury*. But that would still involve intellectualizing, suggesting an explanation in terms of the irrational, suggesting a Freudian order beneath this disorder. Dos Passos stops just in time. As a result of this, past things retain a flavour of the present; they still remain, in their exile, what they once were, inexplicable tumults of colour, sound and passion. Each event is irreducible, a gleaming and solitary *thing* that does not flow from anything else, but suddenly arises to join other things. For Dos Passos, narrating means adding. This accounts for the slack air of his style. "And . . . and . . . and . . ." The great disturbing phenomena—war, love, political movements, strikes—fade and crumble into an infinity of little odds and ends which can just about be set side by side. Here is the armistice:

> In early November rumours of an armistice began to fly around and then suddenly one afternoon Major Wood ran into the office that Eleanor and Eveline shared and dragged them both away from their desks and kissed them both and shouted, "At last it's come." Before she knew it Eveline found herself kissing Major Moorehouse right on the mouth. The Red Cross office turned into a college dormitory the night of a football victory: It was the Armistice.
>
> Everybody seemed suddenly to have bottles of cognac and to be singing, *There's a long long trail awinding* or *La Made-lon pour nous n'est pas sévère.*

These Americans see war the way Fabrizio saw the battle of Waterloo. And the intention, like the method, is clear upon reflection. But you must close the book and reflect.

Passions and gestures are also things. Proust analysed them, related them to former states and thereby made them inevitable. Dos Passos wants to retain only their factual nature. All he is allowed to say is, "In that place and at that time Richard was that way, and at another time, he was different." Love and decisions are great spheres that rotate on their own axes. The most we can grasp is a kind of *conformity* between the psychological state and the exterior situation, something resembling a colour harmony. We may also suspect that explanations are *possible,* but they seem as frivolous and futile as a spider-web on a heavy red flower. Yet, never do we have the feeling of fictional freedom: Dos Passos imposes upon us instead the unpleasant impression of an indeterminacy of detail. Acts, emotions and ideas suddenly settle within a character, make themselves at home and then disappear without his having much to say in the matter. You cannot say he submits to them. He experiences them. There seems to be no law governing their appearance.

Nevertheless, they once did exist. This lawless past is irremediable. Dos Passos has purposely chosen the perspective of history to tell a story. He wants to make us feel that the stakes are down. In *Man's Hope*, Malraux says, more or less, that "the tragic thing about death is that it transforms life into a destiny." With the opening lines of his book, Dos Passos settles down into death. The lives he tells about are all closed in on themselves. They resemble those Bergsonian memories which, after the body's death, float about, lifeless and full of odours and lights and cries, through some forgotten limbo. We constantly have the feeling that these vague, human lives are destinies. Our own past is not at all like this. There is not one of our acts whose meaning and value we cannot still transform even now. But beneath the violent colours of these beautiful, motley objects that Dos Passos presents there is something petrified. Their significance is fixed. Close your eyes and try to remember your own life, try to remember it *that way;* you will stifle. It is this unrelieved stifling that Dos Passos wanted to express. In capitalist society, men do not have lives, they have only destinies. He never says this, but he makes it felt throughout. He expresses it discreetly, cautiously, until we feel like smashing our destinies. We have become rebels; he has achieved his purpose.

We are rebels *behind the looking-glass.* For that is not what the rebel of this world wants to change. He wants to transform Man's *present* condition, the one that develops day by day. Using the past tense to tell about the present means using a device, creating a strange and beautiful world, as frozen as one of those Mardi-Gras masks that become frightening on the faces of real, living men.

But whose memories are these that unfold through the novel? At first glance, they seem to be those of the heroes, of Joe, Dick, Fillette and Eveline. And, on occasion, they are. As a rule, whenever a character is sincere, whenever he is bursting with something, no matter how, or with what:

> When he went off duty he'd walk home achingly tired through the strawberry-scented early Parisian morning, thinking of the faces and the eyes and the sweat-drenched hair and the clenched fingers clotted with blood and dirt . . .

But the narrator often ceases to coincide completely with the hero. The hero could not quite have said what he does say, but you feel a discreet complicity between them. The narrator relates from the outside what the hero would have wanted him to relate. By means of this complicity, Dos Passos, without warning us, has us make the transition he was after. We suddenly find ourselves inside a horrible memory whose every recollection makes us uneasy, a bewildering memory that is no longer that of either the characters or the author. It seems like a chorus that remembers, a sententious chorus that is accessory to the deed.

All the same he got along very well at school and the teachers liked him, particularly Miss Teazle, the English teacher, because he had nice manners and said little things that weren't fresh but that made them laugh. Miss Teazle said he showed real feeling for English composition. One Christmas he sent her a little rhyme he made up about the Christ Child and the three Kings and she declared he had a gift.

The narration takes on a slightly stilted manner, and everything that is reported about the hero assumes the solemn quality of a public announcement: ". . . she declared he had a gift." The sentence is not accompanied by any comment, but acquires a sort of collective resonance. It is a *declaration*. And indeed, whenever we want to know his characters' thoughts, Dos Passos, with respectful objectivity, generally gives us their declarations.

Fred . . . said the last night before they left he was going to tear loose. When they got to the front he might get killed and then what? Dick said he liked talking to the girls but that the whole business was too commercial and turned his stomach. Ed Schuyler, who'd been nicknamed Frenchie and was getting very continental in his ways, said that the street girls were too naive.

I open *Paris-Soir* and read, *"From our special correspondent:* Charlie Chaplin declares that he has put an end to

Charlie." Now I have it! Dos Passos reports all his characters'
utterances to us in the style of a statement to the Press. Their
words are thereby cut off from thought, and become pure
utterances, simple reactions that must be registered as such,
in the behaviourist style upon which Dos Passos draws when
it suits him to do so. But, at the same time, the utterance
takes on a social importance; it is inviolable, it becomes a
maxim. Little does it matter, thinks the satisfied chorus, what
Dick had in mind when he spoke that sentence. What matters
is that it has been uttered. Besides, it was not formed inside
him, it came from afar. Even before he uttered it, it existed
as a pompous sound, a taboo. All he has done is to lend it
his power of affirmation. It is as if there were a Platonic
heaven of words and commonplaces to which we all go to
find words suitable to a given situation. There is a heaven
of gestures, too. Dos Passos makes a pretence of presenting
gestures as pure events, as mere exteriors, as free, animal
movements. But this is only appearance. Actually, in relating
them, he adopts the point of view of the chorus, of public
opinion. There is no single one of Dick's or of Eleanor's
gestures which is not a public demonstration, performed to
a humming accompaniment of flattery.

At Chantilly they went through the château and fed the
big carp in the moat. They ate their lunch in the woods,
sitting on rubber cushions. J.W. kept everybody laughing
explaining how he hated picnics, asking everybody what it
was that got into even the most intelligent women that they
were always trying to make people go on picnics. After
lunch they drove out to Senlis to see the houses that the
Uhlans had destroyed there in the battle of the Marne.

Doesn't it sound like a local newspaper's account of an ex-
servicemen's banquet? All of a sudden, as the gesture dwindles
until it is no more than a thin film, we see that it *counts,* that it
is sacred in character and that, at the same time, it involves
commitment. But for whom? For the abject consciousness of
"everyman," for what Heidegger calls "das Mann." But still,
where does it spring from? Who is its representative as I

read? *I* am. In order to understand the words, in order to make sense out of the paragraphs, I first have to adopt his point of view. I have to play the role of the obliging chorus. This consciousness exists only through me; without me there would be nothing but black spots on white paper. But even while I *am* this collective consciousness, I want to wrench away from it, to see it from the judge's point of view, that is, to get free of myself. This is the source of the shame and uneasiness with which Dos Passos knows how to fill the reader. I am a reluctant accomplice (though I am not even sure that I am reluctant), creating and rejecting social taboos. I am, deep in my heart, a revolutionary again, an unwilling one.

In return, how I hate Dos Passos' men! I am given a fleeting glimpse of their minds, just enough to see that they are living animals. Then, they begin to unwind their endless tissue of ritual statements and sacred gestures. For them, there is no break between inside and outside, between body and consciousness, but only between the stammerings of an individual's timid, intermittent, fumbling thinking and the messy world of collective representations. What a simple process this is, and how effective! All one need do is use American journalistic technique in telling the story of a life, and like the Salzburg reed, a life crystallizes into the Social, and the problem of the transition to the typical—stumbling-block of the social novel—is thereby resolved. There is no further need to present a working man type, to compose (as Nizan does in *Antoine Bloyé*) an existence which represents the exact average of thousands of existences. Dos Passos, on the contrary, can give all his attention to rendering a single life's special character. Each of his characters is unique; what happens to him could happen to no one else. What does it matter, since Society has marked him more deeply than could any special circumstance, since *he is* Society? Thus, we get a glimpse of an order beyond the accidents of fate or the contingency of detail, an order more supple than Zola's physiological necessity or Proust's psychological mechanism, a soft and insinuating constraint which seems to release its victims, letting them go only to take possession of them again without their suspecting, in other words, a statistical determinism. These men, submerged in their own existences, live as they can. They struggle; what comes their way is not determined in advance. And yet, neither their efforts, their faults, nor their most extreme violence can interfere with the regularity of births, marriages and suicides. The pressure exerted by a gas on the walls of its container does not depend upon the individual histories of the molecules composing it.

We are still on the other side of the looking-glass. Yesterday you saw your best friend and expressed to him your passionate hatred of war. Now try to relate this conversation to yourself in the style of Dos Passos. "And they ordered two beers and said that war was hateful. Paul declared he would rather do anything than fight and John said he agreed with him and both got excited and said they were glad they agreed. On his way home, Paul decided to see John more often." You will start hating yourself immediately. It will not take you long, however, to decide that you *cannot* use this tone in talking about yourself. However insincere you may have been, you were at least living out your insincerity, playing it out on your own, continuously creating and extending its existence from one moment to the next. And even if you got caught up in collective representations, you had first to experience them as personal resignation. We are neither mechanical objects nor possessed souls, but something worse; we are free. We exist either entirely *within* or entirely *without*. Dos Passos' man is a hybrid creature, an interior-exterior being. We go on living with him and within him, with his vacillating, individual consciousness, when suddenly it wavers, weakens, and is diluted in the collective consciousness. We follow it up to that point and suddenly, before we notice, we are on the outside. The man behind the looking-glass is a strange, contemptible, fascinating creature. Dos Passos knows how to use this constant shifting to fine effect. I know of nothing more gripping than Joe's death.

Joe laid out a couple of frogs and was backing off towards the door, when he saw in the mirror that a big guy in a blouse was bringing down a bottle on his head held with both hands. He tried to swing around but he didn't have time. The bottle crashed his skull and he was out.

We are inside with him, until the shock of the bottle on his skull. Then immediately, we find ourselves outside with the chorus, part of the collective memory, ". . . and he was out." Nothing gives you a clearer feeling of annihilation. And from then on, each page we turn, each page that tells of other minds and of a world going on without Joe, is like a spadeful of earth over our bodies. But it is a behind-the-looking-glass death: all we really get is the fine *appearance* of nothingness. True nothingness can neither be felt nor thought. Neither you nor I, nor anyone after us, will ever have anything to say about our real deaths.

Dos Passos' world—like those of Faulkner, Kafka and Stendhal—is impossible because it is contradictory. But therein lies its beauty. Beauty is a veiled contradiction. I regard Dos Passos as the greatest writer of our time.

(*August* 1938)

Chapter 8

Individualism and Conformism in the United States

HOW IS ONE TO TALK about 135 million Americans when we have only six weeks to spend here? It would require a ten-year stay. We are set down in a city where we pick up a few details. Yesterday it was Baltimore, today it is Knoxville, the day after tomorrow it will be New Orleans, and then, after admiring the biggest factory or the biggest bridge or the biggest dam in the world, we fly away with our heads full of figures and statistics.

We shall have seen more steel and aluminum than human beings. But can one talk about steel? As to "impressions," they come as they please.

"Stick to facts!" some people tell us.

But what facts? The length of a certain shipyard, or the electric blue of the oxyhydrogen blowpipe in the pale light of a shed? In choosing, I am already making a decision as to what America is.

On the other hand, some people say, "Get some perspective!" But I distrust those perspectives that are already generalizations. I have therefore decided to set forth my personal impressions and interpretations, on my own responsibility. This America may be something I've dreamed up. In any case, I will be honest with my dream: I shall set it forth just as it came to me.

And today I should like to tell you my impressions of two contradictory slogans that are current in Paris: "Americans are conformists" and "Americans are individualists."

Like everyone else, I had heard of the famous American "melting pot" that transforms, at different temperatures, Poles, Italians and Finns into United States citizens. But I did not quite know what the term really meant.

Now, the day after my arrival I met a European who was

in the process of being melted down. I was introduced, in the big lobby of the Plaza Hotel, to a dark man of rather medium height who, like everyone here, talked with a somewhat nasal twang, without seeming to move his lips or cheeks, who would burst out laughing with his mouth, but who didn't laugh with his eyes, and who expressed himself in good French, with a heavy accent, though his speech was sprinkled with Americanisms and barbarisms.

When I congratulated him on his knowledge of our language, he replied with astonishment, "But I'm a Frenchman!" He had been born in Paris, had been living in America for only fifteen years and, before the war, had returned to France every six months. Nevertheless, America already half-possessed him. His mother had never left Paris. When he talked, with a deliberately vulgar accent, about "Paname," he seemed much more like a Yankee bent on displaying his knowledge of Europe than an exiled Frenchman recalling his native land. He felt obliged every now and then to throw a roguish wink in my direction and exclaim: "Aha! New Orleans, pretty girls!" But what he was really doing was living up to the American image of the Frenchman rather than trying to be obliging to a fellow-countryman. "Pretty girls," he said with a forced laugh; I felt Puritanism just round the corner, and a chill ran through me.

I felt as if I were witnessing an Ovidian metamorphosis. The man's face was still too expressive. It had retained the slightly irritating mimicry of intelligence which makes a French face recognizable anywhere. But he will soon be a tree or a rock. I speculated curiously as to the powerful forces that had to be brought into play in order to achieve these disintegrations and reintegrations so surely and rapidly.

But these forces are mild and persuasive. You have only to walk about in the streets, enter a shop or turn on a radio to meet them and feel their effect upon you, like a warm breath.

In America—at least the America with which I'm familiar —you are never alone in the street. The walls talk to you. To left and right of you there are advertisement hoardings, illuminated signs and immense display windows which contain only a big placard with a photographic montage or some statistics. You see a distressed-looking woman offering her lips to an American soldier, or an aeroplane bombing a town and, under the picture, the words, "Bibles, not bombs." The nation walks about with you, giving you advice and orders. But it does so in an undertone and is careful to explain its admonition in minute detail. There is not a single command, whether in a cosmetic advertisement ("Today, more than ever, it is your duty to be beautiful. Take care of your face for *his* return. Buy X . . . Cream") or in a piece of War Bond propaganda, which is not accompanied by a brief comment or explanatory picture.

Yesterday I lunched at a restaurant in Fontana, an artificial town built about a great dam in Tennessee.

Along the busy highway leading to the dam is a big hoarding with a parable, in cartoon form, on the subject of teamwork. Two donkeys tied to each other are trying to reach two hay-stacks which are a certain distance apart. Each donkey is tugging on the halter in an opposite direction. They half-strangle each other. But finally they understand. They come together and start working on the first haystack. When they have eaten it, we see them biting together into the second one.

Obviously the commentary has been deliberately avoided. The passer-by *must* draw the conclusion *himself*. There is no pressure put on him. On the contrary, the cartoon is an appeal to his intelligence. He is obliged to interpret and understand it; he is not bludgeoned with it as with the loud Nazi propaganda posters. It remains in half-tone. It requires his co-operation in order to be deciphered. Once he has understood, it is as though he himself has conceived the idea. He is more than half convinced.

Loudspeakers have been installed in factories everywhere. They are meant to combat the worker's isolation in the presence of matter. At first, when you go through the immense navy yard near Baltimore, you find the human dispersion, that great solitude of the worker, with which we are familiar in Europe. All day long, masked men, bending over steel plates, manipulate their oxyhydrogen blowpipes. But as soon as they put on their helmets they can hear music. And even the music is a kind of guidance that stealthily insinuates itself into them; even the music is a directed dream. And then the music stops, and they are given information about the war or their work.

When we were leaving Fontana, the engineer who had so kindly escorted us all about led us into a little glass-enclosed room in which a new wax disc, already prepared to record our voices, was revolving on a turntable. He explained that all the foreigners who had visited the dam had, on leaving, summed up their impressions before the microphone. Far be it from us to refuse such a kind host; those of us who spoke English said something and the speeches were recorded. The following day they would be broadcast in the yard, the cafeteria and in every house in town, and the workers would be pleased to learn of the excellent impression they had made upon the foreigners and would work with an even greater will.

Add to this the advice given on the radio, the letters to the newspapers, and, above all, the activities of the innumerable organizations whose aims are almost always educational, and you will see that the American citizen is quite hedged in.

But it would be a mistake to regard this as an oppressive tactic on the part of the government or the big American capitalists.

Of course, the present government is at war; it has to use methods like these for war propaganda. In addition, one of the government's principal concerns is education.

In Tennessee, for example, where the farmers had been ruining the soil by planting corn every year, it is trying hard to teach them gradually to let the soil rest by varying the crops from year to year. And in order to achieve its purpose, it has mingled gifts (low-priced electricity, free irrigation) with rational arguments. But there is a much more spontaneous and diffuse phenomenon involved here.

This educative tendency really springs from the heart of the community. Every American is educated by other Americans and educates others in turn. All through New York, in the schools and elsewhere, there are courses in Americanization.

Everything is taught: sewing, cooking, and even flirting. A school in New York gives a course for girls on how to get their boy-friends to propose to them. All of this is directed at forming pure Americans rather than men. But the American makes no distinction between American reason and ordinary reason. All the advice with which his path is marked is so perfectly motivated, so penetrating, that he feels lulled by an immense solicitude that never leaves him helpless or abandoned.

I have known modern mothers who never ordered their children to do anything without first persuading them to obey. In this way they acquired a more complete and perhaps more formidable authority over their children than if they had threatened or beaten them. In the same way, the American, whose reason and freedom are called upon at every hour of the day, makes it a point of honour to do as he is asked. It is when he is acting like everyone else that he feels most reasonable and most American; it is in displaying his conformism that he feels freest.

As far as I can judge, the American nation's characteristic traits are the opposite of those which Hitler imposed upon Germany and which Maurras wanted to impose upon France.

To Hitler (or Maurras), an argument was good for Germany if it was, first of all, German. If it had the slightest whiff of universality, it was always suspect.

The peculiarity of the American, on the other hand, is the fact that he regards his thought as universal. One can discern in this a Puritan influence which I need not go into here. But above all, there is that concrete, daily presence of a flesh and blood Reason, a visible Reason. Thus, most of the people I spoke with seemed to have a naïve and passionate faith in the virtues of Reason. An American said to me one evening, "After all, if international politics were in the hands of well-balanced and reasonable men, wouldn't war be abolished for ever?" Some French people present said that this did not necessarily follow, and he got angry. "All right," he said in scornful indignation, "go and build cemeteries!" I, for my part, said nothing; discussion between us was impossible. I believe in the existence of evil and he does not.

It is this Rousseau-like optimism which, where Nazi Germany is concerned, cuts him off from our point of view. In order to admit the existence of such atrocities, he would have to admit that men can be wholly bad. "Do you think there are two Germanys?" an American doctor asked me. I replied that I didn't.

"I understand," he said. "France has suffered so much that you are unable to think otherwise. It's too bad."

And then there is the machine, which also acts as a universalizing factor. There is generally only one way of using a mechanical object, namely, the one indicated in the accompanying leaflet. The American uses his mechanical corkscrew, his refrigerator or his automobile in the same way and at the same time as all other Americans. Besides, this object is not made to order. It is meant for anyone and will obey anyone, provided he knows how to use it correctly.

Thus, when the American puts a nickel into the slot in the tram or in the underground, he feels just like everyone else. Not like an anonymous unit, but like a man who has divested himself of his individuality and raised himself to the impersonality of the Universal.

It was this complete freedom in conformism that struck me at the very beginning. There is no freer city than New York. You can do as you please there. It is public opinion that plays the role of the policeman. The few Americans I met seemed to me at first to conform through freedom, to be depersonalized through rationalism. They seemed to identify Universal Reason with their own particular nation, within the framework of the same creed.

But almost immediately I discovered their profound individualism. This combination of social conformism and individualism is, perhaps, what a Frenchman will have most difficulty in understanding. For us, individualism has retained the old, classical form of "the individual's struggle against society and, more particularly, against the State." There is no question of this in America. In the first place, for a long time the State was only an administrative body. In recent years it has tended to play another role, but this has not changed the American's attitude towards it. It is "their" State, the expression of "their" nation; they have both a profound respect for it and a proprietary love.[1]

If you merely walk about in New York for a few days you cannot fail to notice the deep link between American conformism and American individuality. Seen flat on the ground from the point of length and width, New York is the most conformist city in the world. From Washington Square north, there is not a single oblique or curving street, with the exception of old Broadway. A dozen long, parallel furrows go straight from the tip of Manhattan to the Harlem River. These are the avenues, which are intersected by hundreds of smaller furrows rigorously perpendicular to them.

This chequerboard is New York. The streets look so much alike that they have not been named. They have merely been given registration numbers, like soldiers.

But if you look up, everything changes. Seen in its height, New York is the triumph of individualism. The tops of the buildings defy all the rules of town planning. They have twenty-seven, fifty-five and a hundred storeys. They are grey, brown or white, Moorish, medieval, renaissance or modern. On lower Broadway, they press against each other, dwarfing the tiny black churches, and then, suddenly, they separate, leaving between them a gaping hole of light. Seen from Brooklyn they seem to have the nobility and solitude of bouquets of palm trees on the banks of rivers in Moroccan Susa—bouquets of skyscrapers which the eye is always trying to assemble and which are always coming undone.

Thus, at first, American individualism seemed like a third dimension. It is not incompatible with conformism, but, on the contrary, implies it. It represents, however, a new direction, both in height and depth, within conformism.

First, there is the struggle for existence, which is extremely harsh. Every individual wants to succeed, that is, to make

---

[1] An R.P.F. gang tried to disrupt a political meeting in which I happened to be participating, and the affair ended in a brawl. An American who shared our ideas was amazed that we did not call in the police. I explained our reluctance, but he remained upset. "Back home," he told me, "the police force belongs to all the citizens. We find it *natural* to turn to them for help."

money. But this is not to be regarded as greed or merely a taste for luxury. In the States, money is, I think, the necessary but symbolic token of success. You must succeed because success is a proof of virtue and intelligence and also because it shows that you enjoy divine protection.

And you must also succeed because only then can you face the crowd as a person. Take the American newspapers. So long as you have not achieved success, you cannot expect your articles to appear in the form in which you have submitted them. They will be cut and pruned. But if you have a money-making name, then everything changes; what you write will go through without cuts. You have acquired the right to be yourself.

The same situation holds in the theatre. A lady very well versed in French literature and known in publishing circles asked me if I should like to have a play of mine done in the States. I replied that I should be delighted were it not for the fact that producers were in the habit of modifying the texts submitted to them. She seemed highly surprised and said: "If they don't, who will? What you have written is meant to be read. But they have to work on it to make understandable." [2]

Thus, in the struggle for life, American individuality is, above all, each person's passionate aspiration toward the state of the individual. There are individuals in America, just as there are skyscrapers. There are Ford and Rockefeller, and Hemingway and Roosevelt. They are models and examples.

The buildings are, in this sense, votive offerings to success. Behind the Statue of Liberty, they are like the statues of a man or an undertaking which has risen above the rest. They are immense publicity ventures, constructed in large part to demonstrate the financial triumph of individuals or groups. The owner occupies only a small part of the premises and rents out the rest. Thus, I was not mistaken in taking them for symbols of New York individualism. They simply demon-

[2] This is the source of the misunderstanding in the Kravchenko case. Since re-writing is an accepted practice in America, Kravchenko is regarded by Americans as the author of his book. We, on the contrary, have some difficulty in considering him as such.

strate that, in the United States, individuality is something to be won. That is probably the reason why New York seemed so passionately attached to a liberal economy.

Yet everyone knows of the power of trusts in the United States, a power which represents another form of controlled economy. But the New Yorker has not forgotten the period when a man could win a fortune by his personal initiative. What he dislikes about the controlled economy is the red tape. Thus, paradoxically enough, the same man who so obediently submits to guidance in public and private life is intransigent where his job is concerned. The reason is that this is the area of his independence, his initiative and his personal dignity.

As for the rest, there are the "associations." In 1930 it was estimated that in Washington there were more than five hundred group and association headquarters. I shall mention only one, the Foreign Policy Association.

On the seventeenth floor of the building we met, "over a cup of tea," a few of those tall, grey-haired, pleasant, but somewhat cold women, intelligent as men, who, ever since the beginning of the war, represent the majority of members of these associations. They told us how, in 1917, a certain number of people, firmly convinced that the United States was entering the war with no knowledge of foreign affairs, had decided to devote their free time to supplying the country with the knowledge it lacked.

The Association now has 26,000 members, with 300 branches in the various states. Its bulletin is sent to more than 500 newspapers. Its publications are consulted by political leaders. It has, moreover, given up the idea of informing the general public; it informs the informers (scholars, teachers, clergymen and journalists). It publishes a weekly bulletin containing a study of an international question and an analysis of happenings in Washington. Every fortnight it issues a bulletin to the newspapers which then reprint it in whole or in part.

Try to imagine an association of this kind in the France of 1939 providing information for Bonnet or Daladier and sending its periodicals to Maurras for *Action Française* and to Cachin for *l'Humanité*.

But I was particularly struck with our hostess' last words. "What we do," she said, "is to protect the individual. Outside the clubs, a man is alone. Inside, he is a person. By belonging to several of them he protects himself against any particular one." The meaning of this individualism is plain to see. The citizen must, first of all, fit himself into a framework and protect himself; he must enter into a social contract with other citizens of his own kind. And it is this small community which confers upon him his individual function and personal worth. Within the association, he can take the initiative, can advocate his personal political views and influence, if he is able to, the line of the group.

Just as the solitary person arouses suspicion in the States, so this controlled, hedged-in individualism is encouraged. This is demonstrated, on quite another level, by industrialists' attempts to encourage self-criticism among their personnel.

When the worker is organized, when the propaganda of government and management has sufficiently integrated him into the community, he is *then* asked to distinguish himself from others and to prove his initiative. More than once near factory entrances we came upon brightly coloured booths in which improvements suggested by employees and snapshots of their inventors, who were frequently rewarded, were displayed behind glass.

I have said enough, I hope, to give some idea of how the American is subjected, from the cradle to the grave, to an intense drive to organize and Americanize him, of how he is first depersonalized by means of a constant appeal to his reason, civic sense and freedom, and how, once he has been duly fitted into the national life by professional associations and educational and other edifying organizations, he suddenly regains consciousness of himself and his personal autonomy. He is then free to escape into an almost Nietzschean individualism, the kind symbolized by the skyscrapers in the bright sky of New York. In any event, it is not based on our kind of individualism, but on conformism. Personality must be won. It is a social function or the affirmation of society.

(*February* 1945)

Chapter 9

American Cities

FOR THE FIRST FEW DAYS I was lost. My eyes were not accustomed to the skyscrapers and they did not surprise me; they did not seem like man-made, man-inhabited constructions, but rather like rocks and hills, dead parts of the urban landscape one finds in cities built on a turbulent soil and which you pass without even noticing. At the same time, I was continually and vainly looking for something to catch my attention for a moment—a detail, a square, perhaps, or a public building. I did not yet know that these houses and streets should be seen in the mass.

In order to learn to live in these cities and to like them as Americans do, I had to fly over the immense deserts of the west and south. Our European cities, submerged in human countrysides that have been worked over mile by mile, are continuous. And then we are vaguely aware that far away, across the sea, there is the desert, a myth. For the American, this myth is an everyday reality. We flew for hours between New Orleans and San Francisco, over an earth that was dry and red, clotted with verdigris bushes. Suddenly, a city, a little checkerboard flush with the ground, arose and then, again, the red earth, the Savannah, the twisted rocks of the Grand Canyon, and the snows of the Rocky Mountains.

After a few days of this diet, I came to understand that the American city was, originally, a camp in the desert. People from far away, attracted by a mine, a petroleum field or fertile land, arrived one fine day and settled as quickly as possible in a clearing, near a river. They built the vital parts of the town, the bank, the town hall, the church, and then hundreds of one-storey frame houses. The road, if there was one, served as a kind of spinal column to the town, and then streets were marked out like vertebrae, perpendicular to the road. It would be hard to count the American cities that have that kind of parting in the middle.

Nothing has changed since the time of the covered wagons; every year towns are founded in the United States, and they are founded according to the same methods.

Take Fontana, Tennessee, which is situated near one of the great T.V.A. dams. Twelve years ago there were pine-trees growing in the mountain's red soil. As soon as the construction of the dam began, the pines were felled and three towns —two white ones of 3000 and 5000 inhabitants each, and one Negro town—sprang from the soil. The workers live there with their families; four or five years ago, when work was in full swing, one birth was recorded each day. Half of the village looks like a pile-dwellers' community: the houses are of wood, with green roofs, and have been built on piles to avoid dampness. The other half is made of collapsible dwellings, "prefabricated houses." They too are of wood; they are constructed about 500 miles away and loaded onto trucks: a single team of men can set one up within four hours after its arrival. The smallest costs the employer two thousand dollars, and he rents them to his workers for nineteen dollars a month (thirty-one dollars if they are furnished). The interiors, with their mass-produced furniture, central heating, electric lamps, and refrigerators, remind one of ship cabins. Every square inch of these antiseptic little rooms has been utilized; the walls have clothes-presses and under the beds there are chests of drawers.

One leaves with a slightly depressed feeling, with the feeling of having seen the careful, small-scale reconstitution of a 1944 flat in the year 3000. The moment one steps outside one sees hundreds of houses, all alike, piled up, squashed against the earth, but retaining in their very form some sort of nomadic look. It looks like a caravan graveyard. The pile-dweller community and the caravan cemetery face one another. Between them a wide road climbs toward the pines. There you have a city, or rather the nucleus of an American city, with all its essential parts. Below is the Woolworth's, higher up the hospital, and at the top, a "mixed" church in which what might be called a minimum service—that is, one valid for all creeds—is conducted.

The striking thing is the lightness, the fragility of these

buildings. The village has no weight, it seems barely to rest on the soil; it has not managed to leave a human imprint on the reddish earth and the dark forest; it is a temporary thing. And besides, it will soon take to the road; in two years the dam will be finished, the workers will leave, and the pre-fabricated houses will be taken down and sent to a Texas oil well or a Georgia cotton plantation, to reconstitute another Fontana, under other skies, with new inhabitants.

This roving village is no exception; in the United States, communities are born as they die—in a day. The Americans have no complaint to make; the main thing is to be able to carry their homes with them. These homes are the collections of objects, furnishings, photographs, and souvenirs belonging to them, that reflect their own image and constitute the inner, living landscape of their dwellings. These are their penates. Like Aeneas, they haul them about everywhere.

The "house" is the shell; it is abandoned on the slightest pretext.

We have workers' communities in France. But they are sedentary, and then they never become real cities; on the contrary, they are the artificial product of neighbouring cities. In America, just as any citizen can theoretically become President, so each Fontana can become Detroit or Minne-apolis; all that is needed is a bit of luck. And conversely, Detroit and Minneapolis are Fontanas which have had luck. To take only one example: in 1905 Detroit had a population of 300,000. Its population is now 1,000,000.

The inhabitants of this city are perfectly aware of this luck; they like to recall in their books and films the time when their community was only an outpost. And that is why they pass so easily from city to outpost; they make no distinction between the two. Detroit and Minneapolis, Knoxville and Memphis were *born temporary* and have stayed that way. They will never, of course, take to the road again on the back of a truck. But they remain at the meeting point; they have never reached an internal temperature of solidification.

Things that would not constitute a change of situation for us are, for the American, occasions for real breaks with his past. There are many who, on going off to war, have sold their apartments and everything else, including their suits. What is the point of keeping something that will be outmoded upon their return? Soldiers' wives often reduce their scale of living and go to live more modestly in other neighbourhoods. Thus, sadness and faithfulness to the absent are marked by a removal.

The removals also indicate fluctuations in American fortunes.

It is customary, in the United States, for the fashionable neighbourhoods to slide from the centre to the outskirts of the city; after five years the centre of town is "polluted." If you walk about there, you come upon tumble-down houses that retain a pretentious look beneath their filth; you find a complicated kind of architecture, one-storey frame houses with entrances formed by peristyles supported by columns, gothic chalets, "Colonial houses," etc. These were formerly aristocratic homes, now inhabited by the poor. Chicago's lurid Negro section contains some of these Greco-Roman temples; from the outside they still look well. But inside, twelve rat- and louse-plagued Negro families are crowded together in five or six rooms.

At the same time, changes are continually made within the same place. An apartment house is bought to be demolished, and a larger apartment house is built on the same plot. After five years, the new house is sold to a contractor who tears it down to build a third one. The result is that in the States a city is a moving landscape for its inhabitants, whereas our cities are our shells.

In France, one hears only from very old people what a forty-year-old American said to me in Chicago. "When I was young, this whole neighbourhood was taken up by a lake. But this part of the lake was filled in and built over." And a thirty-five-year-old lawyer who was showing me the Negro section said: "I was born here. Then it was a white section and, apart from servants, you would not have seen a Negro in the streets. Now the white people have left and 250,000 Negroes are crowded into their houses."

M. Verdier, the owner of the "City of Paris" department store in San Francisco, witnessed the earthquake and fire that

destroyed three quarters of the city. At that time he was a
young man; he remembers the disaster perfectly. He watched
the reconstruction of the city which still had an Asiatic look
around 1913, and then its rapid Americanization. Thus, he
has superimposed memories of three San Franciscos.

We Europeans change within changeless cities, and our
houses and neighbourhoods outlive us; American cities change
faster than their inhabitants do, and it is the inhabitants who
outlive the cities.

I am really visiting the United States in wartime; the vast
life of the American city has suddenly become petrified;
people hardly change their residences any more. But this
stagnation is entirely temporary; the cities have been immobilized like the dancer on the film-screen who stays with
his foot suspended in air when the film is stopped; one feels
all about one the rising of the sap which will burst open the
cities as soon as the war is ended.

First, there are immediate problems; Chicago's Negro
section will have to be rebuilt, for instance. The government
had begun this before Pearl Harbor. But the government-
built apartment houses barely managed to shelter 7000 people.
Now, there are 250,000 to be housed. Then the industrialists
want to enlarge and transform their factories; the famous
abattoirs of Chicago are going to be completely modernized.

Finally, the average American is obsessed by the image of
the "modern house" which is considerably publicized and
which will be, so we are told, a hundred times more com-
fortable than the present dwellings and whose construction
in huge quantities certainly has its place in the plans for
"industrial conversion" which are now springing up almost
everywhere.

When the war is over, America will certainly be seized with
a real construction fever. Today the American sees his city
objectively; he does not dream of finding it ugly, but thinks
it really old. If it were even older, like ours, he could find a
social past, a tradition in it. We generally live in our grand-
fathers' houses. Our streets reflect the customs and ways of
past centuries; they tend to filter the present; none of what
goes on in the Rue Montorgueil or the Rue Pot-de-Fer is

completely of the present. But the thirty-year-old American lives in a house that was built when he was twenty.

These houses that are too young to seem *old* seem merely outdated to them; they lag behind the other tools, the car that can be traded in every two years, the refrigerator or the wireless set. That is why they see their cities without vain sentimentality. They have grown slightly attached to them, as one becomes attached to one's car, but they consider them as instruments, rather than anything else, instruments to be exchanged for more convenient ones.

For us a city is, above all, a past; for them it is mainly a future; what they like in the city is everything it has not yet become and everything it can be.

What are the impressions of a European who arrives in an American city? First, he thinks he has been taken in. He has heard only about skyscrapers; New York and Chicago have been described to him as "upright cities." Now his first feeling is, on the contrary, that the average height of an American city is noticeably smaller than that of a French one. The immense majority of houses have only two storeys. Even in the very large cities, the five-storey apartment house is an exception.

Then he is struck by the lightness of the materials used. In the United States stone is less frequently used than in Europe. The skyscraper consists of a coating of concrete applied to a metal framework, and the other buildings are made of brick or wood. Even in the richest cities and the smartest sections, one often finds frame houses. New Orleans' lovely colonial houses are of wood; many of the pretty chalets belonging to the Hollywood stars and film-directors are made of wood; so are the "California style" cottages in San Francisco. Everywhere you find groups of frame houses crushed between two twenty-storeyed buildings.

The brick houses are the colour of dried blood, or, on the contrary, daubed and smeared with bright yellow, green or raw white.[1] In most of the cities, they are roofless cubes or

---

[1] Kisling and Masson have often complained of the fact that the urban landscape of the United States is not very stimulating to painting. I believe this is partly due to the fact that the cities

rectangular parallelepipeds, with severely flat façades. All these houses, hastily constructed and made expressly to be hastily demolished, obviously bear a strange resemblance to Fontana's "prefabricated houses."

The lightness of these jerry-built houses, their loud colours alternating with the sombre red of the bricks, the extraordinary variety of their decorations which does not manage to conceal the uniformity of their patterns, all give one the feeling, when in the middle of the city, of walking through the suburbs of a watering town, like Trouville or Cabourg or La Baule. Only those ephemeral seaside chalets with their pretentious architectural style and their fragility can convey to those of my French readers who have never seen the States an idea of the American apartment house.

To complete the impression, I should also like to add that sometimes one also thinks of an exposition-city, but an obsolescent, dirty one, like those that ten years later, in some park, survive the celebration that occasioned them. For these shanties quickly grow dirty, particularly in industrial sections.

Chicago, blackened by its smoke, clouded by the Lake Michigan fog, is a dark and gloomy red. Pittsburgh is more gloomy still. And there is nothing more immediately striking than the contrast between the formidable power, the inexhaustible abundance of what is called the "American Colossus" and the puny insignificance of those little houses that line the widest roads in the world. But on second thought, there is no clearer indication that America is not finished, that her ideas and plans, her social structure and her cities have only a strictly temporary reality.

These perfectly straight cities bear no trace of organization. Many of them have the rudimentary structure of a polypary. Los Angeles, in particular, is rather like a big earthworm that might be chopped into twenty pieces without being killed. If you go through this enormous urban cluster, probably the largest in the world, you come upon twenty

have already been painted. They do not have the hesitant colours of our own cities. What is one to do with these tones which already are art, or artifice at least? All one can do is leave them alone.

juxtaposed cities, strictly identical, each with its poor section, its business streets, night-clubs and smart suburb, and you get the impression that a medium-sized urban centre has schizogenetically reproduced itself twenty times.[2]

In America, where the neighbourhoods are added on to each other as the region's prosperity attracts new immigrants, this juxtaposition is the rule. You pass without any transition from a poor street into an aristocratic avenue; a promenade lined with skyscrapers, museums and public monuments and adorned with lawns and trees, suddenly stops short above a smoky station; one frequently discovers at the feet of the largest buildings, along an aristocratic avenue, a "zone" of miserable little kitchen-gardens.

This is due to the fact that these cities that move at a rapid rate are not constructed in order to grow old, but move forward like modern armies, encircling the islands of resistance they are unable to destroy; the past does not manifest itself in them as it does in Europe, through public monuments, but through survivals. The wooden bridge in Chicago which spans a canal two steps away from the world's highest skyscrapers is a survival. The elevated railways, rolling noisily through the central streets of New York and Chicago, supported by great iron pillars and cross-girders, nearly touching the façades of houses on either side, are survivals. They are there simply because no one has taken the time to tear them down, and as a kind of indication of work to be done.

You find this disorder in each individual vista. Nowhere have I seen so many empty lots. Of course they do have a definite function; they are used as car parks. But they break the alignment of the street nonetheless sharply for all that. Suddenly it seems as if a bomb had fallen on three or four houses, reducing them to powder, and as if they had just been swept out: this is a "parking space," two hundred square metres of bare earth with its sole ornament, perhaps, a poster on a big hoarding. Suddenly the city seems unfinished, badly assembled; suddenly you rediscover the desert and the big

---

[2] To convey an idea of this city to the reader, I suggest that he try to imagine, not one Côte d'Azur city, but the entire region between Cannes and Menton.

empty site: noticeable at Fontana. I remember this Los Angeles landscape in the middle of the city, two modern apartment houses, two white cubes framing an empty lot with the ground torn up—a parking space. A few abandoned-looking cars were parked there. A palm tree grew like a weed between the cars. Down at the bottom there was a steep grassy hill, rather like the fortification mounds we use for garbage disposal. On top of the mound was a frame house, and a little below this a string stretched between two little trees, with multi-coloured washing hanging out to dry. When one turned around the block of houses, the hill disappeared; its other side had been built up, covered with asphalt, streaked with tar roads, and pierced with a magnificent tunnel.

The most striking aspect of the American city is the vertical disorder. These brick shanties are of varying heights; I noted at random during a walk in Detroit the following successive proportions: one storey, two storeys, one storey, one storey, three storeys. You find the same proportions in Albuquerque or San Antonio, at the other end of the country. In depth, above this irregular crenellation, you see apartment houses of all shapes and dimensions, long cases, thick thirty-storeyed boxes with forty windows to a storey. As soon as there is a bit of fog the colours fade away, and only volumes remain—every variety of polyhedron. Between them, you have enormous empty spaces, empty lots cut out in the sky.

In New York, and even in Chicago, the skyscraper is on home ground, and imposes a new order upon the city. But everywhere else it is out of place; the eye is unable to establish any unity between these tall, gawky things and the little houses that run close to the ground; in spite of itself it looks for that line so familiar in European cities, the sky-line, and cannot find it. That is why the European feels at first as though he were travelling through a rocky chaos that resembles a city—something like Montpellier-le-Vieux—rather than a city.

But the European makes a mistake in visiting American cities as one does Paris or Venice; they are not meant to be seen that way. The streets here do not have the same meaning as our streets. In Europe, a street is half-way between the path of communication and the sheltered "public place." It is on a footing with the cafés, as proved by the use of the "terrasses" that spring up on the sidewalks of the cafés in fine weather. Thus it changes its aspect more than a hundred times a day, for the crowd that throngs the European street changes, and men are its primary element. The American street is a piece of highway. It sometimes stretches over many miles. It does not stimulate one to walk. Ours are oblique and twisting, full of bends and secrets. The American street is a straight line that gives itself away immediately. It contains no mystery. You see the street straight through, from one end to the other no matter what your location in it. And the distances in American cities are too great to permit moving about on foot; in most of them one gets about almost exclusively in cars, on buses and by underground. Sometimes, while going from one appointment to another, I have been carried like a parcel from underground to escalator, from escalator to elevator, from elevator to taxi, from taxi to bus and, again, by metro and elevator, without walking a step.

In certain cities I noticed a real atrophy of the sidewalk. In Los Angeles, for example, on La Cienega, which is lined with bars, theatres, restaurants, antique dealers and private residences, the sidewalks are scarcely more than side-streets that lead customers and guests from the roadway into the house. Lawns have been planted from the façades to the roadway of this luxurious avenue. I followed a narrow path between the lawns for a long time without meeting a living soul, while to my right, cars streaked by on the road; all animation in the street had taken refuge on the high road.

New York and Chicago do not have neighbourhoods, but they do have a neighbourhood life; the American is not familiar with his city; once he is ten "blocks" away from his home, he is lost. This does not mean that there are no crowds in the business streets, but they are crowds that do not linger; people shop or emerge from the Underground to go to their offices.

I rarely saw an occasional Negro day-dreaming before a shop.

Yet one quickly begins to like American cities. Of course

they all look alike. And when you arrive at Wichita, Saint Louis or Albuquerque, it is disappointing to realize that, hidden behind these magnificent and promising names, is the same standard checkerboard city with the same red and green traffic lights and the same provincial look. But one gradually learns to tell them apart. Chicago, the noble, lurid city, red as the blood that trickles through its abattoirs, with its canals, the grey water of Lake Michigan and its streets crushed between clumsy and powerful buildings, in no way resembles San Francisco, city of air, salt and sea, built in the shape of an amphitheatre.

And then one finally comes to like their common element, that temporary look. Our beautiful closed cities, full as eggs, are a bit stifling. Our slanting, winding streets run head on against walls and houses; once you are inside the city, you can no longer see beyond it. In America, these long, straight unobstructed streets carry one's glance, like canals, outside the city. You always see mountains or fields or the sea at the end of them, no matter where you may be.

Frail and temporary, formless and unfinished, they are haunted by the presence of the immense geographical space surrounding them. And precisely because their boulevards are highways, they always seem to be stopping places on the roads. They are not oppressive, they do not close you in; nothing in them is definitive, nothing is arrested. You feel, from your first glance, that your contact with these places is a temporary one; either you will leave them or they will change around you.

Let us beware of exaggerating; I have spent Sundays in the American provinces that were more depressing than Sundays anywhere else; I have seen those suburban "colonial style" inns where, at two dollars a head, middle-class families go to eat shrimp cocktails and turkey with cranberry sauce in silence while listening to the electric organ. One must not forget the heavy boredom that weighs over America.

But these slight cities, still so similar to Fontana and the outposts of the Far West, reveal the other side of the United States: their freedom. Here everyone is free—not to criticize or to reform their customs—but to flee them, to leave for the desert or another city. The cities are open, open to the world, and to the future. This is what gives them their adventurous look and, even in their ugliness and disorder, a touching beauty.

(*Le Figaro*, 1945)

Chapter 10

New York, the Colonial City

I REALLY KNEW I would like New York, but I thought I'd
be able to like it immediately, as I had liked the red brick of
Venice and London's massive, sombre houses. I didn't know
that, for the newly arrived Euopean, there was a "New York
sickness," like sea-sickness, air-sickness and mountain-sick-
ness.

At midnight, an official bus took me from La Guardia
Field to the Plaza Hotel. I had pressed my forehead against
the window, but had been able to see only red and green
lights and dark buildings. The next day, without any transition, I found myself at the corner of 58th Street and Fifth
Avenue. I walked for a long time under the icy sky. It was
a Sunday in January, 1945, a deserted Sunday. I was looking
for New York and couldn't find it. The further I progressed
along an avenue that seemed coldly mediocre and banal, the
further the city seemed to retreat before me, like a ghost
town. What I was looking for was probably a European city.

We Europeans live on the myth of the big city that we
forged during the nineteenth century. American myths are
not ours, and the American city is not our city; it has neither
the same character nor the same functions. In Spain, Italy,
Germany and France we find circular cities that were originally surrounded by ramparts meant not only to protect the
inhabitants against enemy invasion, but also to conceal the
inexorable presence of Nature. These cities are, moreover,
divided into sections that are similarly round and closed. The
piled-up tangle of houses weighs heavily on the soil. They
seem to have a natural tendency to draw together, so much
so that now and then we have to clear a way through with
an axe, as in a virgin forest. Streets run into other streets.
Closed at both ends, they do not look as though they lead
outside the city. Inside them, you go around in circles. They

126

are more than mere arteries; each one constitutes a social milieu.

You stop along these streets, meet people, drink, eat and linger. On Sundays, you get dressed and take a stroll for the sole pleasure of greeting friends, to see and be seen. These are the streets that inspired Jules Romains' "unanisme." They are filled with a communal spirit that changes from hour to hour.

Thus, my near-sighted European eyes, slowly venturing out, on the watch for everything, vainly tried to find something to arrest them. Anything at all—a row of houses suddenly barring the way, a street corner, or some old, time-mellowed house. But it was no use. New York is a city for far-sighted people, a city in which you can only "adjust" to infinity. My glance met nothing but space. It slid over blocks of identical houses, with nothing to arrest it; it was about to lose itself in empty space, at the horizon.

Céline has remarked of New York that "it is a vertical city." This is true, but it seemed to me, at first, like a lengthwise city. The traffic that comes to a standstill in the side streets is all-priviliged and flows tirelessly down the avenues. How often the taxi-drivers, willing to take passengers from north to south, flatly refuse to take any for the east and west! The side streets have hardly any function other than to mark off the limits of the apartment houses between the avenues. They are cut by the avenues, spread and thrown toward the north. That was why I, a naïve tourist, vainly tried for a long time to find *quartiers*. In France we are surrounded and protected by urban centres; the prosperous districts protect the rich from the poor, and the poor districts protect us from the disdain of the rich, and similarly, the entire city protects us against Nature.

In New York, where the major axes are parallel avenues, I was unable to discover *quartiers* except on Lower Broadway. I could only find filmy atmospheres, longitudinally stretched masses with nothing to mark a beginning or end. I gradually learned to recognize the atmosphere of Third Avenue where, under the shadow of the noisy elevated railway, people meet, smile and chat without even knowing each other; and that

Irish bar in which a German, passing by my table, stopped for a minute to say: "Are you French? I'm a Jerry"; the reassuring comfort of the Lexington Avenue shops; the dreary elegance of Park Avenue; the cold luxury and stucco impassiveness of Fifth Avenue; the gay frivolity of Sixth and Seventh Avenues; the food markets on Ninth Avenue; and the No Man's Land of Tenth Avenue. Each avenue wraps its neighbouring streets in its own atmosphere, but one street down, you're suddenly plunged into another world. Not far from the palpitating silence of Park Avenue where glide the cars of the lords and masters, I come to First Avenue where the earth is constantly trembling under the passing of trucks. How am I to feel safe on one of those endless "north-south" highways when, a few steps away to east or west, other lengthwise worlds await me? Behind the Waldorf-Astoria and the blue and white canopies of "smart" buildings, I glimpse the "Elevated," which carries with it something of the Bowery's poverty.

All of New York is striped this way with parallel and non-communicating significances. These long, perfectly straight lines suddenly gave me the feeling of space. Our cities are constructed to protect us against it; the houses cluster like sheep. But space crosses through New York, quickening and expanding it. The space, the great, empty space of the steppes and pampas, flows through New York's arteries like a draught of cold air, separating one side from the other. An American friend who was showing me about the smart sections of Boston pointed to the left of a boulevard and said, "The 'nice' people live there." And then, pointing to the right side, he added ironically, "No one has ever been able to find out who lives here." The same is true of New York; between the two sides of a given street, you have all of space.

New York is half-way between a pedestrian's and a driver's city. You do not go for walks in New York; you fly through it; it is a city in motion. I feel at ease if I walk quickly; if I stop, I get flustered and wonder, "Why am I in this street rather than in one of the hundreds of others like it?" Why am I standing in front of this drug-store, or this Schrafft's or

Woolworth branch, rather than in front of any other of these thousands of identical ones?

And suddenly pure space looms into view. I imagine that if a triangle could become conscious of its position in space, it would be terrified at the realization of the rigorousness of its defining co-ordinates, but that it would also be terrified to discover that it is merely any triangle, any place. You never lose your way in New York; one glance is enough for you to get your bearings; you are on the East Side, at the corner of 52nd Street and Lexington Avenue. But this spacial precision is not accompanied by any precision of feeling. In the numerical anonymity of the streets and avenues, I am simply anybody, anywhere. No matter where I may be, my position is marked out in longitude and latitude. But no valid reason justifies my presence in this place rather than in any other, since this one is so like another. You never lose your way, and you are always lost.

Is it a city I am lost in, or is it Nature? New York is no protection against Nature's violence. It is an open-skied city. Storms flood its wide streets that take so long to cross when it rains. Hurricanes shake the brick houses and rock the sky-scrapers. They are announced formally over the radio, like declarations of war. In summer, the air vibrates between the houses; in winter, the city is flooded, so that you might think yourself in some Parisian suburb flooded by the Seine, but in America, it is only melting snow.

Nature weighs so heavily on New York that this most modern of cities is also the dirtiest. From my window I see thick, muddy papers, tossed by the wind, flitting over the pavement. When I go out, I walk in a blackish snow, a sort of puffy crust the same colour as the sidewalk, so that it looks as if the sidewalk itself is buckling. From the first of May, the heat crashes down on the city like an atomic bomb. The heat is Evil. People go up to one another and say. "It's murder!" The trains carry off millions of fleeing city-dwellers who, on descending from the train, leave damp marks on the seat, like snails. It is not the city they are fleeing, but Nature. Even in the depths of my apartment, I am open to attack from a mysterious and secretly hostile Nature. I feel as though

I were camping in the heart of a jungle crawling with insects. There is the wailing of the wind, the electric shocks I get each time I touch a doorbell or shake a friend's hand, the cockroaches that scoot across my kitchen, the elevators that make me nauseous and the inextinguishable thirst that rages in me from morning till night. New York is a colonial city, an outpost. All the hostility and cruelty of Nature are present in this city, the most prodigious monument man has ever erected to himself. It is a light city; its apparent lack of weight surprises most Europeans. In this immense and malevolent space, in this rocky desert that will tolerate no vegetation of any kind, millions of brick, wooden and reinforced concrete houses, that all look as if they are about to fly away, have been constructed.

I like New York. I learned to like it. I become accustomed to its massive groupings and its long vistas. My eyes no longer linger over the façades in quest of a house which might, by some remote chance, not be identical with the others. My eyes immediately slip by to the horizon to look for the buildings lost in fog, mere volumes, merely the sky's austere framework. One is rewarded when one has learned how to look at the two rows of apartment houses which, like cliffs, line a great artery; their mission is completed down there, at the avenue's end, in simple, harmonious lines; a scrap of sky floats between them.

New York reveals itself only at a certain height, a certain distance, and a certain speed; these are not the pedestrian's height, distance or speed. This city looks amazingly like the great plains of Andalusia—monotonous when travelled over on foot, magnificent and changing when seen from a car.

I learned to like New York's sky. In European cities where roofs are low, the sky crawls close to the earth and seems tamed. The New York sky is beautiful because the skyscrapers push it back, very far over our heads. Pure and lonely as a wild beast, it guards and watches over the city. And it is not only a local protection; one feels that it stretches out into the distance over all America; it is the whole world's sky.

I learned to like Manhattan's avenues. They are not sober little walks closed in between houses, but national highways.

The moment you set foot on one of them, you understand that it has to go on to Boston or Chicago. It fades away outside the city and the eye can almost follow it into the country. A wild sky over parallel rails, that, more than anything else, is New York. When you are at the heart of this city, you are at the heart of Nature.

I had to get used to it, but now that I have, there is no place in which I feel more free than in the New York crowds. This light, ephemeral city that looks every morning and evening, under the sun's inquisitive rays, like a simple juxtaposition of rectangular parallelepipeds, is never oppressing or depressing. You can experience the anguish of solitude here, but never that of oppression.

In Europe, we become attached to a neighbourhood, to a cluster of houses or a street-corner, and we are no longer free. But hardly have you plunged into New York than your life is completely cut to New York's size. You can gaze down in the evening from the top of the Queensborough Bridge, in the morning from New Jersey, at noon from the seventy-seventh storey of Rockefeller Center, but you will never be captivated by any of the city's streets, because none of them has a distinctive beauty of its own. There is beauty in all of them, as all of America's nature and sky is present in them. Nowhere will you ever have a stronger feeling of the simultaneity of human lives.

New York moves Europeans in spite of its austerity. Of course, we have learned to love our old cities, but their touching quality for us lies in a Roman wall that forms part of an inn's façade, or a house that Cervantes lived in, or the Place des Vosges, or the town hall at Rouen. We like museum-cities, and all our cities are rather like museums in which we wander about amidst ancestral homes. New York is not a museum-city, yet, for Frenchmen of my generation, it already possesses a melancholy of the past. When we were twenty, around 1925, we heard about the skyscrapers. For us they symbolized America's fabulous prosperity. We discovered them with amazement in the films. They were the architecture of the future, just as the cinema was the art of the future and jazz the music of the future. Today we know what to think about jazz. We know that it has more of a past than a future. It is a music of popular, Negro inspiration, capable of limited development and in a process of slow decline. Jazz is outliving its day. The talking film has not fulfilled the promise of the silent one. Hollywood is making no headway in a well-worn rut.

The war has certainly taught the Americans that their country was the greatest power in the world. But the period of easy living is over; many economists fear a new depression. Thus, no more skyscrapers are being built. It seems they are too hard to rent.

The man who walked about in New York before 1930 saw in the big buildings that dominated the city the first signs of an architecture destined to radiate over the whole country. The skyscrapers were alive then. Today, for a Frenchman arriving from Europe, they are already mere historical monuments, relics of a bygone age. They still rear up against the sky, but my mind is no longer with them, and the New Yorkers pass by at their feet without even looking. I cannot think of them without a certain sadness; they tell of an age in which we thought that the very last war had just ended and when we believed in peace. They are already a bit run-down; tomorrow, perhaps, they will be torn down. In any case, their construction required a faith we no longer have.

I walk between the little brick houses the colour of dried blood. They are younger than Europe's houses, but their fragility makes them look much older. Far away I see the Empire State or the Chrysler Building reaching vainly toward the sky, and suddenly I think that New York is about to acquire a History and that it already possesses its ruins.

That is enough to lend a bit of softness to the world's harshest city.

(*Town and Country*, 1946)

Chapter 11

Departure and Return [1]

BRICE PARAIN is a man on the march. He has still to arrive and does not even quite know his goal. But we can now begin to perceive the general direction of his journey. As I see it, it is a return. He himself has called one of his books *Return to France.* He says in this work, "I have learned, after a long period of unrestraint, that the mediating powers have been empowered to forbid man to exceed himself, that they set up barriers at his limits, beyond which he is threatened with destruction."

These few words suffice to date his undertaking. He has gone to extremes. He has tried to go beyond himself, and now he has returned. Does this not sum up all of post- World War I literary history? Men had been filled with great and inhuman ambitions. They had wanted to get at nature, both within man and outside him and to do so unassisted. They had entered the garden on tiptoe to surprise it and see it as it was when no one was there to see it. And then, in the thirties, encouraged, channelized and urged on by publishers, journalists and picture dealers, there was a general return to the human, a return to order. An effort was made to define a modest and practical wisdom in which contemplation would be subordinated to effective and limited action, in which the ambitious values of truth would give way to those of honesty, a wisdom which was neither pragmatism nor opportunism but rather a new compounding of values, illuminating action by knowledge and subduing knowledge to action, subjecting the individual to the social order and refusing to sacrifice it to him; in short, a wisdom of economy whose chief concern was to balance things. The youngest of us have now left it far behind, I fear. Events seem to be requiring both more and less.

[1] Concerning *Investigations into the Nature and Function of Language.*

But, after all, it was an adventure of the mind, as valid as others, such as surrealism or Gidian individualism, and it will have to be judged later on by its consequences. In any case, it was through and in this adventure that Parain chose himself. However, certain things must be made clear. There have been false "returns." Some men, such as Schlumberger, who thought they had never departed simply wanted to force others to return. "We must go back." But it was obvious that the "we" was mere politeness. A sad generation of severe young men, conscious of the shortness of their lives, hastily took their places in the marching ranks, like people of whom we say, with good-humoured indulgence, "they've lost all their illusions without having had any to begin with." There was even an odd kind of sad careerist, reminiscent of some thin-blooded Julien Sorel, like Armand Petitjean, who speculated on this deflation in order to make his way in the world. But Parain returned in earnest. He knew and lived the temptation of the inhuman, and he is now returning to men, slowly and awkwardly, with memories that the young men do not have.

Think of the "return" of Aragon and the surrealist stiffening of his new style, with its sudden flashes reminiscent of the old-time lightning; think of the "return" of Le Fresnaye, back from cubism, revealing a shy and hesitant meaning in his stony heads. Parain is their brother. But his extravagance and repentance, his fits of anger and despair, were always an affair between language and himself. Let us therefore regard *Investigations into the Nature and Function of Language* as a stage of a return to order or, better still, as a *re-descent.* "You go up to the plateau," he writes, "in order to look into the distance as far as the eye can see. You go up to the plateau, where the wind blows . . . where life is solitary. . . . You go down again to the valley, to sea-level, to gardens and houses, where the shops of the blacksmith and wheelwright stand, below the cemetery and the church. You go down at evening, with the falling darkness. . . . Everything rises from the valley only to come down again." [2] We

[2] *Return to France.*

shall try to retrace this itinerary, step by step, first the ascent and then the re-descent.

Parain is a lyricist. By a very special twist of fate, this decent, honest man, with his precise and impartial intelligence, talks about himself, regardless of what he may be saying, and without suspecting that he does. As does everyone else, perhaps. I agree. But at least his testimony is perfectly clear. We shall use it to plot the story of this great and terribly sad re-descent which characterized the second half of the postwar era, the period following what Daniel-Rops has called "the turning years."

I

INTUITION

The beginning of Parain's journey is marked by an intuition; the return is prepared by an experiment. When a man of twenty-five writes: [3] "Signs set up an imperfect communication between men, regulating social relations like a shaky lever," and twelve years later: "There is only one problem . . . the one posed by the non-necessitous nature of language. Owing to language, human energy does not seem to be entirely transmitted in the course of its transformations. . . . There is too much play in the gears," [4] he presents us with a fine example of the continuity of his ideas and the persistence of his metaphors. These comparisons express a fundamental intuition that Parain calls, in his *Essay on Human Wretchedness*, "the giddy feeling of an inexactitude in language." This orients us. Parain does not begin his investigations with the inhuman impartiality of the linguist. He is word-sick and wants to be cured. He suffers at feeling out of gear in relation to language.

That is enough to inform us that this is not the place to expect an objective study of the medium of sound. The linguist usually acts like a man sure of his ideas and concerned

[3] *Essay on Human Wretchedness.*
[4] Unpublished manuscript of November, 1922.

only with knowing whether the old and traditional institution of language renders them accurately. Thus, he may study the "parallelism" of the logial and the grammatical, as if, on the one hand, logic were given in the heaven of ideas and, on the other, grammar were given on earth. Thus, one looks about for a French equivalent for the German word "stimmung," which supposes that the corresponding idea exists for the Frenchman as it does for the German and that the only question that arises is that of its expression. But language thus considered is anonymous. Words are tossed on the table, killed and cooked, like dead fish. In short, the linguist does not study the language as it is spoken; dead words, dead concepts, the word "freedom" as preached in sermons and not the live, heady, irritating and mortal word as it resounds today in an angry or eager mouth.

Parain is concerned with langauge "as it is spoken," that is, he sees it as a link in a chain of concrete action. What interests him is the language of a particular soldier or workman or revolutionary. In such a case, how are we to distinguish the word from the idea? The orator declaims. He says "justice" or "democracy"—and all the listeners applaud. Where is the "thought"? Where is the "verbal material"? What strikes the listener is the whole ensemble, what Claudel has felicitously called "the meaningful mouthful." It is this meaningful mouthful that Parain examines. "Words are ideas," he writes in *Investigations,* for he has placed himself in a perspective which is already practical and political, as has Heidegger, who refuses to distinguish between the body and the soul, a problem of contemplative philosophy, and who would readily say that, from the point of view of action, which is the only real point of view, the soul is the body, and the body the soul.

As a peasant, citizen and "applied warrior" of World War I, Parain deliberately turns his back on contemplative joys. His first essay, which remains unpublished, is concerned with finding an "art of living." "The war," he writes, "gave value to life and urged us not to lose a single moment of it." Ever since, the ethical and the political, which are indissolubly linked, have been his major concern. "A theory of knowledge," he wrote in 1934, "can never be anything but a theory of the reform of the understanding and, in the last analysis, a treatise on ethics." And by this he meant that he accorded the *practical* the primacy over all other domains. Man is a creature that acts. The meaning and scope of science, metaphysics and language are to be found within the narrow limits of this action. It would be tempting to compare Parain and Comte. They have in common this sharp and powerful seriousness, the intention of making no distinction between the ethical and the political, the human sense of human fellowship. But Comte was an engineer. Behind his theory of action we see the machine-tool, the locomotive. Parain is a peasant. He was stirred, like all men of the 1920's, by a great hostility to mechanism. Behind his ethics and his criticism of language can be seen the pick and spade, the work-bench.

At any rate, their primary concern is the same, to think their age through and to do so with ideas that belong to the age. They mistrust the universal and the eternal. Parain studies the language of 1940 and not universal language. He studies the word-sick language in which "peace" means aggression, "freedom" oppression and "socialism" a regime of social inequality. And if he worries about them, he does so in the manner of a doctor and not of a biologist. I mean by this that he is not interested in isolating organs and examining them in a laboratory. He studies the whole organism and means to cure it.

"It is not I," he writes, "who have invented this mistrust of language . . . [It] has been driven home by our entire civilization." [5] He thereby means to date his investigation, just as Hegel dated Hegelianism. But the date is still too roughly approximate. For, after all, neither you nor I am the author of *Investigations;* you may be too old, and I am a little too young. Consider the thinkers born of the recent war. They praise Parain; they approve of his undertaking. But they no longer quite understand it, and they turn his results to their own ends. Blanchot, for example, uses it for purposes of challenging. If we really want to understand this message,

[5] *Essay on Human Wretchedness.*

we must bear in mind that it comes from a man who reached maturity between the two wars. It therefore suffers as the result of being slightly late. Like the work of Proust, which was written before the first war and read after it, it was not transmitted at the right moment, and it is to this delay, to the slight dissonance, that it will owe its fecundity. Parain is a man of forty-six. He is a peasant who was sent to the front during the latter years of the first war. This will explain his primary intuition.

The peasant works alone, in the midst of natural forces which need not be named in order to act. He works in silence. Parain has noted his "stupor" when he returns to the village and hears human voices after working in his field. He has also noted the "social destruction of the individual, which . . . tends to proceed at the present time through the transformation of the peasant into an agricultural worker. . . . To a peasant . . . the earth is the intermediary that solidly attaches his thought to his action, that enables him to judge and act. . . . To a worker, to any member of industrial civilization, this link, this intercessor, is the plan, the scientific hypothesis of construction that provides him with the idea of his place in the whole, that confers upon him his collective utility, his social value, and in his own eyes as well. It is language which is the gesture of intelligence. In moving . . . from a field that is to be tilled, to a part that is to be manufactured, one moves from a thought that is more concrete and nearer its object to one that is more abstract and remote from its object." [6]

Parain, like many another, came to the city. But the first thing he encountered there was not the technical language of shop and factory, but rhetoric. At the Ecole Normale, I knew many such peasant boys who had been taken from the soil because of their exceptional intelligence. They could be as silent as the soil, only to emerge suddenly and hold forth, like the Socrates of *The Clouds,* on the most abstract subjects, taking either side of the question with equal virtuosity and with an amused pedantry. Then they would relapse into

[6] *Essay on Human Wretchedness.*

silence. It was obvious that such intellectual gymnastics were foreign to them. To them, it was a game, a slight bubbling at the surface of their silence.

Parain was one of these students. He himself wrote in November 1922 (he had just taken the examination for the *agrégation* in philosophy): "I have just completed my studies in a university where the art of persuading has replaced the art of living and of thinking." He had been taught the brilliant and weightless language of polemics. A young workman must decide for or against Marx. Parain did not have to decide between Voltaire and Rousseau, but he knew how to set them in opposition, how to reconcile them and how to set them back to back. He has remained a formidable dialectician. He possesses the art of replying quickly and vigorously, of side-tracking, or breaking off, of ending a discussion with a word when it embarrasses him. But he *hears himself* talking, with a kind of outraged amusement. He hears himself talking from the depth of his silence. Hence, an immediate perspective on language. He has always heard words through a thickness of silence, the way fish probably see swimmers at the surface of the water. "When you really hear yourself," he says, "you stop talking." When he is at home, he is silent. What is there to say? Someone is repairing a rickety table, someone else is sewing. About them is the house.

This alternating between rapid discourse and silence is a characteristic trait of his. In 1922, he called this silence *instinct* and contrasted it with speech, which is "eloquence" or "polemics." When you really hear yourself, you stop talking. The lamp is on the table. Everyone is working and feels the silent presence of the others. There is an order of silence. Later on, there was to be for Parain an order of instinct. As for the little verbal bubblings at his surface, they are not his. They have been given to him—or rather loaned. They come from the city. In the fields and in the house, they have nothing to do.

The fact that this peasant fought in a war meant a further rupture. The unified language he had just learned, the language of scholars and industrialists, had seemed, in a way, like an impersonal Reason in which each individual could participate. The war taught Parain that there were several Reasons, that of the Germans, of the Russians, of the French, that each corresponded to an objective system of signs and that there took place among them a test of force.

He learned this lesson amidst another silence, a silence filled with explosions and lacerations, amidst a mute fellowship. But words continued to move over the surface of this silence. To the silent men in the trenches, the articles of Barrès, the communiqués and the patriotic speeches really became *words*. "Words! Words!" They had lost their emotional roots. They no longer flowed into action. But this ineffectualness unmasked them. When the word is a link in a chain—"hand me the . . . the . . . there!"—it is effaced. One obeys it without hearing it, without seeing it. But when it no longer has weight, it exposes itself, it reveals itself *as a word*, just as, to Bergson, it is the indeterminacy in the reaction that sets an image off from the world. It is this language, still fully armed and alive, which issues hot from a human mouth, this language, cut off from all practical application and for that reason all the more haunting, that was henceforth to be the subject of Parain's investigation.

I said earlier that he did not want to indulge in the desiccating experiences of the linguist, that he refused to set words up arbitrarily in an isolated system. But events provided him with what is called in methodological terms a "passive experience." The word isolated itself, spontaneously, though retaining, nevertheless, a human odour. To the peasant, language had meant the city. Now, to the soldier, it meant the rear.

Then he came back. It was as if his entire life were to move to a rhythm of departing and returning. The young intellectual's returning to the fields for the holiday, the demobilized soldier's returning to Paris for the Peace. And this meant submitting language to a new test. Words were all about him, like eager servants. He had only to take them. And yet, no sooner did he want to use them than they betrayed him. If he wished to tell women and old men what war was like, all he needed to do was put out his hand and told hold of such words as "horror," "terror," "boredom."

But, like the message in *Aminadab* that changed meaning on the way, the words were not understood as they were intended. What does "terror" mean to a woman? And what is "boredom"? How was he to infuse into language an experience that occurred outside it? He might at least have depicted himself, have found names with which to name himself, to describe himself. But the instruments he was using in all honesty had unexpected repercussions.

In order to earn a little money, he offered to give lessons to the children of a banker. The banker immediately investigated: *who* was Parain? In 1920, this meant: had he been in the army? and what had he done? What could Parain answer? That he had been a private? It was the truth. No doubt about it, it was a social truth that took its place in a system of filing-cards, notations and signs. But Parain was also a graduate of the Ecole Normale and an *agrégé*. As such, he *should have* been an officer. "In saying 'private', I am saying that to a worker I am a pal and to a banker a suspect . . . perhaps a rebel, at any rate, a problem and not a person to be given immediate confidence." [7] And Parain adds: "If I said 'private', I would think as follows: negligence at the beginning, honesty of being unwilling, despite advantages, to command, because I didn't think I was able to, youthful scruples, also friendships already formed, habits of living, a feeling of confidence that keeps me where I am. Won't (the banker) think: lack of dignity, liking for vulgarity, lack of patriotism? . . . By telling the truth, I deceive him more than by lying." Parain therefore chose to say "lieutenant." Not in order to lie, but so as to be understood. "By saying officer, I am saying that I am one of your kind, someone you can recognize." He therefore meant by officer a non-revolutionary, a truth which he could express only *at the same time* as the other truth, namely, "private."

This was the experience of the demobilized soldier that Parain was to record later on in his *Essay on Human Wretchedness*. "The image of an object . . . evoked by a word is just about identical in the case of two persons, but on

[7] Unpublished essay of 1923.

condition that they speak the same language, that they belong to the same social class and to the same generation, that is, that it fall, at least, within the norm where differences between the two persons may be regarded as practically negligible." [8] Whence he derives the following ethical precept, "If you do not act toward the words of others in accordance with the norms fixed socially by your milieu and your age, you cease to know how to understand and interpret them," [9] and the following first generalization: "The sign taken in isolation has no other relation with the object signified than that of designation . . . it is, so to speak, floating . . . it acquires reality only in an ordered system." [10]

In which system did the word "private" have a meaning? That of the banker or that of the soldier, Parain? But it would have been useless for the soldier Parain to look for a language valid for himself. He was alone. For the time being, there was only one language, that which the bankers, the industrialists and the old men at the rear had in common with the other city-dwellers. He had to choose either to manage with the system that had already been established or to be silent. But the man who remains silent in the city becomes "haggard, half-mad." "Reduce yourselves to silence, even to inner silence, and you'll see how certain bodily desires increase, to the point of obsession, and to what extent you lose the notion of the social, to what point you no longer know how to behave, to what point you cease to understand and begin to feel, to what point you become an idiot, in the Dostoevskian sense of the word. You have separated yourselves from collective experience." [11]

Is it therefore necessary to lie? Exactly what is meant by lying? It means giving up the idea of expressing an impossible truth; it means using words not in order to make yourself understood but to be accepted, to "be loved." Parain, the most honest of thinkers, the last man in the world to abuse words, is also the man who is most indulgent towards lies.

[8] *Essay on Human Wretchedness.*
[9] *Ibid.*
[10] *Ibid.*
[11] *Essay on Human Wretchedness.*

Or rather, it seems to him that there are no lies. It would be too easy if everyone could lie. It would mean that words have rigorous meanings, that they can be composed in such a way as to express a precise truth, and that people prefer deliberately to disregard this truth. To lie would mean to know the true and to reject it, just as doing evil means rejecting good.

But one can no more lie in Parain's world than one can do evil in Claudel's. For the very opposite reasons. For Claudel good is Being. To Parain, being is imprecise, it floats. I cannot reject the True because the True is indeterminate. "Communication is imperfect, not only because thought does not wholly contain the individual it expresses, but also because no word, no phrase, no work has a necessary meaning that imposes itself without a need for someone's interpreting it." [12] Hence, in saying the false may-be when I mean the true, can I be sure of saying the false when I mean to lie? We know of the case of insane persons suffering from a kind of paranoia who complain that someone is "stealing their thoughts," meaning that someone has deflected it within them from its original meaning before it has reached its goal.

They're not so crazy. We all have the same experience. Words drink our thought before we have time to recognize it. We have a vague intention, we clarify it by means of words and suddenly we find ourselves saying something quite different from what we meant. There are no liars. There are only the oppressed who manage with language as best they can. Parain has never forgotten the story of the banker. He still remembers it twenty years later when he talks about his daughter's prevarication: "When my daughter tells me that she has done her homework though she really has not, she does not do so . . . *with the intention* of leading me into error, but rather to indicate to me that she might have done it, that she had wanted to do it, that she should have done it, and that the whole matter is quite unimportant. She therefore tells me that she has done it in order to get rid of a nuisance rather than to speak falsely." [13]

[12] *Ibid.*
[13] *Investigations.*

It was probably such thoughts as these that ran through the head of the demobilized soldier—half-untruthful and half-mute, with a touch of Myshkin and a touch of Julien Sorel—as he left the banker. By the same token, language, that product of cities and of the rear, entered the rank of rich men's privileges. It was loaned to Parain, but it belonged to others, to the bankers, generals and prelates, to all those who handled it carelessly, with an indolent and consummate art, who knew that they would be heard by their peers and heeded by their subordinates. He had the right to use it, but only in the sense and within the limits prescribed by the powers-that-be. By means of words, the bankers and industrialists wormed their way into him and robbed him of his most inner thoughts, misappropriated them for their own purposes. Language was becoming the most insinuating of the instruments of oppression. Worse still, it was becoming the basic intermediary and the essential tool of the unproductive and parasitic class of intermediaries.

This was not a chance discovery. In war, no less than in the fields, Parain had come into contact with the world of labour, for war is hard industrial and agricultural labour. He had returned to peace as the peasant returns to the village, as the miner, after a day's work, returns to the surface of the earth. He came into contact again with the world of ceremony and politeness, the world of intermediaries, where man is involved with man and not with the soil or explosive shells. Language was becoming an intermediary between man and his desire, between man and his work, just as there were intermediaries between producer and consumer. Between man and himself: if I name what I am, I allow myself to be defined within a certain social order, and I become its accomplice. But I cannot remain silent. What, then, must I become?

At about the same time, our age was beginning to engage in an adventure from which it has not yet emerged. And things were moving more quickly than words. Language has its own inertia, just as confidence has. We know that, in periods of inflation, prices remain stable for a time while money drops. The same is true for words. Hence, there was a new discrepancy, which was to affect everyone, bankers and ex-servicemen alike. In vain did words pursue their objects; they had got off to a slow start. What, for example, was to be thought about "Peace"? The Japanese were advancing into the heart of China with cannons and tanks. Nevertheless, they were at peace with the Chinese, for war had not been declared. The Japanese and the Russians were fighting at the Manchurian border and yet peace was maintained, for the Nipponese ambassador remained in Moscow and the Soviet ambassador in Tokyo.

Two countries are at war; a third remains aloof from the operations; am I to say that it is at peace? Yes, if it remains neutral. But what is neutrality? If it furnishes one of the adversaries with supplies, is it neutral? If it suffers from a blockade, is it neutral? Is armed neutrality still neutrality? And what about pre-belligerence? And intervention? And if we decide not to define war as an armed conflict, shall we say that the period between the two wars was a period of war or peace? It's a matter of taste.

What with the blockades and industrial rivalries and class struggle, isn't a man entitled to speak of war? Nevertheless, may I not at the present time feel a legitimate nostalgia for the peace of 1939? There are people who say that war has not ceased since 1914. And they prove it. But others will also prove that it dates from 1939. A peace between two wars? A single war? Who knows—perhaps a single peace? Who is to decide? And I think of the uncertainties of biologists, whose words were intended to designate clear-cut species and who suddenly discovered the continuity of living forms. Are we to leave words rotting where they fall? "Our age needs a dictionary," says Camus, writing about Parain. But Parain would reply that a dictionary supposes a certain discontinuity and a certain stability of meanings. It is therefore impossible to establish one today. "In an age which, like our own, is an age of profound social transformation, in which social values disappear without having yet been replaced by others—and, by analogy, in no age, for there is never a moment that is not in the process of more or less rapid transformation, can anyone know exactly what is meant by other people's words or even by his own." [14]

It was then, when all was lost, that Parain thought he had found a plank to hold on to. There are men who have given up the idea of knowing the world and who want only to change it. Marx wrote: "The question as to whether human thought can arrive at objective truth is not a theoretical question but a practical one. It is in practice that man must prove truth, that is, the reality, the objectivity of his thought. . . . Thus far, philosophers have merely interpreted the world in different ways. The problem now is to change it." [15]

Was not this what Parain meant when he wrote, upon returning from war: "Unable to communicate with exactitude, because I haven't the time—and even if I had, where would I find the talent to do an exhaustive chronological self-description?—unable to confront someone with my entire person, with everything that determines me at the moment, including my current past and my intentions . . . being a particular creature, in other words, different from everyone else and unable, by nature, to define to myself something that might be communicable with precision, that is, something within myself that is identical with something in each person, I choose to express myself in a role. Giving up the idea of being known, I try to be loved." [16] The man who thus abandons the idea of making the word an instrument of knowledge is ready to accept, out of despair, an anti-rationalistic theory of language. Such a theory existed. It was more than a theory; it was a practice. "Lenin did not believe in a universal value of reason and language. He did not believe in exact communication by language. According to him, life went on above and below language. Watchwords, to him, were only forms, which were filled in by activity and animated by the personality; if not by the individual personality, then by the collective one." [17]

With Lenin, the word became the watchword. It would be

[14] *Essay.*
[15] Quoted by Parain (*Investigations*).
[16] *Essay* of 1922.
[17] *Essay.*

futile to expect it to have a pre-established significance. Its only meaning is the one that is given to it. Its value is strictly historical and practical. It is the word of the leader, of the ruling class. It is true if it is verified, that is, if it is obeyed, if it has consequences. This activist conception of language was to represent, for Parain, the great temptation. When you have been straining to open a closed door, a moment comes when you feel like breaking it in. Parain's adherence to the activist doctrine seems as much a matter of anger as it does a matter of resignation. The word, for him, remains an intermediary, but its function is specified: it is a bridge between desire and its fulfilment. "The thing that guides man, at every moment, that musters and orders him, is what he says to himself about himself, about his needs, his desires, his means. These are his watchwords." [18] This is a recognition of the primacy of desire and the emotions. Language is an instrument of fulfilment. Reason is thereby reduced to a more modest role. "Reason is nothing other than the intelligence, which is itself nothing other than the power of constructing a system of signs to be tested, that is, the power of formulating a hypothesis . . . Reason . . . is the attempt that man pursues . . . to provide his desires with an exact and effective means of satisfaction. . . . Its role as servant is quite precise. . . . It must frequently be checked by desires, just as a loafing workman must be ordered to attend to his work." [19] It is here that the shamefulness of language becomes apparent.

If anyone wants to force Parain to adopt the language of the banker, the reason is that the banker is in the saddle. It is not for a poor demobilized soldier either to struggle to understand a language not meant for him—which would lead him into servitude—or to invent a system of signs valid only for himself—which would lead him straight to madness. He has to find a community of oppressed persons eager to take power and to impose its language, a language forged in the silent fellowship of work and suffering. At this point, Parain might say, modifying slightly the words of Marx: "We do not want to understand words; we want to change them."

[18] *Ibid.*
[19] *Ibid.*

But if we are going to go to all that trouble to reinvent a language, it must be rigorous and precise. We must eliminate loose ends and wobbly parts. If the order is to be obeyed, it must be understood down to its last details. And, conversely, to understand is to act. The belts must be tightened, the screws driven home. Since we cannot remain silent, that is, cannot directly and immediately attain being, we must, at least, rigorously control the intermediaries. Parain admits that his youth shuttled back and forth between two dreams. "Symbols lead us to believe that by eliminating all the transmissions we eliminate all the hitches, and also to believe that, on the other hand, if we perfect all this machinery, the gears will work quite smoothly and accidents will become impossible." [20]

The first dream, that of "the idiot," of the soldier on furlough wandering about in the populous cities, of the "haggard and half-mad" demobilized man, had proved to be unrealizable. Parain then plunged into the other dream, that of an authoritarian community of labour, in which language is expressly reduced to its subordinate role of intermediary between desire and action, between leaders and their men, in which everyone understands because everyone obeys, in which the elimination of social barriers results in the elimination of defects in transmission. "That was how, after the experience of an already rigorous social order, namely, war, an order that seemed to me, nevertheless, to allow for many exceptions and privileges, for its mystique was too fragile to predispose us entirely, I came to conceive and desire a social order that was even more rigorous, as rigorous as possible." [21]

We have reached the farthest point of Parain's journey. He went no farther. The rest has been a return. Thus far, he had simply developed the consequences of his original intuition. He adhered to a pragmatic and relativistic authoritarianism, in which the words love and hope received distinct and recognized meanings, like mathematical symbols. Later on, he realized that this revolutionary impulsion involved a sly effort

[20] *Return to France*
[21] *Ibid.*

to destroy language: "If language derives its meaning only from the operations it designates, and if it is these that constitute the object of our thinking, and not essences and their denominations, it should, in the last analysis, appear as useless and even dangerous: useless because we admit that all our thoughts obey the same scheme of action, one which organizes us by itself, without language's playing a decisive role, and because they develop spontaneously, following parallel and therefore harmonious directions; dangerous because language then serves only to furnish pretexts for the negligence and ill will of subordinates who argue instead of obeying." [22]

Thus, though Parain had abandoned the quest of what may be called infra-silence, the silence that is supposed to coincide with some sort of "state of nature" and to exist prior to language, he had not thereby given up his intention of remaining silent. The silence he had now attained extended over the entire realm of language. It became identified with language itself. It was buzzing with murmurs, with orders, with demands. It had been achieved, this time, not through the impossible destruction of words, but by their radical devaluation. He was to say later on, passing judgment on his own attempt, "Bolshevism was then an absolutely anti-rationalistic attitude which completed the ideological destruction of the individual by a destruction, pushed to the point of heroism, of the word that did not end in a total sacrifice."

He was not the only one to pursue these hopeless undertakings. In the glamorous years immediately following the war there were many other young people who rebelled against the human condition and, in particular, against the language that expressed it. The obsession with intuitive knowledge, that is, knowledge without intermediary, which was, as we have seen, Parain's prime motive force, animated surrealism, as did also that profound distrust of speech that Paulhan calls terrorism. But since we must talk, since regardless of what we do, the word is sandwiched in between the intuition and its object, our terrorists were ejected from silence, as was

[22] *Investigations.*

Paulhan himself, and we can follow, throughout the post-war period, an attempt to destroy words by means of words, painting by means of painting, art by means of art.

Surrealism would constitute an interesting subject for an existential analysis. We should have to know what is meant by *destroying*. However, it is clear that destruction was limited, as in the case of Parain, to the Word. This is proved by Max Ernst's famous definition:[23] "Surrealism is the meeting, on a dissecting table, of a sewing machine and an umbrella." Just try to *realize* this meeting. There is nothing in it to excite the mind. An umbrella, a sewing-machine and a dissecting table are sad and neutral objects, tools of human wretchedness. They do not clash with each other, but constitute a reasonable and resigned little gathering, smacking of the hospital and of salaried labour.

It is words that clash, not things—words, with their sonority and overtones. Thus, we get automatic writing and its substitutes, efforts of *speakers* to establish destructive short-circuits between vocables. "Poetry," said Fargue, "the mutual burning of words." But he was satisfied if they merely crackled; the surrealist wanted them to fall to ashes. Bataille defined poetry as "a holocaust of words," just as Parain defined Bolshevism as "a destruction of the word." The latest arrival, M. Blanchot, betrayed the secret of this attempt when he explained to us that the writer must speak *in order to say nothing*.

If words annihilate each other, if they crumble into powder, will not a silent reality finally loom up behind the words? The hesitation at this point is significant. It is Parain's own hesitation. Was the reality that has suddenly made its appearance actually waiting for us, unnamed, behind the words, or is it *our* creation? If I say, with Bataille, "horse of butter," I destroy the word "horse" and the word "butter," but something is there: the horse of butter. What is it? A *nothing;* this is obvious. But is it a nothing that I create or that I reveal?

The surrealist does not choose between these contradictory hypotheses, and perhaps, from his point of view, the choice

[23] After Lautréamont.

is unimportant. Whether the cards have an underside or whether it be I who create this underside, I, in any case, am an absolute, and the burning of the words is an absolute event. Whence the surrealists' flirtation with Bolshevism, in which they saw an effort on man's part to forge his own destiny in absolute fashion. It is here that they join hands with the Parain of 1925 who wrote, "The word must be replaced by a more direct and more effective mode of action, by an immediate mode of action, which takes place without intermediary and which abandons nothing of the disquietude from which it arises." He was impelled, as they were, by the powerful metaphysical pride that was the spirit of the post-war period.

Having followed him, we have arrived at the limit of the human condition, at that point of tension where man tries to see himself as if he were an inhuman witness of himself. In 1930, the rising generation began to record the failure of this attempt. But certain survivors, such as Leiris and Aragon, were to reckon up the situation themselves, each in his own way. Parain is one of these. Let us now follow him on the road back.

II

THE EXPERIMENT

When Parain learned that "the most rigorous social orders taught history, philosophy and literature," he must have felt some of the amazement of the Pythagoreans when they were confronted with the incommensurability of the sides of the right-angled triangle. If a society philosophizes, it means that its mechanism allows for a certain amount of free play, that there is room for the individual dream, for each man's fancy, for questioning and incomprehension. It means, in the last analysis, that there is no perfectly rigorous social order. For Parain regarded literature as the absurd musings of an imperfect language. However, I regard this purely external experience as not very important. For, after all, one can still decide to perfect the most imperfect social order. Will it *never* be rigorous? Or is it *not yet* so? The facts do not speak for themselves. It is up to each individual to decide. Parain's decision seems to me rather to have been dictated by a deeper and more inner experiece, a testing of the self by the self which has more than one feature in common with what Rauh has called "the moral experience." This peasant had taken the paths of pride, the ways of the city and the proletariat, as the result of a misunderstanding.

It would be easy to show the contradictions between Parain's fundamental individualism and the community disciplines to which he has now given his adherence. Parain has probably been aware of them from the very beginning. But these are conflicts that can be resolved, provided that the original mainspring of individualism be the will to power. It is always easy to obey if one dreams of commanding. Parain wants neither to command nor obey. His individualism is nothing less than Nietzschean. It is neither the appetite of a captain of industry, nor the avidity of the oppressed people of the city who are obsessed by the slick and glassy mirage of the shops, but quite simply the simple and humble demand of the small agricultural landowner who wants to remain his own master.

It is the nature of this individualism, more than his own individualism, that tends to separate Parain from his revolutionary friends. It is on the plateaux that language is burned, on the plateaux that one sets fire to the greatest structures of the capitalist order. Parain is a man of the valleys. The destroyers whom he followed briefly are all possessed, in one way or another, of a demiurgic pride. They are Nietzscheans in that they all believe in the plasticity of human nature. If they burn the old Adam, it is in order to hasten the coming of a new man. There is the surrealist man, the Gidian man, the Marxist man, whom we are awaiting at the horizon. They must be revealed and, at the same time, fashioned.

In one sense, the future is empty. No one can predict it. In another sense, the future exists more intensely than the present. The intoxication of these destroyers is their desire to build a world which they do not know and which they will not recognize when they have built it. It is the joy of risking, the joy of not *knowing* what they are doing, the bitter joy of saying to themselves that they will lead men to the threshold of the promised land and that they themselves will remain at the threshold, watching the others move farther off.

These sentiments are quite foreign to Parain. He has no eyes for the future. He does not believe in it. If he does speak of it, it is only to show a world coming apart, a man losing his way. In short, his theory of language should lead him—in fact, did, for a brief moment, lead him—to the idea of human plasticity: change words and you will change man. But in reality, nothing is more remote than this from his most personal thought. The image most deeply rooted in his memory is that of the natural order, the return of the seasons and the birds, the growth of plants and children, the fixed order of the stars and planets. This was the order that he had been secretly constructing against the factitious ordering of discourse. It is to this order that animals are subject, as is man, the talking animal. As we have seen, the word is interpolated between the desire and the act. We must conclude that the word forges the desire.

To give the name "love" to certain agitations and torpors and sudden angers is to bracket them by force, to impose upon them a destiny from without. But Parain has suddenly realized that he was shrinking from this latter consequence. If man *were* what language *makes* him, there would be no problem. Parain maintains a divergence between what I am and what I call myself. Man *is* something apart from discourse. There is a pre-established human order, the silent and humble order of needs. Observe what he says about mothers in the *Essay on Human Wretchedness:*

"There is no woman, even among those who do not at first admit it, who does not want to have children. . . . Rational calculation is against it. The children will be unhappy, they are expensive, they may die . . . the risk is total. Nevertheless . . . their actual energy takes a different direction. For social experience and historical truth are matters of reasoning. This experience is not *their* experience; this truth is not *their* truth. . . . When they reflect, they have something to reflect about, and behind their reflections, their existence is involved, their confidence remains. They are creators in their bodies, in their muscles, in their glands. *They do not flee the struggle because of words, which are cowardly.* . . . What has just been said about children can just as well be said about everything else, about love, honesty, manual labour, sleep, cash payment, everything that civilization has given up and that it longs to regain. . . . We can thus confront what language separates with what life reassembles, what the brain declares impossible with what the flesh maintains. And it becomes evident that the role of language is to record difficulties as fast as they appear . . . whereas the business of man's body—and his appetite for living—is to deny them beforehand so as never to lose the courage to face them. Such is the secret of simple men, of those who, beyond civilization, have retained the same simplicity. It lies in this stubbornness of the body to love and to beget, to transmit its drive and its joy."

There is therefore an order of the body. But obviously this order is not purely biological. It has been set up without words, against words. Nevertheless, it cannot be blind. Parain is well aware of this. He explains that we cannot say "I'm hungry" without saying something more and something other than what we intended. In order for woman, without naming her desire, to be able to have something more than a vague impression of her desire, though without naming it, and to try to satisfy it with absolute security, something other than the ordering of uterine secretions is required. There must be a design, a plan. This design, which is herself and which, nevertheless, is neither her language nor her reflection nor quite her body, but rather a kind of intention and, as it were, entelechy, is, as I see it, a kind of Grace, in the religious sense of the word. And just as the harmonious course of the spheres and the orderly succession of the seasons revealed the designs of the divinity to the peasant stoic of Latium, so, it seems, the meeting within us of this pre-established act reveals to Parain, for the first time, the religious fact.

What a long way we have come from the radical experiments of the post-war period. For what Parain does not say is that this order of the body naturally involves social extension. The society that must correspond to it is what is properly called "conservative." It is no longer a matter of changing man, but of taking the necessary measures to *conserve* the balance of needs. There can be no new man, since there is a natural man. Parain will probably not like my comparing him to Rousseau. But, after all, is not the peasant who, in his "rugged honesty," offers himself to the traps of language really the Noble Savage and the Natural Man? Beneath this radical pessimism lies the optimism of simplicity.

But I see immediately what it is that sets Parain against Rousseau. Though in the eyes of the Protestant order the return to nature may be an impossible undertaking, the individual can at least achieve his balance more or less by himself. Parain is not so sure of himself, and besides, he bears the marks of his Catholic upbringing. He has no Genevan pride. He thinks he is defining man, but he is only describing himself: "Man is an animal that needs assurance. . . . The entire history of man is his effort to establish, to set up within himself a mediating system of co-ordinates, to put himself into the hands of mediating powers." [24] "Man cannot do without mediating powers, just as the earth cannot do without sun. Each man needs a task, a country, children, hope." [25]

Thus, nothing is further removed from him than the destruction in which he was invited to indulge by his contemporaries of 1925. He was surrounded at the time by surrealists, Gidians and communists who kept muttering to him, "Let go!" To let go, to abandon himself, to abandon all orders and all co-ordinates, to find himself alone and naked, a stranger to himself, like Philoctetes when he gave away his bow, like Dimitri Karamazov in prison, like the man who becomes a drug addict out of sheer boredom, like the young man who leaves his social class, family and home and gives himself, naked and alone, to the Party. If he gives everything, he will be exalted. That is what these sirens murmur to him. And this is probably a myth. But Parain does not let go. Quite the contrary. He holds fast. He lashes himself to the mast. We are all familiar with the deep resistance that suddenly mani-

[24] *Return to France.*
[25] *Ibid.*

fests itself when there is a question of losing oneself. We are all familiar too with the amazed remorse, that unsatisfied curiosity, the sullen anger felt by those who have not lost themselves. Parain did not lose himself. He did not want to live without limits. Fields have limits; so do the national and departmental highways. Why should he have lost himself? And what was he asking for? A few acres of land, a decent wife, children, the modest freedom of the craftsman at work, of the peasant in the fields—in short, happiness. Is there any need to lose oneself in order to have these things? He never really wanted to launch himself in a great enterprise. And who can blame him? All he wanted was that a more just and paternal organization assign him his place on earth and, by defining him in terms of rigorous co-ordinates, rid him of the need for security, of the "anxiety that threatened to choke him." [26]

"Man needs a *personal* God. When he cannot sleep or has lost hope and confidence in his strength, when he is beaten, he must turn to something stronger than himself for protection. He has to find security somewhere." [27]

And so, anxiety was present at the beginning, for him as for everyone else. Anxiety and anguish are one and the same. And a choice had to be made. Some chose this very anguish itself, but Parain chose security. Was he right? Was he wrong? Who can judge him? And besides, is not the choosing of anguish often a way of choosing security? All we can do is recognize the fact: thus has he chosen, thus he is, humble and assured, clinging to a few sad and simple truths, surveying the plateaux with insolent modesty and, perhaps, secret dissatisfaction.

But, as a result, the reign of the mediating powers and of language, the first of the intermediaries, returns. To be sure, land would do better. "For a peasant, the land is the intermediary . . . that serves as a common and objective norm." [28] But there are landless peasants, just as there are kings without kingdoms. And Parain is one of these, a rootless man. In

[26] *Return to France.*
[27] *Essay.*
[28] *Ibid.*

a corner of his mind, there is still a certain nostalgia for the totalitarian myth of a harmony that unites the human powers and those of the earth, as the roots of a tree are grounded in the earth that feeds them. Beneath the manner of a grumbling censor, he still harbours the shy and shamefaced naturalism of the native, who is also uprooted. But when he finally had to define and fix himself, it was not to the earth that he returned, but to language. A man must *be*. And for Parain, as for all post-Kantian philosophy, being is synonymous with stability and objectivity. The planet *is,* because its course is set. The tree *is,* because it grows in accordance with fixed laws and without changing place. But man, internally, is "runny," like a cheese. He *is not*. He *will be* only if he knows himself. And, in this case, "knowing oneself" does not mean revealing the truth buried in each man's heart. There is no heart, no truth, simply a monotonous haemorrhage. Knowing oneself means deliberately effecting a transfer of being. I give myself limits. I establish a frame of reference, and then all at once I declare that I *am* these limits and this frame. I *am* a simple private. I *am* a Frenchman. I *am* an *agrégé* and a graduate of the Ecole Normale. This means that I choose to define myself, in the manner of sociologists, in terms of background. Thus, as Halbwachs would say, such and such a man whom one introduces into a drawing-room is so-and-so, the gynaecologist, former interne in the Paris hospitals and medical officer during World War I. Remove the doctor, remove the officer, and all that's left is some dirty water that goes down the drains. It is language that makes the doctor, the magistrate: "We ask it to express what is most intimately personal in a man, most intimately similar to others." [29] We neglect the deliberate aspect of language, that is, its transactions.

We can now see the dialectical movement which has brought Parain back to his starting-point. He was first convinced, like everyone else, of *being*, deep within him, a certain given reality, an individual essence, and he asked language to formulate this essence. But he became aware that he was unable to slip into the socialized forms of speech.

[29] *Investigations.*

He did not recognize himself in the mirror of words. It was then that a double movement revealed to him a double fluidity: if he placed himself in the midst of words, in the city, he saw them melt and flow away, lose their meaning as they passed from one group to another, become more and more abstract, and he set up against them the myth of a natural order of human necessities (love, work, maternity, etc.). If the former could no longer express the latter, it was precisely because that which changes cannot account for that which remains, because vocables that have been deliberately made cannot be applied to nature, because the city cannot speak of the fields.

Language then seemed to him to be a destructive power that separated man from himself. But if he tried to desert words and return to his silence, then the fixed order of desires which he thought he had found immediately vanished again, revealing a fluidity without memory or consistency, a moving and disorderly image of nothingness. Seen from within this fluidity, words seemed, on the contrary, to be as fixed as stars. When one is plunged into the little morass known as love, when one feels tossed about by uncertain emotions, the word love is indeed lovely, what with the ceremonies that go with it, the feelings of tenderness and desire and jealousy, as if one desired to *be* what it *says*. Parain then tried to keep before him, at the same time, the double flow. This was his expressionistic and revolutionary period: language is not; it must be made; the individual is not; he must be named. But in the face of these endless and boundless whirls, he lost heart and turned away. He clung fast. Besides, this universal fluidity made any solution contradictory.

In order for an individual to find within himself enough coherence and force to recreate language, he must first be fixed, in other words, he must first be named. Expressionism is thus a vicious circle. "Action [is not] the measure of our language. . . . Does it not, on the contrary, presuppose an order that provokes it, therefore a word? Can its movement originate from its own self?" [30] And so Parain started shut-

---

[30] *Investigations.*

tling back and forth again. In the *Essay on Human Wretchedness,* he exposes, in the name of the order of needs, the mobility of language. In *Return to France,* on the other hand, the word is fixed and reëstablished in its function of intercessor; it is we who flow without bounds. But a solution begins to appear, an attempt at a modest and positive synthesis and, at the same time, a recourse to God. This solution, which was later developed in *Investigations,* can, I believe, be summed up in four articles:

(1) Having to set a batch of experiences in order, Parain deliberately chose one of them and made it *his* original experience. That was how he constructed his personal history. He defined it as follows, "Man can no more do without language than he can direct it."

(2) He gave it currency by his theory of objectivity. It is the act of naming that gives form to the universal fluidity of sensations and stabilizes it as "things": "The insect probably moves about in his universe of actions and reactions, without representing to himself the external world as an object independent of this universe, which remains homogeneous. Would we not be in the same state of ignorance if we did not have language? . . . I observe how cleanly the object detaches itself from me as soon as I name it. From that moment on, I can no longer refuse to allow it to be an object. Philosophers have rightly observed that every perception is constituted by a judgment. But have they sufficiently stressed the fact that it is the naming that is the first judgment and that this is the decisive moment of the perception?" [31] Words are ideas. This means that man does not create ideas; he assembles them. We have been told again and again, over a long period of time, that man is not God and that he cannot create anything in the universe. He composes and arranges. But coal, oil and marble are simply present. At least, however, he still had his thoughts, which he was allowed to produce by a kind of emanation.

Parain takes them away from him; they are within words. As a result, I am *"situated in language."* [32] Words thereby

[31] *Return to France.*
[32] *Investigations.*

become things. Parain does, of course, tell us that language is "neither subject nor object, adhering neither to one nor the other. Subject when I speak, object when I listen to myself . . . distinct, nevertheless, from other beings; likewise distinct from myself." But despite this prudence, he is obliged to recognize that language, which is the foundation of objectivity, is itself objective: "Subject when I speak, object when I listen to myself." But I never speak without listening to myself, as is proved by the example of the deaf-and-dumb, who are dumb because they are deaf. And how can Parain really accept the notion that words are "subjects"? How could they confer objectivity if they did not already have it? If the word seems to be a subject when I speak, the reason is that I slip into the word; in this sense, the hammer or spoon is also a subject when I use it and when it is not to be distinguished from my action. A moment later, when I lay it down on the table and contemplate it, it is an object.

Thus, as a result of having denied the thing-ness of perception and reduced the sun, wall and table to fleeting and subjective organizations of sensations, Parain deliberately accepts a thing-ness of language. The word is that strange being: an idea-thing. It possesses both the impenetrability of the thing and the transparence of the idea, the inertia of the thing and the active force of the idea. We can take it up as if it were a thing, between our fingers; we can carry it about. But it escapes and betrays us, suddenly regains its independence and arranges itself with other words, in accordance with affinities that escape us. Though individual and dated, like the thing, it expresses only the universal, like the idea. Our relation to it is that of the sorcerer's apprentice to his master's broom; we can set it in motion but cannot guide or stop it. We are completely responsible, in one sense, since we do speak, and completely innocent, in another, since we do not know what we are saying. We are as incapable of lying as of speaking the truth, since it is words that teach us what we mean by words.

Our allusion here to the sorcerer's apprentice is quite intentional. Did not Alain say that magic is "mind lingering amidst things"? Parain's language is the reign of magic.

Blinded ideas, plugged by matter, matter possessed by mind and in revolt against mind. Not Descartes' Evil Spirit, but the Evil Spirit in reverse.

(3) Nevertheless, Parain did not bring himself to abandon his expressionist attitude completely. In a sense, language is no doubt the magical and capricious anti-reason that sometimes offers its services to man and sometimes escapes him. There can be no question as to its really being *the reverse side of an unknown being's reason.*

But Parain cannot overlook the historical life of words. He asserts, as he did earlier, that words change meaning in accordance with the collectivity that uses them. How are we to reconcile this objectivity with this relativity? Are there transcendent and fixed meanings, or is it the social act that gives the word its meaning? Neither one nor the other, because words have open meanings, in the sense that Bergson speaks of "open" societies. Words are both "germs of being" and promises. "Any sign that, either alone or in its system, ends in fulfilment, any promise that is scrupulously kept, may be regarded as concrete. . . . Man must no longer regard his language as a simple notation of facts and laws . . . but rather as an actual involvement in the life that it supports and recreates at every moment." [33] In a way, their meaning lies before them, "to be filled in." But if they are "to be filled in," it is in the manner of a form that a hotel clerk hands us. There is one entire part that is variable and another that is fixed. It is our action that concretizes them, but the abstract scheme and the general line of this action are given in advance in each word: "I declare to a woman that I love her. . . . Have I not simply promised, is it not simply understood between us, that this word will have the meaning that we shall give it in living together? We are going to recreate it. This is a great work. Has it been waiting for us in order to have the meaning that we shall give it? And if it is our intention to give it a meaning, this means that we are going to work for it and not for ourselves. This means, therefore, that it is our master." [34]

[33] *Essay.*
[34] *Investigations.*

This situation has incalculable moral consequences: if the word is a promise, if its meaning remains to be made, then the ambitious quest for *truth*, that is, for a deeply buried treasure that must be unearthed, loses all meaning; there is nothing anywhere, on earth or beneath the earth, nothing that awaits us, nothing with which we can confront the phrases that we shape. But if the main lines of my promise are already laid down in words, if the word is like an impersonal questionnaire to be filled in with my life, work and blood, then the deep and discreet virtue that was hidden in our love of truth is not lost, then *honesty* is not lost. With the expressionist "watchword," honesty gave way to the arbitrary powers of invention, of disordered action, in short, to force. Truth was measured by success, and success was merely a result of chance.

By allowing words an explosive charge, a potential, by allowing them to mortgage the future, Parain reserves a role in the world for man. He also banishes the marvellous and contradictory power of seeing the absolute in silence—and the wild inventiveness that rolls words merrily along as if they were pebbles. In exchange, he preserves for man the power of setting up a human order: commitment, work, fidelity. This is what is restored to us. And it is not enough to be honest, once the promise has been made. We must also be painstaking in the choice of promises, and we must promise little so as to be sure of keeping our word.

There are words that are wild or drunken or outlandish, words of which we must beware. And there are also simple words: work, love, family, words which retained Parain's confidence and affection even at the height of his crisis. They are on a human scale. It is by these words that I must let myself be defined, though it is understood that this definition is not the consecration of a state of fact, but the announcement of a new duty. If I keep my promises, if I "fulfil" my commitments, if having asserted that I love, I carry out this undertaking properly, then I *shall be* what I *say*. "The identity of man and his expression through language . . . is not bestowed as a birth-right. It is the achievement of the individual who, to attain it, cannot do without the aid of society.

Just as a man can believe in it naïvely when he is mature, so an adolescent is bound to reject it. . . . This is our task. It arises from our need for honesty. It means happiness and faith, but only after long wandering." [35] When a man expresses himself, he always says more than he intends, for we think we are expressing the individual, whereas we are really saying the universal: "I'm hungry. It is I who say I'm hungry, but it is not I who am being heard. I have disappeared between the two moments of my statement. Once I have uttered it, all that remains of me is the man who is hungry, and this man belongs to everyone. . . . I have entered the order of the impersonal, that is, the way of the universal." [36]

But since to speak is to commit oneself, the meaning of this ethic is manifest: it means, as in the system of Kant, achieving the universal in one's own flesh. But the universal is not given at the beginning, as in the *Critique of Practical Reason,* nor is it the universal that defines man at the beginning. I am "situated" in language. I cannot be silent. In speaking, I cast myself into this unknown and foreign order, and I suddenly become responsible for it. I must *become* universal. My only possibility, the sole commandment, is to realize with humility and caution, by means of my own flesh, the universality into which I first cast myself heedlessly. I have said that I love; that is the promise. Now I must sacrifice myself so that through me the word love may take on meaning, so that there may be love on earth. At the end of this long enterprise, I shall be rewarded by becoming *he who loves,* that is, I shall finally deserve the name I have given myself. Parain's ethics proposes that I beware of words and their magical powers, that I attach myself only to a few of them, the simplest and most familiar, that I speak little, that I name things with caution, that I say nothing about myself that I am not sure of being able to live up to, that I apply myself throughout my life to fulfilling my promises.

It seems an austere and somewhat timorous ethics. The author does not question it. The reason is that it is located between an original anxiety and a terminal resignation. Parain

[35] *Essay.*
[36] *Investigations.*

has, in fact, always been concerned with "preserving the initial anxiety";[37] he is convinced that "man ends with a certain resignation." [38] We easily perceive the ups and downs of this lost soul: the constant oscillation from the individual to the universal, from the historical to the eternal, the constant disappointments that suddenly reveal the universal at the heart of the individual and, *vice versa,* disclose, to those who thought themselves rooted in the heart of the eternal, the trickery and sham of history, the contradictory and anguished desire of a rigorous social order that nevertheless preserves the dignity of the individual, and, lastly, the resigned affirmation that the fulfilment of the individual lies in the sacrifice wherein he destroys himself so that the universal may exist.

What is this if not the hopeless dialectic which Hegel has demonstrated under the name of *unhappy conscience?* I am a nothingness in the face of the compact immobility of words. It is a question of *being.* But first who is to decide the meaning of being? Each individual. And each will choose himself precisely in so far as he has made a choice of the nature and meaning of being in general. To Parain, being means fixity, dense plenitude, universality. Such is the ideal that he has assigned, from the very beginning and by free choice, to his existence. But how can nothingness be?

(4) We have given up everything. We limit our ambition to adapting ourselves progressively to words which we have not made. However, this resignation cannot save us. If words move, the balance achieved with such difficulty is upset. But they do move. There are word-quakes more dangerous than earthquakes. We are thus thrown into a state of universal mobility, for we hitch the rapid and restless landslide of our individual life to the slower and more massive landslide of language.

There is only one source of help against this peril: God. If words come from society, they are born and die with it, and we are tricked. Happily, "the reasons whereby it is usually proved that language cannot have been invented by man are

[37] *Return to France.*
[38] *Essay.*

irrefutable." [39] If language does not come from man, it therefore comes from God: "Man can no more do without language than he can direct it. He can only accord it his confidence, trying, by the human means at his disposal and the seriousness of his individual experience, not to abuse it. This law of our thought is the best proof of the existence of God; it is parallel to those advanced by theologians, though located in a narrower and thereby more impregnable domain." [40] Parain does not formulate this proof. Perhaps he is reserving it for another work. In any case, we can get a glimpse of it. God appears in it as both author of and warrant for language. He is its author, that is, the order that, in spite of everything, shows through, cannot be due to man.

From this point of view, the proof is linked with the physico-theological argument: it is the ordering beheld in the course of words, in the course of the stars, that compels us to conclude in favour of the existence of a transcendent finality. But since, in another sense, this order is postulated rather than perceived, since the most important thing is to save man from despair by letting him hope for a fixity hidden in the mobile life of words, it may also seem that we are dealing with what is known as the ethical proof, which concludes in favour of the existence of God from our great need of Him. The truth is that it is both ethical and teleological; it is both an exigence and a prayer.

Descartes had limited his ambitions to thinking by means of clear and distinct ideas. Nevertheless, they required a guarantee. Thus, God appeared in his philosophy as a necessary function. Similarly for Parain, who limits himself to thinking with simple words, to "making language serve only those ends for which its imprecision presents the least danger." [41] Nevertheless, a warrant is needed for these simple words. Not of their truth, for this remains to be made and it is for us to make it. Nor of their absolute fixity, since they live and die. But rather of a certain stability preserved within their mobility itself. Hegel says somewhere, concerning law,

[39] *Investigations.*
[40] *Return to France.*
[41] *Ibid.*

that it is the immobile image of movement. And it is laws that Parain asks of God.

It matters little that everything changes so long as words, which are germs of being, have a fixed value, so long as there exists somewhere an immobile and silent image of their fluidity. And this must be so. Otherwise, everything will sink into the absurd: things, which do not exist if they are not named; discourse, which peters out; and our human condition, since "we are not creatures of silence, but logical beings." And just as there is a God for Descartes, because we cannot go wrong when our will is drawn into expressing an opinion, in spite of itself, in like manner there is a God for Parain because we are animals whose chief function is to talk.

This is indeed a strange God, moreover, closer to that of Kafka and Kierkegaard than that of Saint Thomas. He suffers from a quite modern impotence. The messages He sends to men are jammed, or rather they reach us in a jumble. They start from within silence and from a thinking that governs matter, and we receive them in the form of a plurality of sounds; and it is matter that becomes subjected to their meanings. This God does not speak to man. He suggests His silence by means of sounds and words. He reminds me of Kafka's emperors, all-powerful yet unable to communicate with their subjects. Moreover, God too is a word; God is *also* a word, and, as such, a promise, a germ of being. "God must be . . . applied in accordance with the exigence that language bears within itself and brings to us." [42] This is perhaps the clearest part of this theology: there is the *word* God, which both suggests to us and masks from us the *fact* of God. And we must honestly, by faith and works, recreate the meaning of this word.

Parain, who started from silence, now returns to silence. But it is not the same silence. His point of departure was an infra-silence, a violent muteness of the moment that broke through language: "When I go walking, I sometimes do not speak. I mean that I sometimes do not speak to myself. There are times when, as I watch the mist over the Seine, seeing

[42] *Return to France.*

human forms in the sky, sometimes a policeman's uniform or a dancing man or a beautiful woman, I suddenly pull up, I grow suddenly timid. Such emotions constitute the only circumstances in which we feel ourselves existing." [43] But he realized that silence had meaning only through language, which names and sustains it.[44] Since words are a foundation of objectivity, if I see in the sky a policeman's uniform or a dancing man, I do so because I have at my disposal the words man, uniform, policeman and dancing. To be silent is to imply the words and that is all. However, such is Parain's love of silence that he discovers another silence, an ultra-silence, that gathers within itself all of language and pervades it, as the Heideggerian nothingness embraces the world, as the non-knowing of Blanchot and Bataille envelops knowledge and supports it.

Here it is simply a matter of one of the many surprises held in store for us by *totalization*. To challenge is to totalize. The totality of knowledge is non-knowing, because it appears at a point of view that transcends knowledge. And the totality of language is silence, for one must be situated in the midst of language in order to speak. However, in the case with which we are concerned, totalization is impossible for man, since it would have to be achieved by means of words. And Parain's silence is only a big optimistic myth—a myth which, if I am not mistaken, he has now left behind.[45]

Shall I offer a criticism of these theses? I have known Parain for ten years. I have often argued various matters with him. I have witnessed all the turns of this upright and rigorous thinking. I have often admired his knowledge and

[43] Unpublished manuscript.
[44] Compare what Bataille says of the *word* silence in *The Inner Experience*.
[45] This likening of a linguistic totality to silence had already begun to tempt him when he spoke to me about the late works of Tolstoy which, according to him, could be likened to "an old man's great silence." A writer is God in that he creates his own language and that one can totalize his words, can speak of the language of Plato and Shakespeare. He thereby reveals himself beyond his words, and his work may be likened to silence. This is reminiscent of Blanchot.

dialectical skill. To avoid any misunderstanding, I should like to make it clear that my objections seem to me a stage in the long and friendly dialogue we have been carrying on all these years. He will probably reply tomorrow. And so it will go back and forth between us, and meanwhile his thinking will follow its course. He will change his position, and, in all probability, I shall do likewise. We shall approach or move away from each other. Another Parain and another Sartre will carry on the discussion.

But since the function of the critic is to criticize, that is, to take a stand for or against and to situate himself by situating, let me say that I accept roughly the greater part of Parain's analyses. I challenge only their scope and their place. The question at issue between us, one that often arises in the history of philosophy, is that of the beginning. Parain may be reproached with not beginning with the psychology of the man who speaks. But this is not my opinion. He is also a Comtist in that he is deeply suspicious of psychology. He has no desire to enter into analyses of those "verbal images" or "verbo-motive processes" with which psychologists bombarded us during the early years of the twentieth century. He is right. If there are wordless thoughts, such as Messer's and Bühler's subjects discovered within themselves, what interest have they for us? For it would have to be proved that these wordless thoughts are not bounded, limited and conditioned by the whole of language. And there is no point in describing the empirical transition from the idea to the word, for what does it teach us? We would have to be sure that the idea is not simply the dawn of a word.

Parain boasts that, with needs and speech, he can reconstruct a whole man. And if he means the empirical man that psychology claims to have attained, he may not be wrong. In the same way, sociologists maintained that physiological and social facts were enough to compose the human order. This may be granted; all depends on the definition of the social and physiological. But is there no other beginning than introspective psychology?

Someone speaks to me. The word "pellet" strikes my ear. We have here a dated, localized event, an individual one, in short. If we take a rigorous view of the matter, it is not the word "pellet" that I hear but rather a certain highly particular sound, uttered by a soft or hoarse voice and lifted up in a whirlwind, amidst lights that penetrate it, odours that impregnate it, and a sadness or gaiety that colours it. Three hours go by. Whereupon, I, in turn, utter the word "pellet." Can I be said to hear myself? Not quite, since, if my voice is recorded, I do not recognize it. It is a case of a quasi-hearing, which there is no need to go into here. And if the word that I *eat*, that fills my mouth with its pulp, resembles the one I heard a while before, it does so only in so far as both are individual events.

Take another individual event: I am looking at the page of a book which is glazed, as it were, by a cold sun. I inhale an odour of mushroom that rises from the paper to my nose, and, among other particularities, I see a few particular strokes drawn on a line: "pellet." I now ask Parain where is the *word* "pellet," that non-temporal and non-extended reality that is both on the page of the book, in the vibration of the air, in that moist mouthful I swallow and that does not let itself be absorbed by any of these particular phenomena. Where is *that* word which was neither yesterday nor the day before, which is not today and which will not be tomorrow, but which manifests itself yesterday, today and tomorrow in such a way that each time I hear it, I perceive the auditory phenomena as one of its embodiments and not as an absolute event? In short, if language is the basis of objectivity, what is at the basis of the objectivity of language? I see before me a white worm. According to Parain, I need the words "white worm" to endow it with a certain permanence, a future, a past, qualities, relationships with the other objects of the world. But when I open this book about meteors, I see the little black scrawl that composes the vocable "pellet," exactly as I see the white worm. If it is true, that, without the denomination, the latter is only a label grouping of sensations, the former cannot exist differently. Do we therefore need a word to denominate the word "pellet"? But then what will denominate this word in turn? And so on *ad infinitum*.

This means that the simple act of naming, therefore of

speaking, has become impossible. This is the "third man" that Aristotle used against Plato. It is not unanswerable if it is applied to pure ideas, since Plato cites it himself, not without irony, in the *Parmenides*. But the reason is that the idea does not need an idea in order to be understood. It is nothing other than the pure act of intellection. When, on the other hand, I consider the word, I see that it has a body and that it manifests itself to me by means of this body, amidst a host of other bodies. But where does it get its privileged character? Shall we say that it gets it from God or from society? But this is a lazy solution. Or rather we are in an area where neither God nor society can any longer intervene.

Let us grant that, by divine grace, the word "pellet" is preserved and endowed with a kind of permanence and that it is the *same word* that struck me yesterday and that strikes me today. After all, the inkwell, the desk and the tree that I saw a while ago and that I see now are the same. We therefore must admit that even in this unrealizable conjecture, the *external* identity of the word pellet would be of no use to me, for however identical it might be physically, I would still have to recognize it, that is, to extract it from the flux of phenomena and stabilize it. I would still have to refer it to its appearances of yesterday and the day before and establish between these different moments a synthetic place of identification.

Of what importance is it that this inkwell is the same outside me? If I have no memory, I shall say that there are ten inkwells, a hundred inkwells, as many inkwells as there are appearances. Or rather I won't even say that there is an inkwell. I won't say anything at all. In like manner, for the word "pellet": knowledge and communication are possible only if there is *a* word pellet. But even if the word did exist in the bosom of God, I must produce it by the operation known as "synthesis of identification." And now I realize that the word had no privileged stature. For I must also make the table and the tree and the white worm exist as permanent syntheses of relatively stable properties. It is not by naming them that I endow them with objectivity. But I can name them only if I have constituted them as independent wholes, that is, if I objectify the thing and the word that names it in one and the same synthetic act. I hope that no one will think of replying that God maintains *within us* the identity of the word. For if God thinks within me, I vanish. God remains alone. And Parain would certainly not go so far as that. No, it is I who, either in listening or speaking, establish the word with one of the elements of my experience.

Before dealing with language, Parain should have asked himself how the experience is possible, for there is an experience of language. He has meditated upon Descartes, Leibnitz and Hegel. Well and good. But he says nothing about Kant. And this enormous gap in the *Investigations* is no accident. It means simply that Parain has been mistaken in the order of his thoughts. For if I constitute my experience and my words within this experience, it is not on the level of language but on that of the synthesis of identification that the universal appears. When I say that "I'm hungry," the word universalizes. This is taken for granted. But in order to universalize, *I* must first universalize, that is, I must disengage the word "hungry" from the disorderly confusion of my present impressions.

But we must go even further back. Parain has not hesitated to reproduce a weak analysis of the Cartesian *cogito* that he found in *The Will to Power*. We know that Nietzsche was not a philosopher. But why does Parain, who is a professional philosopher, quote this crackbrained nonsense? Does he think he can get by with this so easily? It doesn't matter what Descartes *says* of the *cogito*. What counts is that when I understand a word, I must evidently be conscious of understanding it. If I am, both word and understanding vanish into darkness.

Parain says that language interpolates itself between me and my self-knowledge. This may be so, but on condition that the relation I maintain with myself begins with knowledge. But when I am conscious of understanding a word, no word is interpolated between me and myself. The word, the single word in question, is there *before* me, as *that which is understood*. Where else would you put it? In consciousness? You might as well introduce into it a tree or a wall that would cut it off from itself. And yet it must be understood; otherwise it is merely an idle sound. After this, what difference is it to me whether one argues on and on about the "I" of the *cogito*? This merely concerns syntax and grammar, and perhaps logic. But the effectiveness, the eternity, of the *cogito* lies in the fact that it reveals a type of existence defined as the state of being present to oneself without intermediary. The word is interpolated between my love and myself, between my courage or cowardice and myself, not between my understanding and my consciousness of understanding. For the consciousness of understanding is the law of being of understanding. I shall call this the silence of consciousness.

This is a far cry from the flux of sensory impressions to which Parain wants to reduce us. However, I know his answer to this: I grant what you say about consciousness, but as soon as you try to *express* what you are, you get bogged down in language. I agree. However, I know what it is that I want to express because I *am* it without intermediary. Language may resist and mislead me, but I shall never be taken in by it unless I want to, for I can always come back to what I am, to the emptiness and silence that I am, through which, nevertheless, there is a language and there is a world. The *cogito* escapes Parain's clutches, as do the synthesis of identification and the universal. And that was the beginning.

The fact remains that the *Other* is present and that he understands my words, if he wishes, or can refuse to understand them. And it seems to me that the Other is not sufficiently present in the work of Parain. He intervenes occasionally, but I don't know where he comes from. This too is a problem of beginning. Who is first? The Other or language? If language, then the Other disappears. If the Other must appear before me only when he is named, then it is the word that makes the Other, just as it makes the white worm or the pellet. And it is also the word that can remove him. I cannot escape solipsism: amidst the flux of my sensations, the word *Other* isolates a certain unit which it endows with a certain universal meaning. It cannot be a matter of an exceptional experience. But then I am talking to myself. The supposed interventions of the Other are only reactions of my language upon my language. If, on the contrary, when I speak, I have the agonizing certainty that words escape me and that they will take on elsewhere, outside me, unexpected aspects and unforeseen meanings, does not this mean that it is inherent in the very structure of language to be understood by a free individual other than myself? In short, is it not the Other who makes language, is it not the Other who comes first? Parain acknowledges this, almost in spite of himself, since he refers to that quintessence of the Other, namely God. But why is God needed? To explain the origin of language? But a problem arises only if man first exists, alone, naked, silent and finished, and if he speaks *afterwards*. It is then that we can ask ourselves how he came to speak. But if I exist originally only by and for the Other, if, as soon as I appear, I am thrust before his eyes, and if the Other is as certain to me as I myself am, then I am a language, for language is only existence in the presence of another.

Take, for example, the case of a woman who stands watching me shrewdly, full of hatred, without saying a word, as I move about the room. All my gestures are immediately alienated from me, stolen from me. They form a horrible composition of whose existence I am unaware. There, in the fire of her gaze, I am clumsy and ridiculous. I pull myself together. I fight against that foreign chill which numbs me. And then I become too offhand, too conceited, even more ridiculous.

There you have language in a nutshell; it is precisely this silent and desperate dialogue. Language is being-for-another. What need have we for God? The Other is sufficient, any other. He enters, and I cease to belong to myself. It is he who interpolates himself between me and myself, not in the silent privacy of the *cogito,* but between myself and all that I am on earth, happy or unhappy, handsome or ugly, low or magnanimous. For I need the co-operation of the Other in order to be all that. But if it is true that to speak means to act in front of the Other, the great problems of language may turn out to be only a regional specification of the great ontological problem of the existence of the Other. If the Other does not understand me, is it because I speak or because he is another? And if language betrays me, is this due to a characteristic malignity, or does it not rather do so because it is the mere surface of contact between me and the Other? In short, in order for there to be a problem of language, the Other must first be assumed.

In opposition to Parain, we must therefore maintain the priority of the *cogito,* of the universalizing synthesis,[46] of the immediate experience of the Other. Thus, we restore language to its true place. But if its power is thereby limited from above, it is also, as I see it, limited from below, not only by the human reality that names and understands, but also by the objects that are named. "When I feel certain inner disturbances and then say that I am hungry, I am not communicating my sensations to the persons I am addressing. I am merely indicating to them that I have a desire to eat, or rather that I think I need to eat. I have thought that my restlessness would be calmed if I took some food. In doing this, I have advanced an hypothesis concerning my state. But I may be mistaken. Amputees actually feel cold in the leg that has been cut off." [47]

Parain is still under the influence of nineteenth-century psychology which allows only for emotional states that have been experienced and to which our generation attaches meanings from without as a matter of habit. Isn't this rather premature? Ought he not first to have taken a stand on the phenomenological conception of affectivity, which makes of each desire an intentional "Erlebnis," that is, one which is directly grounded in its object?

I once knew a young woman who had a stomach ulcer. When she had gone a long time without food, she would feel a sharp pain and would thereby gather that she had to eat.

[46] I have simplified the problem of synthesis by presenting it in its Kantian form. We ought, perhaps, to speak of "passive syntheses," as does Husserl, or to show that human reality, by temporalizing itself, makes use of complexes that have already been *synthesized.* In any case, the argument remains the same: what holds for language holds for any object, for language is also an object.
[47] *Investigations.*

We have here a case of "emotional states" or "sensations," such as Parain postulates. However, the young woman did not say that she was hungry. Nor did she think that she was. She thought that the pains she suffered would disappear if she fed herself. To be hungry, on the other hand, means to be conscious of being hungry. It means being thrust into the world of hunger. It means seeing bread and meat gleam with a painful brilliance in shop windows. It means finding oneself dreaming of a chicken. "The doctor," says Parain, "may reject my diagnosis." But there is no diagnosis—that is, no random induction tending to interpret the mute data—and the doctor has nothing to say here. He may explain to me that I ought not to eat, that this hunger is ambiguous, that it corresponds to a certain state of my organism far removed from inanition. But he cannot impugn my hunger.

What would a joy of suffering of sexual desire be like if it needed language to assure it that it was what it was? Language would no doubt dangerously extend its scope, would indicate to me that it was a "universal desire," would suggest an appropriate line of conduct for satisfying it. But a desire which did not reveal itself as a desire would in no way distinguish itself from indifference or resignation. When I have a headache, I *suppose* that an aspirin will calm my suffering. But my headache is not at all a desire for an aspirin. However, when I desire a woman, my desire does not want to be calmed but rather satisfied, and I do not have to set up a hypothesis to know how I can satisfy it. The desire is simply there, for those arms and that throat. It is a desire for this woman or else no desire at all.

But, it may be argued, there remains the external object: the tree, the table, that night. There is no denying that here language forms a constitutive stratum of the thing. But it is not language that gives it its cohesion, form or permanence. In this case, too, it seems to me that Parain's psychological presuppositions date somewhat. Why speak of sensations here? Sensation has long since been relegated to the storeroom. It is a dream of psychology, a mere word. The Gestalt experiments reveal, on the contrary, a positive cohesion of objects,

176 / **Literary and Philosophical Essays**

laws of structure, and dynamic and static relationships which surprise and bewilder the observer and do not need to be named.

At night, if I see a bright spot on the wheel of a bicycle, it describes a cycloid. During the day, the same spot seems to me animated with a circular movement. Words have nothing to do with the matter. Something quite different is involved. A fly does not speak, says Parain, and therefore "its sensations remain in a state of blur." [48] I find this rather rash. What does he know about the fly? He affirms what he has to prove. The experiments of the Gestaltists tend to show that the less evolved animals behave in accordance with the perception of *relationships* and not in accordance with alleged sensations. A chick, a bee and a chimpanzee interpret *the lightest colour* as a signal, and not a particular grey or green.[49] Does Parain challenge these experiments? If he does, he should say so.

The trouble is that his knowledge is that of his generation. He is unfamiliar with contemporary German psychologists and philosophers, or else he does not understand them. He does not know much about Hegel. He has not read the unpublished writings of Kant. The recent works of Gelb and Goldstein on aphasia have escaped him. Thus, without realizing it, he is thrashing about amidst outmoded problems. He draws conclusions from the French philosophical movement that went from Ribot to Bergson to Brunschvicg. He liquidates matters and makes a final reckoning. For us, all these names are dead and the liquidation has taken place painlessly and noiselessly. We have been brought up otherwise.

Language is located between stable and concrete objects which have not waited for it in order to reveal themselves (intentional desires, forms of external perception), and human realities which are articulate by nature and, by virtue of this fact, are located outside speech, for they attain each other directly and are thrust together without intermediary. Consequently, it can lie, mislead, falsify and make improper generalizations. The questions it raises are technical, political,

[48] *Investigations.*
[49] Cf. Guillaume, *Psychology of Form.*

aesthetic and moral. In this area Parain's analyses are to the point. But there is no metaphysical problem of language. In Parain's writings are to be found all the theories that sum up the attitudes that man has taken in the modern world toward himself and his destiny. I find Descartes and rationalism, Leibnitz, Hegel, Nietzsche, pragmatism. But I am constantly embarrassed, for it seems to me that Parain does much more than interpret them. He translates them into his own language. Descartes places confidence in clear and distinct ideas, and Parain translates this into confidence in words. Nietzsche attempts a *logical* criticism of the *cogito;* Parain writes that he "poses perfectly the problem of language, while *thinking that he poses* only that of logic." Modern pragmatism is inspired by the following line of Faust:

Im Anfang war die Tat,

and Parain translates: "Action is the measure of our language." The Platonic "logos" becomes discourse, and so on. Is this not bias? Is he not forcing the truth? Does the Greek word "logos" have only one meaning? And may I not, in turn, amuse myself by *translating* Parain's thoughts? Can I not say that this man, after despairing of knowledge and reason, after adhering for a time, in an age when man wanted to forge his destiny, to a kind of radical pragmatism, has returned, with his contemporaries, to a reliance on a transcendent order which delivers him from his anxiety? What becomes of language in all that? And if he translates, then I will translate his translation. And so on endlessly. Is it not better to let everyone say what he meant to say? As Breton said to a commentator of Saint-Pol-Roux, "If Saint-Pol-Roux had *meant to say* 'water-bottle,' he would have said it." Does not the same hold true for Descartes or Hegel?

It is in our hearts that Parain's books resound most deeply. When he writes, for example, "I feel that I am responsible for a world I have not created," [50] we give him our unreserved adherence. Parain is a man for whom man exists—

50 *Investigations.*

man, not human *nature,* that ready-made reality, but man in given conditions, the being who derives his being from his limits only. We like his resigned but militant wisdom, his gravity, his readiness to look things in the face, his brave and proud honesty and, above all, his great charity. The theoretical principles of his work may seem to us a bit outmoded, but in his ethics he is akin to the youngest of us. I am thinking especially of Camus. For Camus, man's response to the absurdity of his condition does not lie in a great romantic rebellion, but in daily effort. Our *true* revolt lies in seeing things clearly, keeping our word and doing our job. For there is no reason for me to be faithful, sincere and courageous. And *that is precisely why* I must show myself to be such. Parain asks nothing else of us. No doubt he does hint at a kind of divine sanction, but his God is so far away that He doesn't bother us. Will the young people of this difficult age find satisfaction in this ethics, or is it only a necessary stage in the exploration of the limits of the human condition? And will Parain himself, and Camus, be satisfied with it? Parain readily agrees that the bias towards scrupulous honesty in the choice of words leads the novelist easily into populism. For the words bread, piece-work, plough and school are more familiar to us than those of love, hatred, freedom and destiny. And yet he loathes this grey, drab, horizonless world.

In like manner, the human person of Camus seems to burst the seams of his doctrine. What will they do? We must wait. Schlumberger's remarks about Corneille apply admirably to the post-war period, even though he professes to despise it, as well as to the return that followed it, and perhaps also to what will follow this return.

"There is no great movement that does not have its point of departure in a creation . . . with all the brutality, haste and even artificiality that this implies. Nor is there any great movement that is not followed, after one has lived for a longer or shorter period by these new modes, by the need for a more minute clarification, a 'return to nature,' that is, to average modes. The alternating of the two disciplines is necessary. What a relief it is when a sound and modern work restores to their rightful places the great, exalted figures who have become, with time, empty puppets. But how we start when a peremptory affirmation makes possible a new departure in a stagnant age in which analysis becomes more and more meticulous, refined and pedestrian, when a man sets to work again on that most difficult of undertakings, the effort to invent man." [51]

[51] *Outline of French Literature* (Gallimard); "Corneille," by Jean Schlumberger.

Chapter 12

Cartesian Freedom

FREEDOM IS ONE and indivisible, but it manifests itself in a variety of ways, according to circumstances. The following question may be asked of all philosophers who set up as its defenders: in connection with what exceptional *situation* have you experienced your freedom? It is one thing to test your freedom in the realm of action, of social or political activity, or of artistic creation, and another thing to test it in the act of understanding and discovering. A Richelieu, a Vincent de Paul or a Corneille would, had they been metaphysicians, have had certain things to tell us about freedom because they grasped it by one end, at a moment when it manifested itself by an absolute event, by the appearance of something new, whether poem or institution, in a world that neither asked for it nor rejected it. Descartes, who was primarily a metaphysician, grasped things by the other end: his primary experience was not that of creative freedom "ex nihilo" but of autonomous thinking which discovers by its own power intelligible relationships among existing essences. That is why we Frenchmen, who have been living by Cartesian freedom for three centuries, understand implicitly by "free will" the practice of independent *thinking* rather than the production of a creative act, and our philosophers have finally come, like Alain, to identify freedom with the act of judging.

The fact is that the exhilaration of understanding always includes the joy of feeling ourselves responsible for the truths we discover. Regardless of who the teacher is, there always comes a moment when the pupil confronts the mathematical problem unaided. If he does not bring his mind to grasp the relationships, if he himself does not produce the conjectures and diagrams which are to be applied like cipher-stencils to the figure under consideration and which reveal the major features of its construction, if he does not finally acquire a decisive insight, the words remain dead signs; everything has been learned by rote. Thus, if I examine myself, I can feel that intellection is not the mechanical result of a pedagogic procedure, but rather that its origin lies solely in my deliberate willing, my application, my refusal to be distracted or hurried, in the undivided attention of my mind—to the radical exclusion of all external forces. And such indeed was Descartes' primary intuition. He was more fully aware than anyone else that the slightest act of thinking involves all thinking, an autonomous thinking that posits itself—in each of its acts—in its full and absolute independence.

But, as we have seen, this experience of *autonomy* does not coincide with that of *productivity*. The reason is that thought must obviously have *something* to understand, whether it be the objective relationships among essences and among structures, or the sequence of ideas, in short, a pre-established order of relationships. Thus, as a counterpart to freedom of intellection, nothing is more rigorous than the path that lies ahead: "As there is but one truth concerning each thing, whoever finds it knows all that can be known about it. For example, a child who has been taught arithmetic and who has done a sum in accordance with its rules can be certain that, as far as the sum which he examined is concerned, he has found all that the human mind can find. For the method which teaches how to follow the true order and to indicate exactly all the circumstances of what is sought, contains everything that gives certainty to the rules of arithmetic." [1]

Everything is stated: the object to be discovered and the method. The child who sets himself to doing a sum in accordance with the rules does not enrich the universe with a new truth. He merely repeats an operation that has been performed by a thousand others before him and that he will never be able to push beyond the same point they have reached. The attitude of the mathematician is therefore a rather striking paradox. His mind is like that of a man who walks on a very narrow path where each of his steps and the very posture of his body are rigorously conditioned by the

[1] *Discourse on Method,* Part II.

nature of the ground and the necessities of the walking, but who is nevertheless imbued with the unshakable conviction that he is performing all these acts freely. In short, if we start with mathematical intellection, how shall we reconcile the fixity and necessity of essences with freedom of judgment? The problem is particularly difficult owing to the fact that, in Descartes' time, the order of mathematical truths seemed to all right-thinking people the product of the divine will. And since this order could not be eluded, Spinoza preferred to sacrifice human subjectivity to it: he showed the true as developing and asserting itself by its own power *through* these incomplete individualities, these finite modes. Confronted with the order of essences, subjectivity can be only the simple freedom of adhering to the true (in the sense that, for certain moralists, we have no other *right* than to do our *duty*) or else it is only a jumbled thought, a mutilated truth, the development and elucidation of which dissipate its subjective character. In the second case, man disappears. There remains no difference between thought and truth. The true is the totality of the system of thoughts. If anyone wants to save man, the only thing to do, since he cannot *produce* any idea but only contemplate it, is to provide him with a simple negative power, that of saying *no* to whatever is not true. Thus, we find in Descartes, under the appearance of a unitary system, two rather different theories of freedom, according to whether he is considering this power of understanding and judging which is his or whether he simply wants to save the autonomy of man when confronted with the rigorous system of ideas.

His spontaneous reaction is to affirm the responsibility of man in the presence of the true. Truth is a human thing, since I must affirm it in order for it to exist. Before my *judgment,* which is an adherence of my will and a free commitment of my being, there exist only neutral and floating ideas which are neither true nor false. Man is thus the being through whom truth appears in the world. His task is to commit himself totally in order that the natural order of existants may become an order of truths. He must ponder the world, must will his thinking and must transform the order of being into a system of ideas. Ever since the *Meditations,* he has appeared as the "ontico-ontological" being of whom Heidegger speaks. Descartes therefore begins by providing us with entire intellectual responsibility. At every moment, he experiences the freedom of his thought, and his solitude as well, in the face of the sequence of essences. As Heidegger has said, nobody can die for me. But Descartes had said earlier that nobody can understand for me. In the end, we must say yes or no and decide alone, for the entire universe, on what is true. This adherence is a metaphysical and absolute act. Commitment is not relative. It is not a matter of an approximation that can be called into question again. But just as Kant's moral man acts as a legislator for the community of ends, Descartes, as a scientist, decides as to the laws of the world. For this "yes," which must finally be uttered in order for the reign of the true to come into being, requires the commitment of an infinite power that is given in its entirety all at once. We cannot say a "partial" yes or a "partial" no. And man's "yes" is no different from God's. "Only the will do I perceive within me to be so great that I cannot conceive the idea of anything wider or more far-reaching, so that it is chiefly the will which enables me to know that I bear the image and likeness of God. For, though it is incomparably greater in God than in myself, either because of knowledge and power, which, being joined to it, make it more stable and more efficacious, or because of its object . . . nevertheless it does not seem to me greater, if I consider it strictly and precisely in itself."

It is evident that, precisely because this entire freedom is not a matter of degree, it belongs equally to every man. Or rather—for freedom is not a quality among other qualities—it is evident that every man *is* a freedom. And the famous assertion that common sense is the most common thing in the world does not mean only that every man has the same seeds in his mind and the same innate ideas, but also that "it bears witness to the fact that the power to judge soundly and to distinguish the true from the false is equal in all men."

A man cannot be more of a man than other men because freedom is similarly infinite in each individual. In this sense, no one has shown better than Descartes the connection between the spirit of science and the spirit of democracy, for universal suffrage cannot be founded on anything other than this universal faculty of saying yes or saying no. We can, no doubt, observe a wide difference among men. One man has a better memory, another a richer imagination, another understands things more quickly, another embraces a wider field of truth. But these qualities are not constitutive of the notion of man. They are to be regarded as corporeal accidents. The only thing that characterizes us as human creatures is the use that we freely make of these gifts. It makes no difference whether we have understood more or less quickly, since understanding, however it come, must be total for all or it does not exist. If Alcibiades and the slave understand the same truth, they are entirely alike in that they understand it. In like manner, the situation of a man and his powers cannot increase or limit his freedom. Descartes has here made, after the Stoics, an essential distinction between freedom and power. To be free is not to be able to do what one wants but to want what one can: "There is nothing that is entirely in our power, save our thoughts, at least if you use the word thinking, as I do, for all the operations of the soul, so that not only acts of meditation and of will, but even the functions of seeing, hearing, determining to perform one movement rather than another, etc. . . . , in so far as they depend upon it, are thoughts. . . . I did not mean thereby that external things are not at all in our power, but simply that they are so only in so far as they can follow from our thoughts, and not *absolutely* or *entirely*, because there are other powers outside us which can interfere with the results of our intentions." [2]

Thus, with a variable and limited power, man has total freedom. Here we perceive the negative aspect of freedom. For if I do not have power to perform such and such an action, I must abstain from desiring to perform it: "I must always try to conquer myself rather than fortune and to change my desires rather than the order of the world." In short, I must practise Επόχη in the moral realm. Nevertheless, the

[2] To M***, March 1638.

fact remains that freedom, in this primary conception, has a certain "efficacity." It is a positive and constructive freedom. It probably cannot change the quality of the movement that is in the world, but it can modify the direction of this movement. "The main seat of the soul is in the small gland which is in the middle of the brain, from which it radiates throughout the rest of the body by the agency of the [animal] spirits, the nerves and even the blood. . . . And the entire action of the soul consists in this, that merely by willing something, it makes the small gland to which it is closely joined move in the way requisite for producing the effect relating to this desire." [3]

It is this "efficacity," this constructiveness of human freedom that we find at the origin of the *Discourse on Method*. For the method is *invented:* "Certain paths," says Descartes, "have led me to considerations and maxims from which I have formed a method." [4] Better still, each rule of the Method (except the first) is a maxim of action or invention. Does not the analysis prescribed by the second rule call for a free and creative judgment which produces schemes and which conceives hypothetical divisions which it verifies shortly afterwards? And must not the order recommended in the third rule be sought and prefigured in the midst of disorder before we submit to it? The proof is that it will be invented if it does not actually exist: "Supposing even that there is order between [those objects] which do not naturally precede each other." And do not the listings of the fourth precept suppose a power of generalization and classification characteristic of the human spirit? In short, the rules of the Method are on the level of Kantian schematism. They represent, in sum, very general directives for free and creative judgment. Was not Descartes, at a time when Bacon was teaching the English to look to experience, the first to call upon the physicist to give precedence to hypothesis? We thus discover in his works a splendid humanistic affirmation of creative freedom, which constructs the true, piece by piece, which at every moment anticipates and prefigures the real relationships among es-

[3] *Treatise on the Passions of the Soul,* Articles 34 and 41.
[4] *Discourse on Method,* Part I.

sences by producing hypotheses and *schemata* which equal for God and for man, equal for all men, absolute and infinite, forces us to assume a fearful task, *our* task par excellence, namely, to cause a truth to exist in the world, to act so that the world is true—and which causes us to live with *generosity,* a "sentiment that each one has of his own free will and that is joined to the resolution never to be lacking in it."

But the established order intervenes at once. For a philosopher like Kant, the human mind constitutes the truth. For Descartes, it merely discovers it, since God has fixed for all time all the relationships which essences maintain among themselves. In addition, however the mathematician has chosen to handle his problem, he cannot doubt the result once it has been reached. The man of action who contemplates his enterprise can say, "This is mine." But not the scientist. As soon as the truth is discovered, it becomes foreign to him. It belongs to everyone and no one. He can merely recognize it, and, if he has a clear view of the relationships that constitute it, he cannot even doubt it. Transpierced by an inner illumination that animates his entire being, he can only give his adherence to the theorem that has been discovered and thereby to the order of the world. Hence, the judgments "two and two are four" and "I think, therefore I am" have value only inasmuch as I affirm them, but I cannot help but affirm them. If I say that I do not exist, I am not even shaping a fiction. I am assembling words whose meanings destroy each other, just as if I spoke of squared circles or three-sided cubes. Thus, the Cartesian will is forced to affirm. "For example, examining recently whether anything really existed in the world, and knowing that by virtue of the fact that I was examining the question, it very manifestly followed that I myself existed, I could not help but judge that a thing which I conceived clearly was true, not that I found myself forced to do so by any external cause, but only because the great light that was in my understanding was followed by a great inclination in my will." [5]

Descartes persists in using the word "free" to qualify this

[5] *Fourth Meditation.*

irresistible adherence to evidence, but he does so because he is here giving a quite different meaning to the word freedom. The adherence is free because it is not caused by the pressure of any constraint external to us, that is, it is not caused by a movement of the body or by a psychological impulsion. We are not in the realm of the passions of the soul. But if the *soul* remains independent of the body during the unfolding of the evidence *of the soul,* and if, in the terms of the definitions in the *Treatise on the Passions,* we may call the affirmation of relationships that are clearly and distinctly conceived an action of the thinking substance taken in its totality, these terms cease to have meaning if we consider the will in relation to the understanding. For we have called freedom the will's self-determined possibility of saying yes or no to ideas conceived by the understanding, which meant, in other terms, that the die had never been cast, that the future had never been foreseeable. Whereas at present, the relation of understanding to will, as concerns evidence, is conceived in the form of a rigorous law in which the clarity and distinctness of the idea play the role of determining factor in relation to the affirmation. In short, Descartes is here much closer to philosophers such as Spinoza and Leibnitz who define the freedom of a human being by the development of his essence, apart from any external action, though the moments of this development follow on each other's heels with rigorous necessity. It is at this point that he goes so far as to deny the freedom of indifference or rather so far as to make it the lowest degree of freedom: "In order for me to be free, it is not necessary that I be indifferent to choosing one of two alternatives, but rather, the more I incline toward one, whether because I know from evidence that the true and good meet there or because God thus disposes the inner working of my thinking, the more freely do I choose and embrace it." [6]

The second term of the alternative, "whether God thus disposes the inner working of my thinking," concerns faith in the strict sense of the term. In this domain, as the understanding cannot be the sufficient reason of the act of faith,

[6] *Fourth Meditation.*

the entire will is shot through and illuminated by an inner and supernatural light that is called grace. We may be shocked to see this autonomous and infinite freedom suddenly *affected* by divine grace and *disposed* to affirm what it does not see clearly. But, at bottom, is there a great difference between natural light and this supernatural light which is grace? In the second case, there can be no doubt that it is God Who affirms, through the intermediary of our will. But does not the same obtain in the first case? If ideas have being, they do so insofar as they come from God. Clarity and distinctness are only signs of the inner cohesion and the absolute density of being of the idea. And if I am irresistibly inclined to affirm the idea, it is exactly insofar as it weighs on me with all its being and all its absolute positiveness. It is this pure and dense being, flawless and entire, which affirms itself within me by its own weight. Thus, since God is the source of all being and all positivity, this positivity, this fullness of existence which is itself a true judgment, cannot have its source in me, who am nothing, but in Him. And let us not regard this theory merely as an effort to reconcile a rationalistic metaphysics with Christian theology. It expresses, in the vocabulary of the time, the consciousness that the scientist has always had of being a pure nothingness, a simple beholder in the face of the obstinate and eternal consistency, the infinite weight of the truth he contemplates.

Three years later, in 1644, Descartes did return to concede to us the freedom of indifference. "We are," he says, "so certain of the freedom and indifference that are within us that there is nothing we know more clearly. Consequently, the omnipotence of God should not prevent us from believing in them." [7] But this is a simple precaution. The tremendous success of the *Augustinus* had worried him, and he did not want to run the risk of being condemned by the Sorbonne. We must rather point out that this new conception of freedom without free will began to extend to all subjects on which he reflected. He wrote to Mersenne: "You reject what I have said, *that it is sufficient to judge correctly in order to act*

[7] *Principles*, Para. 41.

correctly; and yet it seems to me that the common scholastic doctrine is *Voluntas non fertur in malum, nisi quatenus ei sub aliqua ratione boni repraesentatur ab intellectu,* whence the saying: *omnis peccans est ignorans;* with the result that if ever the understanding proposed to the will anything which was not a good thing, the will could not fail to make the proper choice." The thesis is now complete. The clear vision of the Good entails the act as the distinct vision of the True entails assent. For the Good and the True are one and the same thing, namely, Being. And if Descartes is able to say that we are never so free as when we do Good, it is in doing so that he substitutes a definition of freedom by the *value* of the act— the freest act being that which is the best, the one most in conformity with the universal order—for a definition by autonomy. And this is in accordance with the logic of his doctrine: if we do not invent *our* Good, if Good has an *a priori,* independent existence, how could we perceive it without doing it?

Nevertheless, we find in the quest for the True, just as we do in the pursuit of the Good, a veritable autonomy of man, but only insofar as he is a nothingness. It is as a nothingness and insofar as he is involved in Nothingness, Evil and Error that man escapes God. For God, Who is infinite fullness of being, can neither conceive nor govern nothingness. He has placed that which is positive within me. He is the author who is responsible for everything in me which is. But because of my finiteness and my limits, because of that side of me which is in shadow, I turn away from Him. If I retain freedom of indifference, I do so in relation to what I do not know or what I know imperfectly, in relation to fragmentary, mutilated and obscure ideas. I, who am a nothingness, can say *no* to all these nothingnesses. I am able *not* to decide to act or affirm. Since the order of truths exists outside of me, that which will define me as an autonomy is not creative invention but refusal. It is by refusing to the point of being unable to refuse any more that we are free. Thus, methodical doubt becomes the very model of the free act: *"Nihilominus . . . hanc in nobis libertatem esse experimur, ut semper ab iis credendis, quae non plane certa sunt et explorata possimus abstinere."* And elsewhere he writes: *"Mens quae propria libertate utens supponit ea omnia non existere, de quarerum existentia vel minimum potest dubitare."*

This power of escaping, disengaging oneself and withdrawing is recognizable as a prefiguration of Hegelian negativity. Doubt strikes at all propositions which affirm something that is outside our thought, that is, I can place all existants between parentheses; I am exercising my freedom fully when I, who am myself a nothingness and a void, make of everything that exists a nothingness. Doubt is a breaking of contact with being. Through doubt, man has a permanent possibility of disentangling himself from the existing universe and of suddenly contemplating it from above as a pure succession of phantasms. In this sense, it is the most magnificent affirmation of the reign of the human. The hypothesis of the Evil Genius shows clearly that man can escape from all traps and illusions. There is an order of the true because man is free, and even if this order does not exist, it would be enough for man to be free for there never to be a reign of error, because man, who is a pure negation, a pure suspension of judgment, can, provided he remains motionless, like someone holding his breath, withdraw at any moment from a false and faked nature. He can even withdraw from everything within himself which is nature, from his memory, his imagination, his body. He can withdraw even from time and take refuge in the eternity of the moment. Nothing reveals more clearly the fact that man is not a being of "nature." But at the very moment that he attains this unequalled independence, against the omnipotence of the Evil Spirit, and even against God, he discovers that he is a pure nothingness. Confronted with the *being* that is placed, in its entirety, between parentheses, all that remains is a simple *no,* bodiless and without memories, without knowledge and without *anyone.*

It is this translucent refusal of everything that is achieved in the *cogito,* as the following passage testifies: *"Dubito ergo sum, vel, quod idem est; Cogito ergo sum."* [8] Although this

---

[8] *The Search After Truth.*

doctrine is patterned on the Stoic Ἐποχή, no one before Descartes had stressed the connection between free will and negativity. No one had shown that freedom does not come from man as he is, as a fullness of existence among other fullnesses in a world without lacunae, but rather from man as he *is not*, from man as a finite, limited being. However, this freedom can in no way be creative, since it is *nothing*. It has no power to produce ideas, for an idea is a reality, that is, it possesses a certain *being* that I cannot confer upon it. In addition, Descartes himself limited its scope, since, according to him, when being finally appears— absolute and perfect being, infinitely infinite—we cannot refuse it our adherence. We can thus see that he did not push his theory of negativity to the limit: "Since truth consists in *being* and falsehood in *non-being* only." [9] Man's power of refusal lies only in his refusing the false, in short, in saying no to non-being. If we are able to withhold our assent to the works of the Evil Spirit, it is not because they are true or false—they have at least, insofar as they *are* our conceptions, a minimum of being—but insofar as they are not, that is, insofar as they relate falsely to objects that do not exist. If we can withdraw from the world, it is not insofar as it exists in its full and high majesty, like an absolute affirmation, but insofar as it appears to us confusedly through the mediation of the senses and insofar as we ponder it imperfectly by means of a few ideas, the foundations of which escape us. Thus, Descartes constantly wavers between the identification of freedom with the negativity or negation of being—which would be the freedom of indifference—and the conception of free will as a simple negation of negation. In short, he failed to conceive negativity as productive.

A strange freedom. It ends by decomposing into two phases. In the first, it is negative and an autonomy, but confines itself to refusing our assent to error or confused thoughts. In the second, it changes meaning; it is a positive adherence, but the will then loses its autonomy, and the great clarity which exists in the understanding penetrates and determines the will.

[9] To Clerselin, April 23rd, 1649.

Is this what Descartes wanted, and does the theory he constructed really correspond to this proud and independent man's primary feeling about his free will? This does not seem to be the case. This individualist, whose very person plays such an important role in his philosophy, whether he is tracing the history of his thinking in the *Discourse on Method* or whether he is encountering himself, as an unshakable fact, on the path of his doubting, conceived a freedom that disembodied and deindividualized, for, if we are to believe him, the thinking subject is at first *nothing* but a pure negation, a nothingness, a slight trembling of air which alone escapes the act of doubting and which is *nothing other* than the doubt itself, and, when it emerges from this nothing, it does so in order to become a pure assumption of being.

There is not much difference between the Cartesian scientist, who is, in the last analysis, only the simple *vision* of eternal truths, and the Platonic philosopher, dead to his body and dead to his life, who has become only the contemplation of Forms and who ends by being identified with science itself. But *man,* in Descartes, had other ambitions. He conceived his life as an undertaking. He wanted science to be *made* and to be made by him; but his freedom did not allow him to "make" it. He wanted the passions to be cultivated, provided they were put to good use. He perceived, to a certain extent, the paradoxical truth that there are *free* passions. He prized true generosity above all things, defining it as follows: "I think that true generosity, which leads a man to esteem himself as highly as he can legitimately do so, consists only partly in his knowing that there is nothing that really belongs to him but the free disposing of his will nor any reason why he should be praised or blamed except for his using it well or badly, and partly in his feeling within him a firm and constant resolution to use it well, that is, never to lack the will to undertake and execute all things which he judges to be best: which is to follow virtue perfectly." [10] This freedom, which he invented and which can

[10] *Treatise on the Passions,* Para. 53.

only restrain desires until the clear vision of Good determines the resolutions of the will, cannot justify his proud feeling of being the veritable author of his acts and the continuous creator of free enterprises, any more than it gives him the means of inventing operative schemata in accordance with the general rules of the Method.

The reason is that Descartes, who was a dogmatic scientist and a good Christian, allowed himself to be crushed by the pre-established order of eternal truths and by the eternal system of values created by God. If man does not invent his God, if he does not construct Knowledge, he is only nominally free. Cartesian freedom here joins hands with Christian freedom, which is a false freedom. Cartesian man and Christian man are free for Evil, but not for Good, for Error, but not Truth. God takes them by the hand and, through the conjunction of natural and supernatural lights which He dispenses to them, leads them to the Knowledge and Virtue He has chosen for them. They need only let themselves be guided. The entire merit in this ascension reverts to Him. But insofar as they are nothingness, they escape Him. They are free to let go of His hand on the way and to plunge into the world of sin and non-being. *Per contra,* they can, of course, always beware of intellectual and moral Evil. They can beware and preserve themselves, can suspend judgment, can check their desires and stop their acts in time. In short, they are only asked not to hinder God's intentions. But Error and Evil are, in the last analysis, non-beings. Man has not even the freedom to produce anything in this domain. If he persists in his vice or his prejudices, what he creates will be a *nothing*. The universal order will not even be ruffled by his stubborness. "The worst," says Claudel, "is not always sure." In a doctrine that confuses being and perception, the only field of human initiative is the "bastard" terrain of which Plato speaks, the terrain that "is never seen except in dream," the borderline between being and non-being.

But since Descartes warns us that God's freedom is no more entire than that of man and that one is in the image of the other, we have a new means of investigation for determining more exactly his personal exigences, exigences which philosophic postulates have not allowed him to satisfy. If he conceived divine freedom as being quite like his own freedom, then it is of his own freedom, such as he would have conceived it without the fetters of Catholicism and dogmatism, that he speaks when he describes the freedom of God. We have here an obvious phenomenon of sublimation and transposition. The God of Descartes is the freest of the gods that have been forged by human thought. He is the only creative God. He is subject neither to principles—not even to that of identity—nor to a sovereign Good of which He is only the executor. He had not only created existants in conformity with rules which have imposed themselves upon His will, but He has created both beings and their essences, the world and the laws of the world, individuals and first princples:

"The mathematical truths which you call eternal have been established by God and are entirely dependent upon Him, as are all other creatures. To say that these truths are independent of God is to speak of Him as one speaks of Jupiter or Saturn and to subject Him to the Styx and the fates . . . It is God Who has established these laws in nature, as a king establishes the laws of his kingdom . . .[11] As for eternal truths, I repeat that they are indeed true or possible because God knows them as true or possible and that they are not, on the other hand, known as true by God as if they were true independently of Him. And if men quite understood the meaning of their words, they would never say without blasphemy that the truth of something precedes God's knowledge of it, for to God willing and knowing are one. With the result that by virtue of His willing a thing He knows it and by that very fact the thing is true. It should therefore not be said that if God did not exist, these truths would nevertheless be true." [12]

"You ask who obliged God to create these truths; and I say that He was as free not to make all the lines drawn from the centre to the circumference not equal as not to create the world. And it is certain that these truths are not more neces-

[11] Letter to Mersenne, April 15th, 1630.
[12] Letter to Mersenne, May 6th, 1630.

sarily co-existent with His essence than other created things. . . ." [13] "And though God wished that some truths be necessary, this does not mean that He wished them necessarily, for it is one thing to wish them to be necessary and quite another thing to wish necessarily or to be the necessity of wishing." [14]

The meaning of the Cartesian doctrine is revealed here. Descartes realized perfectly that the concept of freedom involved necessarily an absolute autonomy, that a free act was an absolutely new production, the germ of which could not be contained in an earlier state of the world and that consequently freedom and creation were one and the same. The freedom of God, though similar to that of man, loses the negative aspect that it had in its human envelope; it is pure productivity; it is the extra-temporal and eternal act by which God brings into being a world, a Good and eternal truths. Thenceforth, the root of all Reason is to be sought in the depths of the free act. It is freedom which is the foundation of the true, and the rigorous necessity that appears in the order of truths is itself supported by the absolute contingency of a creative free will. This dogmatic rationalist might say with Goethe, not "in the beginning was the word," but "in the beginning was the act." As for the difficulty of maintaining freedom in the face of truth, he glimpsed a solution to it in conceiving a creation which is at the same time an act of intellection, as if the thing created by a free decree somehow encounters the freedom that sustains it in being and thereby yields to understanding. In God, willing and intuition are one and the same; the divine consciousness is both constitutive and contemplative. And, in like manner, God invented Good. He is not disposed by His perfection to decide what is the best; rather, that which He has decided is, as a result of His decision itself, absolutely Good. For Descartes, the divine prerogative is, in the last analysis, an absolute freedom which invents Reason and Good and which has no limits other than itself and its fidelity to itself. But, on the other hand, there is

[13] Letter to Mersenne, May 27th, 1630.
[14] Letter to Mesland, May 2nd, 1644.

nothing more in this freedom than in human freedom, and he is aware, in describing his God's free will, that he has merely developed the implicit content of the idea of freedom. If we examine the matter closely, we shall see that this is why human freedom is not limited by an order of freedoms and values which might offer themselves to our assent as eternal *things*, as necessary structures of being. It is the divine will that has laid down these values and truths and that supports them. Our freedom is limited only by the divine freedom. The world is only the creation of a freedom that preserves it for an indefinite time. Truth is nothing if it is not willed by this infinite and divine power and if it is not taken up, assumed and confirmed by human freedom. The free man is alone in the face of an absolutely free God. Freedom is the foundation of being, its secret dimension. Freedom, in this rigorous system, is the inner meaning and the true face of necessity.

Thus, in his description of divine freedom, Descartes ends by rejoining and explicating his primary intuition of his own freedom, of which he says that it is "known without proof and merely by our experience of it." It matters little to us that he was forced by the age in which he lived, as well as by his point of departure, to reduce the human free will to a merely negative power to deny itself until it finally yields and abandons itself to the divine solicitude. It matters little that he hypostasized in God the original and *constituent* freedom whose infinite existence he recognized by means of the *cogito* itself. The fact remains that a formidable power of divine and human affirmation runs through and supports his universe. It took two centuries of crisis—a crisis of Faith and a crisis of Science—for man to regain the creative freedom that Descartes placed in God, and for anyone finally to suspect the following truth, which is an essential basis of humanism: man is the being as a result of whose appearance a world exists. But we shall not reproach Descartes with having given to God that which reverts to us in our own right. Rather, we shall admire him for having, in a dictatorial age, laid the groundwork of democracy, for having followed to the very end the demands of the idea of *autonomy* and for having understood,

long before the Heidegger of *Vom Wesem des Grundes,* that
the sole foundation of being is freedom.[15]

[15] Simone Pétremont takes me to task, in *Critique,* for having
overlooked, in the present essay, "freedom against oneself." The
fact is that she herself is unaware of the dialectic of freedom.
To be sure, there is freedom against the *self.* But in order for it
to be a "self" it must first be freedom. Otherwise, nature is only
an externality, therefore a radical negation of the person. Even
disarray, that is, the external imitation of externality, even *insanity,*
presuppose freedom.

Chapter 13

Materialism and Revolution[1]

1

THE REVOLUTIONARY MYTH

YOUNG PEOPLE OF TODAY are uneasy. They no longer recognize their right to be young. It is as though youth were not an age of life, but a class phenomenon, an unduly prolonged childhood, a spell of irresponsibility accorded to the children of the well-to-do. The workers go without transition from adolescence to manhood. And it really does look as though our age, which is in the process of eliminating the various European bourgeoisies, is also eliminating that abstract and metaphysical period of which people have always said, "It will have its fling." Most of my former students have married early because they felt ashamed of their youth and of the leisure that was once the fashion.

They have become fathers before they have finished their studies. They still receive money from their families at the end of each month, but it is not enough. They have to give lessons or do translations or odd jobs. They are part-time workers. In one way, they are like kept women and, in another, like "home-workers." They no longer take the time, as we did at their age, to play about with ideas before adopting one set in particular. They are fathers and citizens, they vote, they must commit themselves. This is probably not a bad thing. It is fitting, after all, that they be asked to choose immediately for or against man, for or against the masses. But if they choose the first side, their difficulties begin, because they are persuaded that they must strip themselves of their

[1] As I have been unfairly reproached with not quoting Marx in this article, I should like to point out that my criticisms are not directed against him, but against the Marxist scholasticism of 1949. Or, if you prefer, against Marx *through* Neo-Stalinist Marxism.

subjectivity. If they consider doing this, it is for reasons which remain subjective, as they are still inside. They take counsel with *themselves* before plunging *themselves* into the water and, as a result, the more seriously they contemplate abandoning subjectivity, the greater the importance it assumes in their eyes. And they realize, with annoyance, that their notion of objectivity is still subjective. Thus they go round and round, unable to choose sides, and if they do come to a decision, they jump in with their eyes shut, out of weariness or impatience.

However, that is not the end of it. They are now told to choose between materialism and idealism; they are told that there is nothing in between and that it must be one or the other. Now, to most of them, the principles of materialism seem philosophically false; they are unable to understand how matter could give rise to the *idea* of matter. Nevertheless, they protest that they utterly reject idealism. They know that it acts as a myth for the propertied classes and that it is not a rigorous philosophy but a rather vague kind of thinking whose function is to mask reality or to absorb it into the idea. "It doesn't matter," they are told. "Since you are not materialists, you will be idealists in spite of yourselves, and if you rebel against the quibbling of the professors, you will find yourselves the victims of a more subtle and all the more dangerous illusion."

Thus, they are hounded even in their thoughts, which are poisoned at the source, and they are condemned to serve unwillingly a philosophy they detest or to adopt out of discipline a doctrine in which they are unable to believe. They have lost the carefree quality characteristic of their age without acquiring the certainty of maturity. They are no longer at leisure and yet they cannot commit themselves. They remain at the threshold of communism without daring either to enter or to go away. They are not guilty; it is not their fault if the very people who at present invoke the dialectic wish to force them to choose between two opposites and reject, with the contemptuous name of "Third Party," the synthesis which embraces them. Since they are deeply sincere and hope for the coming of a socialist regime, since they are prepared to serve the Revolution with all their might, the only way to help them is to ask oneself, as they do, whether materialism and the myth of objectivity are really required by the cause of the Revolution and if there is not a discrepancy between the revolutionary's action and his ideology. I shall therefore turn back to materialism and attempt to re-examine it.

It seems as though its first step is to deny the existence of God and transcendent finality; the second, to reduce the action of mind to that of matter; the third, to eliminate subjectivity by reducing the world, and man in it, to a system of objects linked together by universal relationships. I conclude in all good faith that it is a metaphysical doctrine and that materialists are metaphysicians. But they immediately stop me. I am wrong. There is nothing they loathe so much as metaphysics; it is not even certain that philosophy finds favour in their eyes. Dialectical materialism is, according to M. Naville, "the expression of a progressive discovery of the world's interactions, a discovery which is in no way passive but which implies the activity of the discoverer, seeker and struggler." According to M. Garaudy, dialectical materialism's first step is to deny the existence of any legitimate knowledge apart from scientific knowledge. And for Madame Angrand, one cannot be a materialist without first rejecting all *a priori* speculation.

This invective against metaphysics is an old acquaintance. It goes back to the writings of the positivists of the last century. But the positivists, who were more logical, refused to take a stand as to the existence of God because they considered all possible conjecture on the subject to be unverifiable, and they abandoned, once and for all, all speculation on the relation between body and mind because they thought that we could not know anything about it. It is indeed obvious that the atheism of M. Naville or Madame Angrand is not "the expression of a progressive discovery." It is a clear and *a priori* stand on a problem which infinitely transcends our experience. This is also my own stand, but I did not consider myself to be any the less a metaphysician in refusing existence to God than Leibnitz was in granting it to Him. And by what miracle is the materialist, who accuses idealists of indulging in metaphysics when they reduce matter to mind, absolved from the same charge when he reduces mind to matter? Experience does not decide in favour of his doctrine— nor, for that matter, does it decide in favour of the opposing one either. Experience is confined to displaying the close connection between the physiological and the psychological, and this connection is subject to a thousand different kinds of interpretation. When the materialist claims to be *certain* of his principles, his assurance can come only from intuition or *a priori* reasoning, that is, from the very speculation he condemns. I now realize that materialism is a metaphysics hiding positivism; but it is a self-destructive metaphysics, for by undermining metaphysics out of principle, it deprives its own statements of any foundation.

It thereby also destroys the positivism under which it takes cover. It was out of modesty that Comte's disciples reduced human knowledge to mere scientific knowledge alone. They confined reason within the narrow limits of our experience because it was there only that reason proved to be effective. The success of science was for them a fact, but it was a *human* fact. From the point of view of man, and for man, it is true that science succeeds. They took good care not to ask themselves whether the universe *in itself* supported and guaranteed scientific rationalism, for the very good reason that they would have had to depart from themselves and from mankind in order to compare the universe as it *is* with the picture of it we get from science, and to assume God's point of view on man and the world. The materialist, however, is not so shy. He leaves behind him science and subjectivity and the human and substitutes himself for God, Whom he denies, in order to contemplate the spectacle of the universe. He calmly writes, "The materialist conception of the world means simply the conception of nature as it is, without anything foreign added." [2]

What is involved in this surprising text is the elimination

[2] Marx and Engels; *Complete Works;* Ludwig Feuerbach, Volume XIV, p. 651, Russian edition. I quote this passage in order to show the use made of it *today*. I plan to show elsewhere that Marx had a much deeper and richer conception of objectivity.

of human subjectivity, that "addition foreign to nature." The materialist thinks that by denying his subjectivity he has made it disappear. But the trick is easy to expose. *In order* to eliminate subjectivity, the materialist declares that he is an *object*, that is, the subject matter of science. But once he has eliminated subjectivity in favour of the object, instead of seeing himself as a thing among other things, buffeted about by the physical universe, he makes of himself an *objective beholder* and claims to contemplate nature as it is, in the absolute.

There is a play on the word objectivity, which sometimes means the passive quality of the object beheld and, at other times, the absolute value of a beholder stripped of subjective weaknesses. Thus, having transcended all subjectivity and identified himself with pure objective truth, the materialist travels about in a world of objects inhabited by human objects. And when he returns from his journey, he communicates what he has seen: "Everything that is rational is real," he tells us, and "everything that is real is rational." Where does he get this rationalistic optimism? We can understand a Kantian's making statements about nature since, according to him, reason constitutes experience. But the materialist does not admit that the world is the product of our constituent activity. Quite the contrary. In his eyes it is we who are the product of the universe. How then could we know that the real is rational, since we have not created it and since we reflect only a tiny part of it from day to day? The success of science may, at the most, lead us to think that this rationality is *probable*, but it may be a matter of a local, statistical rationality. It may be valid for a certain order of size and might collapse beyond or under this limit.

Materialism makes a certainty of what appears to us to be a rash induction, or, if you prefer, a postulate. For materialism, there is no doubt. Reason is within man and outside man. And the leading materialist magazine calmly calls itself "*Thought* (*La Pensée*), the organ of modern rationalism." However, by a dialectical reversal which might have been foreseen, materialist rationalism "passes" into irrationalism and destroys itself. If the psychological fact is rigorously conditioned by the biological, and the biological fact is, in turn, conditioned by the physical state of the world, I quite see how the human mind can express the universe as an effect can express its cause, but not in the way a thought expresses its object. How could a captive reason, governed from without and manœuvred by a series of blind causes, still be reason? How could I believe in the principles of my deductions if it were only the external event which has set them down within me and if, as Hegel says, "reason is a bone"? What stroke of chance enables the raw products of circumstances to constitute the keys to Nature as well? Moreover, observe the way in which Lenin speaks of our consciousness: "It is only the reflection of being, in the best of cases an approximately exact reflection." But who is to decide whether the present case, that is, materialism, is "the best of cases"? We would have to be within and without at the same time in order to make a comparison. And as there is no possibility of that, according to the very terms of our statement, we have no criterion for the reflection's validity, except internal and subjective criteria: its conformity with other reflections, its clarity, its distinctness and its permanence. Idealistic criteria, in short. Moreover, they determine only a truth *for man,* and this truth not being constructed like those offered by the Kantians, but experienced, will never be more than a faith without foundation, a mere matter of habit.

When materialism dogmatically asserts that the universe produces thought, it immediately passes into idealist scepticism. It lays down the inalienable rights of Reason with one hand and takes them away with the other. It destroys positivism with a dogmatic rationalism. It destroys both of them with the metaphysical affirmation that man is a material object, and it destroys this affirmation by the radical negation of all metaphysics. It sets science against metaphysics and, unknowingly, *a* metaphysics against science. All that remains is ruins. Therefore, can I be a materialist?

It may be objected that I have understood nothing of the matter, that I have confused the naïve materialism of Helvetius and Holbach with *dialectical* materialism. There is, I am told, a dialectical movement within nature whereby opposites which clash are suddenly surmounted and reunited in a new synthesis; and this new product "passes" in turn into its opposite and then blends with it in another synthesis. I immediately recognize the characteristic movement of the Hegelian dialectic, which is based entirely on the dynamism of Ideas. I recall how, in Hegel's philosophy, one Idea leads to another, how every Idea produces its opposite. I know that the impulse behind this immense movement is the attraction exerted by the future on the present, and by the whole, even when it does not exist, on its parts. This is as true of the partial syntheses as of the absolute Totality which finally becomes Mind.

The principle of this Dialectic is, thus, that a whole governs its parts, that an idea tends of itself to complete and to enrich itself, that the forward movement of consciousness is not linear, like that which proceeds from cause to effect, but synthetic and multi-dimensional, since every idea retains within itself and assimilates to itself the totality of antecedent ideas, that the structure of the concept is not the simple juxtaposition of invariable elements which might, if necessary, combine with other elements to produce other combinations, but rather an organization whose unity is such that its secondary structures cannot be considered apart from the whole without becoming "abstract" and losing their essential character.

One can readily accept this dialectic in the realm of ideas. Ideas are naturally synthetic. It appears, however, that Hegel has inverted it and that it is, in reality, characteristic of matter. And if you ask what *kind* of matter, you will be told that there is only one kind and that it is the matter of which scientists talk. Now the fact is that matter is characterized by its inertia. This means that it is incapable of producing anything by itself. It is a vehicle of movements and of energy, and it always receives these movements and this energy from without. It borrows them and relinquishes them. The mainspring of all dialectics is the idea of totality. In it, phenomena are never isolated appearances. When they occur together, it is always within the high unity of a whole, and they are bound together by inner relationships, that is, the presence of one modifies the other in its inner nature. But the universe of science is quantitative, and quantity is the very opposite of the dialectical unit. A sum is a unit only in appearance. Actually, the elements which compose it maintain only relations of contiguity and simultaneity; they are there together, and that is all. A numerical unit is in no way influenced by the co-presence of another unit; it remains inert and separated within the number it helps to form. And this state of things is indeed necessary in order for us to be able to count; for were two phenomena to occur in intimate union and modify one another reciprocally, we should be unable to decide whether we were dealing with two separate terms or with only one. Thus, as scientific matter represents, in a way, the realization of quantity, science is, by reason of its inmost concerns, its principles and its methods, the opposite of dialectics.

When science speaks of forces that are applied to a point of matter, its first concern is to assert their independence; each one acts as though it were alone. When science studies the attraction exerted by bodies upon one another, it is careful to define the attraction as a strictly external relationship, that is to reduce it to modifications in the direction and speed of their movements. Science does occasionally employ the word "synthesis," for example, in regard to chemical combinations. But it never does so in the Hegelian sense; the particles forming a combination retain their properties. If an atom of oxygen combines with atoms of sulphur and hydrogen to form acid, it retains its identity. Neither water nor acid is a real whole which changes and governs its composing elements, but simply a passive resultant, a *state*. The entire effort of biology is aimed at reducing the so-called living syntheses to physico-chemical processes. And when M. Naville, who is a materialist, feels the need to construct a scientific psychology, he turns to "behaviourism" which regards human conduct as a sum of conditioned reflexes. Nowhere in the universe of science do we encounter an organic totality. The instrument of the scientist is analysis. His aim is to reduce the complex to the simple, and the recomposition which he afterwards effects is only a counterproof, whereas the dialectician, on principle, considers these complexes as irreducible.

Of course Engels claims that "the natural sciences . . . have proved that, in the last analysis, Nature proceeds dialectically, that it does not move in an eternally identical circle that perpetually repeats itself, but that it has a real history." In support of his thesis, he cites the example of Darwin: "Darwin inflicted a severe blow to the metaphysical conception of Nature by demonstrating that the entire organic world . . . is the product of a process of development that has been going on for millions of years." [3] But, first of all, it is obvious that the notion of *natural history* is absurd. History cannot be characterized by change nor by the pure and simple action of the past. It is defined by the deliberate resumption of the past by the present; only human history is possible. Besides, if Darwin has shown that the species derive from one another, his attempt at explanation is of a mechanical and not dialectical order. He accounts for individual differences by the theory of small variations, and he regards each of these variations as the result not of a "process of development," but of mechanical chance. In a group of individuals of the same species, it is statistically impossible that there not be some who are superior in weight, strength or some particular detail. As to the struggle for existence, it cannot *produce* a new synthesis through the fusion of opposites; it has strictly negative effects, since it *eliminates* definitively the weaker elements. In order to understand it, all we need do is compare its results with the really dialectical ideal of the class struggle. In the latter case, the proletariat will absorb the bourgeoisie within the unity of a classless society. In the struggle for existence, the strong simply cause the weak to disappear. Finally, the chance advantage *does not develop:* it remains inert and is transmitted unchanged by heredity; it is a *state,* and it is not this state which will be modified by an inner dynamism to produce a higher degree of organization. Another chance variation will simply be joined to it from without, and the process of elimination will recur mechanically. Are we to conclude that Engels is irresponsible or dishonest? In order to prove that Nature has a history, he

[3] Engels.

uses a scientific hypothesis that is explicitly meant to reduce all natural history to mechanical series.

Is Engels more responsible when speaking of physics? "In physics," he tells us, "every change is a transition from quantity to quality, from the quantity of movement—of any form whatever—inherent in the body or communicated to the body. Thus, the temperature of water in the liquid state is, at first, unimportant, but if you increase or diminish the temperature of the water, there comes a moment when its state of cohesion is modified and the water is transformed, in one case into vapour and in another into ice." But he is tricking us; it is all done with mirrors. The fact is that scientific investigation is not in the least concerned with demonstrating the transition from quantity to quality; it starts from the perceptible quality, which is regarded as an illusory and subjective appearance, in order to find behind it the quantity which is regarded as the truth of the universe. Engels naïvely regards temperature as if it were, as a matter of *primary* data, a pure quantity. But actually it appears first as a quality; it is the state of discomfort or of contentment which causes us to button up our coats or else to take them off. The scientist has reduced this perceptible quality to a quantity in agreeing to substitute the measurement of cubic expansions of a liquid for the vague information of our senses. The transformation of water into steam is for him an equally quantitative phenomenon or, if you prefer, it exists for him only as quantity. He defines steam in terms of pressure or of some kinetic theory which reduces it to a certain quantitative state (position, speed) of its molecules. We must therefore choose. Either we remain within the domain of perceptible quality, in which case steam is a quality and so is temperature; we are not being scientific; we witness the action of one quality on another. Or else we regard temperature as a quantity. But then the transition from the liquid to the gaseous state is scientifically defined as a quantitative change, that is, by a measurable pressure exerted on a piston or by measurable relationships among molecules. For the scientist, quantity gives rise to quantity; laws are quantitative formulas and science possesses no symbol for the expression of quality as such. What Engels claims to present as a scientific procedure is the pure and simple movement of his mind which passes from the universe of science to that of naïve realism and back again to the scientific world and the world of pure sensation. And besides, even if we were to allow him this, does this intellectual coming-and-going in the least resemble a dialectical process? Where does he see a progression? Let us concede that the change of temperature, regarded as quantitative, produces a qualitative transformation of water; water is changed into vapour. What then? It will exert a pressure on an escape-valve and raise it; it will shoot up into the air, grow cold and become water again. Where is the progression? I see a cycle. To be sure, the water is no longer contained in the recipient, but is outside, on the grass and the earth, in the form of dew. But in the name of what metaphysics can this change of place be regarded as a progress? [4]

It will perhaps be objected that certain modern theories—like that of Einstein—are synthetic. We know that in his system there are no longer any isolated elements; each reality is defined in relation to the universe. There is considerable matter for discussion here. I shall confine myself to observing that there is no question of a synthesis, for the relations which can be established among the various structures of a synthesis are *internal* and *qualitative,* whereas the relations which, in Einstein's theory, enable us to define a position or a mass remain *quantitative* and *external.* Moreover, the question lies elsewhere. Whether the scientist be Newton, Archi-

---

[4] Let no one hope to get out of the difficulty at this point by talking of intensive quantities. Bergson long ago demonstrated the confusion and error of this myth of intensive quantity which was the undoing of the psychophysicists. Temperature, as we feel it, is a quality. It is not warmer today than it was yesterday, but warm in a different way. And, conversely, the *degree,* measured according to cubic expansion is a pure and simple quantity, to which there remains attached, in the mind of the layman, a vague idea of perceptible quality. And modern physics, far from retaining this ambiguous notion, reduces heat to certain atomic *movements.* What becomes of intensity? And what are the intensities of a sound or a light, if not mathematical relationships?

medes, LaPlace or Einstein, he studies not the concrete totality, but the general and abstract conditions of the universe. Not the *particular* event which catches and absorbs into itself light, heat and life and which we call the "glistening of the sun through leaves on a summer's day," but light in general, heat phenomena, the general conditions of life. There is never any question of examining *this particular* refraction through *this particular* piece of glass which has its history and which, from a certain point of view, is regarded as the concrete synthesis of the universe, but the conditions of possibility of refraction *in general*. Science is made up of *concepts,* in the Hegelian sense of the term. Dialectics, on the other hand, is essentially the play of notions. We know that for Hegel the notion organizes and fuses concepts together in the organic and living unity of concrete reality. The Earth, the Renaissance, Colonization in the eighteenth Century, Nazism, are objects of *notions;* being, light and energy are abstract concepts. Dialectical enrichment lies in the transition from the abstract to the concrete, that is, from elementary concepts to notions of greater and greater richness. The movement of the dialectic is thus the reverse of that of science.

"It is true," a Communist intellectual admitted to me, "that science and dialectics pull in opposite directions. But that is because science expresses the bourgeois point of view, which is an analytical one. Our dialectic is, on the other hand, the very thought of the proletariat." That is all very well—even though Soviet science does not seem to differ much in its methods from that of the bourgeois countries—but why, in that case, do the Communists borrow arguments and proofs from science in order to support their materialism? I agree that the basic spirit of science is materialist. But on the other hand it is presented to us as being analytic and bourgeois. The positions are thereby reversed, and I distinctly see two classes struggling. One, the bourgeoisie, is materialist; its method of thinking is analysis, and its ideology is science. The other, the proletariat, is idealist; its method of thinking is synthesis, and its ideology is dialectic. And as there is a struggle between the classes, the ideologies should be incompatible. But this is not the case. It seems that the dialectic is the crown of science and makes full use of its results. It seems that the bourgeoisie, availing itself of analysis and then reducing the higher to the lower, is idealist, whereas the proletariat—which thinks synthetically and is guided by the revolutionary idea—even when affirming the irreducibility of a synthesis to its elements, is materialist. What are we to make of this?

Let us come back to science which, whether bourgeois or not, has at least proved itself. We know what science teaches us about matter. A material object is animated from without, is conditioned by the total state of the world, is subject to forces which always come from elsewhere, is composed of elements that unite, though without interpenetrating, and that remain foreign to it. It is exterior to itself. Its most obvious properties are statistical; they are merely the resultant of the movements of the molecules composing it. Nature, as Hegel so profoundly remarked, is externality. How are we to find room in this externality for the dialectic, which is a movement of absolute interiorization? Is it not obvious that, according to the very idea of synthesis, life cannot be reduced to matter and human consciousness cannot be reduced to life? There is the same discrepancy between modern science, which is the object of materialist love and faith, and the dialectic which the materialists claim to be their instrument and method, as we observed earlier between their positivism and their metaphysics; the one destroys the other. Thus, they will sometimes tell you, and with the same imperturbability, that life is only a complex chain of physico-chemical phenomena and, at other times, that it is an irreducible moment in the dialectic of nature. Or rather, they dishonestly try to think both ways at the same time.

One feels throughout their confused discourse that they have invented the slippery and contradictory notion of reducible irreducibles. M. Garaudy is satisfied with this. But when we hear him speak, we are struck with his wavering; at one moment he affirms, in the abstract, that mechanical determinism has had its day and that it must be replaced by the dialectic and, at another, when he tries to explain a concrete situation, he reverts to causal relationships, which are linear and presuppose the absolute externality of the cause in relation to its effect. It is this notion of *cause*, perhaps, which best indicates the great intellectual confusion into which the materialists have fallen. When I challenged M. Naville to define within the framework of the dialectic this famous causality which he is so found of employing, he seemed troubled and remained silent. How well I understand him! I would even say that the idea of cause remains suspended between scientific relationships and dialectical syntheses. Since materialism is, as we have seen, an *explanatory* metaphysics (it tries to *explain* certain social phenomena in terms of others, the psychological in terms of the biological, the biological in terms of physico-chemical laws), it employs on principle the scheme of causality.

But as materialism sees in science the explanation of the universe, it turns to science and observes with surprise that the causal link is not scientific. Where is the cause in Joule's law or Mariotte's law or in Archimedes' principle or in Carnot's? Science generally establishes functional relationships between phenomena and selects the independent variable that suits its purpose. It is, moreover, strictly impossible to express the qualitative relationship of causality in mathematical language. Most physical laws simply take the form of functions of the type $y = f(x)$. Some set up numerical constants, and others give us phases of irreversible phenomena, but without our being able to tell whether one of these phases is a *cause* of the following one. (Can one say that nuclear dissolution in mitosis is a *cause* of the segmentation of the protoplasmic filament?) Thus, materialist causality remains suspended in air. The reason is that its origin lies in the metaphysical intention of reducing mind to matter and explaining the psychological by the physical. Disappointed because science offers *too little* to bolster his causal explanations, the materialist reverts to the dialectic. But the dialectic contains *too much;* the causal link is linear and the cause remains external to its effect. In addition, the effect never contains more than the cause; if it did, this residue would, according to the perspectives of causal explanation, remain unexplained. Dialectical progress is, on the contrary, cumulative; at each new stage, it turns back to the ensemble of positions transcended and embraces them all. And the transition from one state to another is always a process of enrichment. The synthesis always contains *more* than the united thesis and antithesis. Thus, the materialist cause can neither draw its support from science nor hang on to dialectic; it remains a vulgar and practical notion, the sign of materialism's constant effort to bend one towards the other and to join by force two mutually exclusive methods; it is the very type of the false synthesis and the use of it is dishonest.

This is nowhere more evident than in the Marxists' efforts to study "superstructures." For them, these are, in a sense, the "reflections" of the mode of production. "If," writes Stalin, "under a regime of slavery we encounter certain ideas and social theories, certain opinions and political institutions, while under feudalism we find others, and under Capitalism still others, this is not to be explained by 'nature' or by the 'properties' of ideas, theories, opinions and political institutions themselves, but by the different conditions of the material life of society at different periods of social development. The state of society and the conditions of its material existence are what determine its ideas, theories, political opinions and political institutions." [5]

The use of the term "reflection" and the verb "determine," as well as the general tone of this passage are sufficiently revealing. We are on deterministic ground; the superstructure is completely supported and conditioned by the social situation of which it is the reflection; the relationship of the mode of production to the political institution is that of cause to effect. Thus, we have the case of the simple-minded thinker who regarded Spinoza's philosophy as a direct reflection of the Dutch wheat trade. But at the same time, for the very purposes of Marxist propaganda, ideologies must be, to a certain extent, self-sufficient and be able to act in turn upon the social situation that conditions them. That means, in short, a certain autonomy in relation to the sub-structures. As a result, the Marxists fall back on the dialectic and make of the

[5] Stalin, *Dialectical Materialism and Historical Materialism.*

superstructure a synthesis that does, to be sure, proceed from conditions of production and of material existence, but whose nature and laws of development have a real "independence." In the same pamphlet, Stalin writes, "New social ideas and theories arise only when the development of the material existence of society confronts society with new tasks. . . . If new social theories and ideas arise, they do so because they are necessary to society, because without their organizing, mobilizing and transforming action, the solution of urgent problems entailed by the development of the material existence of society is *impossible*." [6]

In this text, as is apparent, necessity has assumed a completely different aspect; an idea arises because it is necessary to the carrying out of a new task. This means that the task, even before it is carried out, *calls forth* the idea which "will facilitate" its being carried out. The idea is postulated and worked by a vacuum which it then fills. The word "evoked" is actually the one which Stalin uses a few lines later. This action of the future, this necessity which is one with finality, this organizing, mobilizing and transforming power of the idea very clearly leads us back to the terrain of the Hegelian dialectic. But how can I believe in both of Stalin's affirmations at once? Is the idea "determined by the state of society" or "evoked by the new tasks to be carried out"? Am I to think, as he does, that "society's mental life is a reflection of objective reality, a *reflection* of being," that is a derived and borrowed reality which has no *being* of its own, something analogous to the "lecta" of the Stoics? Or, on the contrary, am I to declare, with Lenin, that "ideas become living realities when they live in the consciousness of the masses"? Which am I to accept, a causal and linear relationship implying the inertia of the effect, of the reflection, or a dialectical and synthetic relationship which would imply that the last synthesis turns back to the partial syntheses which have produced it in order to embrace them and absorb them into itself, and, consequently, that the mental life, although proceeding from the material conditions of society, turns back to

[6] My italics.—J.-P.S.

them and completely absorbs them? The materialists are unable to decide: they waver between one and the other. They assert abstractly the existence of dialectic progression, but their concrete studies are limited, for the most part, to Taine's explanations in terms of environmental determinism and the historical moment.[7]

That is not all. What exactly is this concept of *matter* that the dialecticians employ? If they borrow it from science, the poorer concept will fuse with other concepts in order to arrive at a concrete notion, the richer one. This notion will finally include within it, as one of its structures, the concept of matter, but far from being explained by it, the contrary will occur: the notion will explain the concept. In this case, one can start with matter as the emptier of the abstractions. One can also start from Being, as Hegel does. The difference is not very great, though the Hegelian point of departure, being more abstract, is the happier choice. But if we must really *invert* the Hegelian dialectic and "stand it on its feet again" it must be admitted that matter, chosen as a point of departure for the dialectical movement, does not appear to the Marxists to be the poorer concept, but the richer notion. It is identified with the whole universe; it is the unity of all phenomena; life, thoughts and individuals are merely its modes. It is, in short, the great Spinozist totality.

But if this be the case and if Marxist matter be the exact counterpart of Hegelian spirit, we arrive at the following paradoxical result: that Marxism, in order to stand the dialectic on its feet again, has set the richer notion at the point of departure. And certainly for Hegel the spirit exists from the start, but as a virtuality, as a summons; the dialectic is one with its history. For the Marxists, on the other hand, it is all of matter, as act, that is given in the first place, and the dialectic, whether applied to the history of species or to the evolution of human societies, is merely the retracing of the partial development of one of the modes of this reality. But then if the dialectic is not the very generating of the world, if it is not an act of progressive enriching, it is nothing

[7] Only they define the environment more precisely in terms of the material conditions of existence.

at all. In obligingly dismissing the dialectic, Marxism has given it its death-blow. "Save me from my friends," one thinks. You may wonder how this could have passed unnoticed. Because our materialists have dishonestly constructed a slippery and contradictory concept of "matter." At times it is the poorest of abstractions and at others the richest of concrete totalities, depending on their needs. They jump from one to the other and mask one with the other. And when they are finally cornered and can no longer escape, they declare that materialism is a method, an intellectual orientation. If you pushed them a bit further, they would say it is a style of living. They are not far wrong in this, and I, for my part, certainly regard it as one of the forms of the conventional mentality and of flight from one's own self.

But if materialism is a *human attitude,* with all the subjective, contradictory and emotional aspects involved in such an attitude, it ought not to be presented as a rigorous philosophy, as the doctrine of objectivity. I have witnessed conversions to materialism; one enters into materialism as into a religion. I should define it as the subjectivity of those who are ashamed of their subjectivity. It is, of course, also the irritation of those who suffer physically and who are familiar with the reality of hunger, illness, manual work and everything that can sap a man's strength. It is, in a word, a doctrine of the first impulse. Now, the first impulse is perfectly legitimate, particularly when it expresses the spontaneous reaction of an oppressed person—but that does not mean that it is the correct impulse. It always contains an element of truth, but goes beyond it. To affirm the crushing reality of the material world in opposition to idealism is not necessarily to be a materialist. We will return to this.

Furthermore, how did the dialectic retain its necessity in its fall from heaven to earth? Hegelian consciousness has no need to set up the dialectical *hypothesis:* it is not a pure, objective witness observing the generating of ideas from without; it is itself dialectical; it is self-generating in accordance with the laws of synthetic progression. There is no need for it to *assume* necessity in relationships; it *is* this necessity; it experiences this necessity. And its certainty does not come from some evidence that is more or less open to criticism, but from the progressive identification of the dialectic of consciousness with the consciousness of the dialectic. If, on the other hand, the dialectic represents the way in which the material world develops, if consciousness, far from wholly identifying itself with the whole dialectic, is but a "reflection of being," a partial product, a moment of synthetic progress, if, instead of taking part in its own generation from within, it is invaded from the outside by feelings and ideologies which have their roots elsewhere and if it is influenced by them without producing them, it is merely a link in a chain whose beginning and end are very far apart. And what can it say with *certainty* about the chain, unless it be the whole chain? The dialectic deposits a few effects in it and pursues its way.

On considering these effects, one may conclude that they bear witness to the probable existence of a synthetic mode of progression. Or else one may form conjectures on the consideration of exterior phenomena. In any case, one must be content with regarding the dialectic as a working hypothesis, as a method to be tried, a method which is justified if proved successful. How is it that the materialists regard this method of research as a structure of the universe and that some of them declare that "the reciprocal relationships and conditioning of phenomena, established by the dialectical method, constitute the necessary laws of matter in motion" [8] since the natural sciences proceed in a spirit contrary to this and use rigorously opposite methods, since the science of history is only in its primary stages? It is obviously because in transferring the dialectic from one world to the other they did not want to forego the advantages it had enjoyed in the first world. They retained its necessity and certainty, while removing the means they had of checking them. They wished, thus, to give matter the mode of synthetic development which belongs only to the idea and they borrowed from the reflection of the idea in itself a kind of certainty which has no place in the world's experience. But matter itself thereby becomes an idea; it nominally retains its denseness, inertia and exteriority, but it

[8] Stalin, *Ibid.*, p. 13.

presents, in addition, a perfect translucency—since one can decide, with complete certainty and on principle, about its internal processes—it is a synthesis, it progresses through constant enrichment.

Let us make no mistake; there is no simultaneous transcendence of materialism and idealism here;[9] denseness and transparency, exteriority and interiority, inertia and synthetic progression are simply juxtaposed in the spurious unity of "dialectical materialism." Matter has remained that which is revealed to us by science. There has been no combination of opposites, for lack of a new concept which might establish them within itself, something which is not exactly matter nor exactly idea. Their opposition cannot be surmounted by surreptitiously attributing the qualities of one of these opposites to the other. Actually, it must be admitted that materialism, in claiming to be dialectical, slides into idealism.

Just as the Marxists claim to be positivists and destroy their positivism through the use they implicitly make of metaphysics, just as they proclaim their rationalism and destroy it by their conception of the origin of thought, so, at the very moment they posit it, they deny their basic principle, materialism, by a furtive recourse to idealism.[10]

[9] Although Marx sometimes claimed there was. In 1844 he wrote that the antinomy between idealism and materialism would have to be transcended, and Henri Lefebvre, commenting on his thinking, states in *Matérialisme Dialectique* (pp. 53, 54), "Historical materialism, which is clearly expressed in *Deutsche Ideologie*, attains the unity of idealism and materialism foreshadowed and announced in the Manuscripts of 1844." But then why does M. Garaudy, another spokesman for Marxism, write in *Les Lettres Françaises*, "Sartre rejects materialism and claims, nevertheless, to avoid idealism. That is where the futility of that impossible 'third party' reveals itself . . ." How confused these people are!

[10] It may be objected that I have not spoken of the common source of all transformations in the universe, which is energy, and that I have taken up my position on the ground of mechanism in order to appraise dynamic materialism. My reply is that energy is not a directly perceived reality, but a concept fashioned in order to account for certain phenomena, that scientists are familiar with it through its effects rather than through its nature, and that at the most they know, as Poincaré said, that "something remains." Besides, the little we can state about energy is in rigorous oppo-

This confusion is reflected in the materialist's attitude towards his own doctrine; he claims to be *certain* of his principles, but he asserts more than he is able to prove. "The materialist *grants* . . . ," says Stalin. But why does he grant it? Why grant that God does not exist, that mind is a reflection of matter, that the world's development proceeds through the conflict of opposite forces, that there is an objective truth, that there are no unknowable things in the world, but only things that are still unknown? We are not told why. But if it is true that "new ideas and social theories called forth by the new tasks imposed by the development of society's material existence spring up, become the heritage of the masses which they mobilize and organize against society's decadent forces, thus promoting the overthrowing of these forces which hinder the development of society's material existence," it seems clear that these ideas are adopted by the proletariat because they account for its present situation and needs, because they are the most efficient instrument in its struggle against the bourgeoisie. "The failure of the Utopians, including the populists, anarchists, and revolutionary socialists, can be explained, among other ways," says Stalin in the forementioned work, "by the fact that they do not recognize the major role of material conditions in the development of society. Fallen into idealism, they base their practical activity, not on the needs of the development of material existence in society, but independently and in defiance of these needs, on 'ideal levels' and 'universal projects' detached from the real life of society.

"The strength and vitality of Marxism-Leninism lies in the fact that it bases its practical activity on precisely those needs

---

sition to the demands of dialectical materialism. Its total quantity is conserved, it is transmitted in discrete quantities, it undergoes a constant reduction. This last principle, in particular, is incompatible with the demands of a dialectic which claims to be enriched with each step. And let us not forget, moreover, that a body always receives its energy from without (even intra-atomic energy is so received); it is within the framework of the general principle of inertia that we are able to study the problem of equivalence of energy. To make energy the vehicle of the dialectic would be to transform it by violence into *idea*.

of the development of the material existence of society without ever detaching itself from the real life of society." Though materialism may be the best instrument for action, its truth is of a pragmatic kind. It is true for the working class, because it is good for it, and since social progress is to be brought about by the working class, it is truer than idealism, which served the interests of the bourgeoisie for a while when it was a rising class, and which today can only obstruct the development of the material existence of society. But when the proletariat will finally have absorbed the bourgeoisie and brought about the classless society, new tasks will make their appearance, tasks which will "give rise to" new ideas and social theories.

Materialism will have had its day, since it is the mode of thought of the working class and the working class will no longer exist. Regarded objectively as an expression of class needs and tasks, materialism becomes an *opinion*, that is, a mobilizing, transforming and organizing force whose objective reality is measured in terms of its power of action. And this opinion which claims to be certitude carries within it its own destruction, for it is obliged, in the very name of its principles, to regard itself as an objective fact, as a reflection of being, as an object of science, and, at the same time, it destroys the science which should analyze and establish it— at least as an opinion. The circle is obvious, and the whole system remains suspended in air, perpetually floating between being and nothingness.

The Stalinist extricates himself through faith. If he "grants" materialism, it is because he wants to act and to change the world. When one is engaged in so vast an enterprise, one hasn't the time to be too particular about the choice of principles justifying it. He believes in Marx, Lenin and Stalin, he admits of the principle of authority, and, finally, he retains the blind and tranquil faith in the certitude of Marxism. This conviction will influence his general attitude towards all ideas proposed to him. Scrutinize closely one of his doctrines or one of his concrete assertions and he will say that he has no time to waste, that the situation is urgent, that he has to act, to attend to first things first and to work for the revolution.

Later on we will have the leisure to challenge principles—or rather they will challenge themselves. But for the moment, we have to reject all argument, because it is liable to have a weakening effect. That is quite all right, but when it's his turn to attack and to criticize bourgeois thinking or a particular intellectual position that he judges to be reactionary, he then claims to possess the truth.

The same principles which he just told you could not be disputed at the time suddenly became patent facts. They pass from the level of useful opinions to that of truths. "The Trotskyists," you say to him, "are wrong, but they are not, as you claim, police informers. You *know perfectly well* they are not." "On the contrary," he will reply, "I know perfectly well that they are. What they really think is a matter of indifference to me. Subjectivity does not exist. But *objectively* they play into the hands of the bourgeoisie. They *behave* like provocateurs and informers, because playing into the hands of the police and deliberately assisting it come to the same thing." You reply that it does not come to the same thing, and that in all *objectivity*, the behaviour of the Trotskyist and that of the policeman are not alike. He retorts that one is as harmful as the other and that the effect of both is to hinder the advancement of the working class. And if you insist, if you demonstrate to him that there are several ways of hindering this advancement and that they are not equivalent, even in their results, he replies proudly that these distinctions, even if true, do not interest him. We are in a period of struggle; the situation is simple and the positions clearly defined. Why be over-subtle? The militant Communist must not encumber himself with so many nuances. So we are back to the useful. Thus, the proposition, "the Trotskyist is an informer," wavers perpetually between the state of useful opinion and that of objective truth.[11]

Nothing demonstrates this ambiguity in the Marxist notion

[11] This is a résumé of conversations about Trotskyism that I have had time and again with Communist intellectuals, and not the least important of them. They always follow the pattern I have just indicated.

Materialism and Revolution / 221

of truth better than the ambivalence of the Communist attitude towards the scientist. The Communists claim to derive
from him; they exploit his discoveries and make his thinking
the only kind of valid knowledge. But their mistrust of him
remains guarded. In so far as they lean on the rigorously
scientific idea of *objectivity*, they have need of his critical
spirit, his love of research and challenging, his lucidity, which
rejects the principle of authority and refers constantly to
experience or rational proof. But in so far as they are believers
and science challenges all beliefs, they are suspicious of these
virtues. If the scientist brings his scientific qualifications with
him into the Party, if he claims the right to examine principles, he becomes an "intellectual"; his dangerous freedom
of thought which is an expression of his relative material
independence, is countered by the faith of the militant worker
who, because of his very situation, *needs* to believe in his
leaders' orders.[12]

This, then, is the materialism they want me to choose, a
monster, an elusive Proteus, a large, vague, contradictory
semblance. I am asked to choose, this very day, in all intellectual freedom, in all lucidity, and that which I am to choose
freely and lucidly and with all my wits about me is a doctrine
that destroys thought. I know that man has no salvation other
than the liberation of the working class; I know this *before*
being a materialist and from a plain inspection of the facts.
I know that our intellectual interest lies with the proletariat.
Is that a reason for me to demand of my thinking, which has
led me to this point, that it destroy itself? Is that a reason for
me to force it henceforth to abandon its criteria, to think in
contradictions, to be torn between incompatible theses, to lose
even the clear consciousness of itself, to launch forth blindly
in a giddy flight that leads to faith? "Fall to thy knees and
thou shalt believe," says Pascal. The materialist's effort is very
closely akin to this.

[12] As can be seen in the Lysenko case, the scientist who recently
provided Marxist politics with a groundwork by guaranteeing the
truth of materialism, has to submit, in his research, to the demands
of this politics. It is a vicious circle.

Now, if it were only a matter of my falling to my knees, and if by this sacrifice I could assure man's happiness, I ought certainly to agree to it. But what is involved is everyone's relinquishing the right to free criticism, the right to facts, the right to truth. I am told that this will all be restored to us later, but what proof is there of this? How am I to believe in a promise made in the name of mutually destructive principles? I know only one thing, that my mind has to relinquish its independence this very day. Have I fallen into the inacceptable dilemma of betraying the proletariat in order to serve truth or betraying truth in the name of the proletariat?

If I consider the materialist faith, not in its content but in its history, as a social phenomenon, I clearly see that it is not a caprice of intellectuals nor a simple error on the part of philosophers. As far back as I go, I find it bound up with the revolutionary attitude. The first man who made a deliberate attempt to rid men of their fears and bonds, the first man who tried to abolish slavery within his domain, Epicurus, was a materialist. The materialism of the great philosophers, like that of the "intellectual societies," contributed not a little to the preparation of the French Revolution; finally, the Communists, in defence of their thesis, readily made use of an argument which bears a strange resemblance to that which the Catholic employs in the defence of his faith. "If materialism were erroneous," they say, "how do you explain the fact that it is responsible for the unity of the working class, that it has enabled it to be led into battle and that during the last fifty years it has brought us, in spite of the most violent repression, this succession of victories?" This argument, which is scholastic, and which offers an *a posteriori* proof in terms of success, is far from insignificant.

It is a fact that materialism is now the philosophy of the proletariat precisely in so far as the proletariat is revolutionary. This austere, false doctrine is the bearer of the purest and most ardent hopes; this theory which constitutes a radical denial of man's freedom has become the most radical instrument of his liberation. That means that its content is suited to "mobilizing and organizing" revolutionary forces and, also, that there is a deep relationship between the *situation* of an oppressed class and the materialist *expression* of this situation. But we cannot conclude from this that materialism is a philosophy, and still less that it is *the* truth.

In so far as it permits of coherent action, in so far as it expresses a concrete situation, in so far as millions of men find in it hope and the image of their condition, materialism certainly must contain some truth. But that in no way means that it is wholly true as doctrine. The truths contained in it can be shrouded and drowned in error; it is possible that in order to attend to first things first, and to get back to these truths, revolutionary thinking has sketched out a rapid and temporary structure, what dressmakers call a basted garment. In that case, materialism offers much more than is required by the revolutionary. It also offers a good deal less, for this hasty and forced joining of elements of truth prevents them from organizing spontaneously among themselves and from attaining true unity. Materialism is indisputably the *only* *myth* that suits revolutionary requirements.

The politician goes no further; the myth is useful and so he adopts it. But if his undertaking is a long-range affair, it is not a myth that he needs but the *Truth*. It is the philosopher's business to make the truths contained in materialism hang together and to build, little by little, a philosophy which suits the needs of the revolution as exactly as the myth does. And the best way of spotting these truths within the error in which they are steeped is to determine these requirements on the basis of a careful examination of the revolutionary attitude, to reconstruct, in each case, the path by which they have led to the demand for a materialist representation of the universe, and to see whether they have not, each time, been deflected and diverted from their primary meaning. If they are freed from the myth which crushes them and which hides them from themselves, perhaps they may plot the main lines of a coherent philosophy which will be superior to materialism in being a *true* description of nature and of human relationships.

II

THE PHILOSOPHY OF REVOLUTION

The game of the Nazis and their collaborators was to blur ideas. The Pétain regime called itself a revolution, and things reached such a point of absurdity that one day the following headline appeared in the *Gerbe:* "The motto of the National Revolution is—*hold fast.*" It is fitting, then, that we bear in mind a few basic truths. In order to avoid any presuppositions, we shall adopt the *a posteriori* definition of revolution given by a historian, A. Mathiez. In his opinion, revolution takes place when a change in institutions is accompanied by a profound modification in the property system.

We shall call revolutionary the party or the person in the party whose acts intentionally prepare such a revolution. The first observation to be made is that not anyone can become a revolutionary. The existence of a strong and organized party whose object is revolution can, to be sure, exert its attraction upon individuals or groups of any origin, but the organization of this party can belong only to people of a certain social condition. In other words, the revolutionary is *in a situation.* It is obvious that he is to be found only among the oppressed, but it does not suffice to be oppressed to choose to be a revolutionary. The Jews can be classed with the oppressed—and the same holds true for racial minorities in certain countries —but many of them are oppressed within the bourgeoisie and, as they share the privileges of the class which oppresses them, they are unable, without contradiction, to work for the destruction of these privileges.

In the same way, we cannot call the feudal colonial nationalists or the American Negroes revolutionaries, though their interests may coincide with those of the party which is working for the revolution. They are not completely integrated into society. The former ask for the *return* to an earlier state of things; they want to *regain* their supremacy and to cut the bonds which attach them to the colonizing society. What the American Negroes and the bourgeois Jews want is an equality of rights which in no way implies a change of structure in the property system. They wish simply to share the privileges of their oppressors, that is, they really want a more complete integration.

The situation of the revolutionary is such that he cannot share in these privileges in any way whatever. The only way he can get what he wants is by the destruction of the class that oppresses him. This means that the oppression is not, like that of the Jews or the American Negroes, a secondary and, as it were, lateral characteristic of the social regime under consideration, but that it is, on the contrary, a constituent one. The revolutionary is, thus, both an oppressed person and the keystone of the society which oppresses him. In other words it is as an oppressed person that he is indispensable to this society. That is, the revolutionary belongs to those who *work* for the dominant class.

The revolutionary is necessarily a worker and one of the oppressed, and it is as a worker that he is oppressed. This double character of producer and oppressed person is sufficient to define the revolutionary's situation, but not the revolutionary himself. The silk-weavers of Lyons and the workers of June, 1848, were not revolutionaries, but rioters; they were fighting for particular improvements and not for a radical transformation of their existence. That means that they were hemmed in by their situation and that they accepted it as a whole. They accepted being hirelings, working at machines of which they were not the owners; they recognized the rights of the propertied class; they were obedient to its morality. They were simply demanding an increase of salary within a state of things which they had neither transcended nor even recognized.

The revolutionary, on the other hand, is defined by his *going beyond* the situation in which he is placed. And because he does go beyond it towards a radically new situation, he can grasp it in its synthetic wholeness, or, if you like, he makes it exist for himself as totality. Thus it is by means of his thrust toward the future and from the point of view of the future that he *realizes* it. Instead of appearing to him, as it does to a resigned victim, as a definitive and *a priori* structure, it is for him only a moment of the universe. Since he wants to change it, he must consider it immediately from a historical point of view and he must consider himself an historical agent.

Thus, from the very beginning, as a result of this projection of the self into the future, he escapes from the society that crushes him and turns back towards it in order to understand it. He sees a human history which is one with man's destiny and of which the change he wishes to bring about is, if not the end, at least an essential stage. He sees history as progress, since he judges the state toward which he wishes to lead us to be better than that in which we are at present. At the same time, he sees human relationships from the point of view of work, since work is his lot. Now, work is, among other things, a direct link between man and the universe, man's hold on Nature and, at the same time, a primary kind of relation between men.

It is, therefore, an essential attitude of human reality which, within the unity of a self-same project, both "exists" and causes his relation with nature and his relation with others to exist in their mutual dependence. And in so far as he demands his liberation *as* a worker, he knows perfectly well that it cannot be brought about by a simple integration of himself with the privileged class. What he hopes for, quite to the contrary, is that the relationships of solidarity which he maintains with other workers will become the very model of human relationships. He hopes, therefore, for the liberation of the entire oppressed class; unlike the lonely rebel, the revolutionary understands himself only in his relationships of solidarity with his class.

Thus, because he becomes conscious of the social structure upon which he depends, the revolutionary demands a philosophy which considers his situation, and, as his action has meaning only if it brings man's fate into question, this philosophy must be total, that is, it must produce a total explanation of the human condition. And since he himself is, as a worker, an essential structural unit of society and the link between man and Nature, he has no need of a philosophy which does not express, primarily and essentially, the original relation of man to the world, which is precisely the co-ordinated action of one upon the other.

Finally, since this philosophy is born of a historical enter-prise and must represent for him who requires it a certain mode of historicizing which he has chosen, it must neces-sarily present the course of history as being oriented or as being, at least, capable of being oriented. And as it is born of action and reconsiders, so as to clarify it, the action which necessitated it, this philosophy is not a contemplation of the world, but ought, itself, to be an action. We must understand that this philosophy does not come to tack itself on to the revolutionary effort, but that it is indistinguishable from this effort; it is embodied in the original plan of the worker who joins the revolutionary party, and is implicit in his revolu-tionary attitude, for any plan for changing the world is inseparable from a certain understanding which reveals the world from the viewpoint of the change one wishes to bring about in it.

The task of the philosopher of revolution will therefore consist in indicating, and elaborating upon, the great, guiding themes of the revolutionary point of view. And this philo-sophical effort is in itself an act, for it cannot elucidate these themes without taking its place within the very movement which begets them, namely, the revolutionary movement. It is an act also because once the philosophy is made clear it makes the militant revolutionary more conscious of his destiny, of his place in the world, and of his ends.

Thus revolutionary thinking is a *thinking within a situa-tion;* it is the thinking of the oppressed in so far as they rebel together against oppression; it cannot be reconstructed from the outside; you can come to know it, once it has been devel-oped, by reproducing within yourself the revolutionary move-ment and by considering it on the basis of the situation from which it arises. It should be noted that the thinking of phi-losophers of the ruling class also constitutes action. Nizan has clearly demonstrated this in his *Chiens de Garde* (*Watch Dogs*). It aims at defending, conserving and repelling. But its inferiority to revolutionary thinking is due to the fact that the philosophy of oppression tries to conceal its pragmatic character; as it is aimed not at changing the world, but at maintaining it, it claims to *contemplate* the world as it *is*. It regards society and nature from the viewpoint of pure knowledge, without admitting to itself that this attitude tends to perpetuate the present state of the universe by implying that the universe can be known rather than changed and that if one actually does want to change it, one must first know it.

The theory of the primacy of knowledge, unlike any philosophy of work which grasps the object through the action that modifies it by using it, exerts a negative and inhibiting influence by conferring a pure and static essence upon the object. But the theory contains within itself a negation of the action it involves, since it affirms the primacy of knowledge and rejects all pragmatic conceptions of truth. The superiority of revolutionary thinking consists in its first proclaiming its active nature; it is conscious of being an act, and if it presents itself as a total comprehension of the universe, it does so because the oppressed worker's scheme is a total point of view toward the entire universe. But as the revolutionary needs to distinguish between the true and the false, this indissoluble unity of thought and action calls for a new and systematic theory of truth. The pragmatic conception of truth will not do, for it is subjectivist idealism, pure and simple.

That is why the materialist myth was invented. It has the advantage of reducing thought to nothing more than one of the forms of universal energy and of stripping it of its wan will-o'-the-wisp look. In addition, it presents thought, in each particular case, as one objective mode of conduct among others, that is, as occasioned by the state of the world and turning back upon that state in order to modify it. But we saw earlier that the idea of a conditioned thinking is self-destructive; I shall presently show that the same holds true for the idea of a determined action. It is not a question of inventing a cosmogonic myth which will present thinking-action in symbolic form, but of abandoning all myths and reverting to the real revolutionary necessity, which is to unite action with truth and thought with realism.

What is needed is, in a word, a philosophical theory which shows that human reality is action and that action upon the universe is identical with the understanding of that universe as it is, or, in other words, that action is the unmasking of reality, and, *at the same time*, a modification of that reality.[13] As we have seen, the myth of materialism is, in addition, the representation in image form and within the unity of a cosmology and of historical movement, of the relation of man to matter. The representation, therefore, of the relation between men, and, in short, of all the revolutionary themes. We must revert to the skeletal structure of the revolutionary attitude and examine it in detail so as to see whether it does not call for something other than a mythical representation, or if, on the contrary, it calls for the groundwork of a rigorous philosophy.

Any member of the ruling class is a man of divine right. Born into a class of leaders, he is convinced from childhood that he is born *to* command and, in a certain sense, this is true, since his parents, who do command, have brought him into the world to carry on after them. A certain social function, into which he will slip as soon as he is of age, the metaphysical reality, as it were, of his person, awaits him. Thus, in his own eyes, he is a person, an *a priori* synthesis of legal right and of fact. Awaited by his peers, destined to relieve them at the appointed time, he exists because he *has the right* to exist.

This sacred character which the bourgeois has for his fellow and which manifests itself in ceremonies of *recognition* (the greeting, the formal announcement, the ritual visit, etc.) is what is called human dignity. The ideology of the ruling class is completely permeated with this idea of dignity. And when men are said to be "the lords of creation," this expression is to be taken in its strongest sense; they are its monarchs by divine right; the world is made for them; their existence is the absolute and perfectly satisfying value to the mind which gives its meaning to the universe. That is the original meaning of all philosophical systems which affirm the primacy of the subject over the object and the composition of Nature through the activity of thought. It is self-evident that man,

[13] This is what Marx, in his "theses on Feuerbach" calls "practical materialism." But why "materialism"?

under these conditions is a supra-natural being; what we call Nature is the sum-total of that which exists without having the right to do so.

For the sacrosanct, the oppressed classes are part of Nature. They are not to command. In other societies perhaps, the fact of a slave's being born within the *domus* also conferred a sacred character upon him, that of being born *to* serve, that of being the man of divine duty in relation to the man of divine right. But the same cannot be said in the case of the proletariat. The worker's son, born in an outlying working-class district, living among the crowd, has no direct contact with the propertied élite; he has no personal duty save those that are defined by law. It is not even forbidden him, should he possess that mysterious grace we call merit, to gain access, under certain circumstances and with certain reservations, to the upper class. His son or grandson will became a man of divine right. Thus, he is only a living being, the best organized of the animals. Everyone has felt the contempt implicit in the term "native," used to designate the inhabitants of a colonized country.

The banker, the manufacturer, even the professor in the home country, are not natives of any country; they are not natives at all. The oppressed person, on the other hand, feels himself to be a native; each single event in his life repeats to him that he has not the right to exist. His parents have not brought him into the world for any particular purpose, but rather by chance, *for no reason;* at best, because they liked children or because they were open to a certain kind of propaganda, or because they wanted to enjoy the advantages accorded to large families. No special function awaits him and, if he has been apprenticed, it was not done so as to prepare him to exercise the priesthood of a profession, but only to enable him to continue the unjustifiable existence he has been leading since his birth. He will work in order to live, and to say that the ownership of the fruits of his labour is stolen from him is an understatement. Even the meaning of his work is stolen from him, since he does not have a feeling of solidarity with the society for which he produces.

Whether he be a fitter or an unskilled labourer, he knows

perfectly well that he is not irreplaceable; the worker is actually characterized by interchangeability. The doctor's or jurist's work is appreciated for its quality, the "good" worker's only for its quantity. He becomes conscious of himself through the circumstances of his situation as a member of a zoological species, the human species. So long as he remains on this level, his condition will seem natural to him; he will go on with his life as he began it, with sudden rebellions, if the oppression makes itself more severely felt, but these will be merely sporadic. The revolutionary goes beyond this situation because he wishes to change it, and considers it from the point of view of this will to change.

It should be observed, first of all, that he wishes to change the situation for his whole class and not for himself; if he were thinking only of himself, he could, as a matter of fact, leave the realm of the species and embrace the values of the ruling class. It stands to reason, then, that he would accept *a priori* the sacrosanct character of the men of divine right for the mere purpose of benefiting by it in turn. But as he cannot dream of claiming this divine right for his *entire class,* since the origin of this right lies in the very oppression that he wishes to destroy, his first step will be to contest the rights of the ruling class.

Men of divine right do not exist in his eyes. He has not approached them, but he senses that they lead the same existence as he does, an existence that is equally vague and unjustifiable. Unlike the oppressors, he does not seek to exclude the members of the other class from the community of men. But he wishes, first of all, to strip them of that magical aspect which makes them formidable in the eyes of those they override. By a spontaneous impulse he also denies the values they originally set up.

If it were true that their Good had an *a priori* existence, then the essence of revolution would be polluted; to set oneself up against the oppressors would mean setting oneself up against Good in general. But he does not dream of replacing this Good with another *a priori* Good, for he is not at a constructive stage. He wants only to free himself of all the values and rules of conduct that the ruling class has invented, because these values and rules act only as checks to his behaviour and, by their very nature, aim at prolonging the *status quo*. And since he wants to change the organization of society, he must first reject the idea that it was established by Providence. Only if he considers it as a fact can he hope to replace it with another fact that suits him better. At the same time, revolutionary thinking is humanistic.

The declaration that "we too are men" is at the bottom of any revolution. And the revolutionary means by this that his oppressors are men. Certainly he will do violence to them, he will try to break their yoke, but if he must destroy some of their lives, he will always try to reduce this destruction to a minimum, because he needs technicians and experts. Thus, in spite of everything, the bloodiest of revolutions involves coalition.

It is, above all, an absorption and an assimilation of the oppressing class by the oppressed. Unlike the turncoat or the persecuted minority which wishes to raise itself to the level of the privileged and to be identified with them, the revolutionary wishes, by denying the validity of their privileges, to bring them down to his level. And as the constant feeling of his own contingent nature inclines him to recognize himself as an unjustifiable fact, he regards the men of divine right as simple facts like himself. Thus, the revolutionary is not a man who demands rights, but rather a man who destroys the very idea of rights, which he regards as a product of force and custom. His humanism is not based on human dignity, but, on the contrary, denies man any particular dignity.

The unity into which he wants to merge himself and his fellows is not that of the human kingdom, but of the human species. There is a human species, a contingent and unjustifiable phenomenon; the circumstances of its development have brought about a state in which there is a kind of lack of inner balance; the revolutionary's task is to help it to achieve a more rational balance beyond its present state. Just as the species has taken possession of the man of divine right and absorbed him, so Nature takes possession of man and absorbs him. Man is a fact of nature and humanity one species among others.

Only in this way can the revolutionary think of being able to escape the hoaxes of the privileged class. The man who identifies himself with the natural can never again be taken in by an appeal to an *a priori* ethics. Materialism seems at this point to offer its aid; it is the epic of the factual. The links established throughout the materialistic world are probably necessary, but necessity appears within an original contingency. If the universe exists, its development and the succession of its states can be regulated by laws. But it is not *necessary* that the universe exist, nor is it necessary that being, in general, exist, and the contingency of the universe is communicated through all the links, even the most rigorous, to each particular fact. Each state, governed from without by the preceding one, can be modified, if one acts upon its causes. And the new state is neither more nor less *natural* than the preceding one—if we mean thereby that it is not based upon rights and that its necessity is merely relative.

At the same time, since the imprisonment of man in the world is involved, materialism has the advantage of offering a crude myth about the origin of the species whereby the more complex forms of life proceed from the simpler ones. The question is not one of merely replacing the end with the cause in each individual case, but of presenting a stereotyped image of a world in which ends are everywhere substituted for causes. It is apparent, even in the attitude of the first and most naïve of the great materialists, that materialism has always had this function.

Epicurus recognizes the possibility of an infinite number of equally valid explanations that might account no less precisely for phenomena, but he challenges us to find one which will liberate man more completely from his fears. And Man's basic fear, especially when he suffers, is less the fear of death or of the existence of a harsh God, but simply rather that the state of things from which he suffers might have been produced and may be maintained for transcendental and unknowable ends.

In this case, any effort to modify it would be vain and wrong. A subtle discouragement would insinuate itself into his judgments and prevent his hoping for or even conceiving of any improvement. Epicurus reduced death to a fact by removing the moral aspect it acquired from the fiction of seats of judgment in the nether world. He did not do away with ghosts but regarded them as strictly physical phenomena. He did not dare do away with the gods, but reduced them to a mere divine *species,* unrelated to us; he removed their power of self-creation and showed that they were the products of the play of atoms, just as we were.

But, once again, is the materialistic myth, which may have been useful and encouraging, really necessary? The revolutionary's conscience demands that the privileges of the oppressor class be unjustifiable, that the primordial contingency he finds in himself also be a constituent part of his oppressor's very existence, that the system of values set up by his masters, the purpose of which is to confer *de jure* existence upon *de facto* advantages, may be transcended towards an organization of the world which does not yet exist and which will exclude, both in law and in fact, all privileges. But his attitude toward the *natural* is obviously ambivalent. In a way, he plunges into Nature, dragging his masters with him.

But, on the other hand, he proclaims that he wants to substitute a rational adjustment of human relationships for what has been produced blindly by Nature. The Marxist expression for designating the society of the future is *antiphysis.* This means that Marxists want to set up a human order whose laws will constitute the negation of natural laws. And we are probably to understand by this that this order will be produced only by obeying the prescriptions of Nature. But the fact is that this order must *be conceived* within a Nature that denies it; the fact is that in the anti-Natural society the conception of law will precede the establishment of law, whereas, at present, law, according to materialism, conditions our conception of it.

In short, transition to antiphysis means the replacement of the society of laws by the community of ends. And there is no doubt that the revolutionary distrusts values and refuses to recognize that he is trying to achieve a better organization of the human community. He fears that a return to values, even by an indirect path, may open the door to further chicanery.

But on the other hand, the mere fact that he is ready to sacrifice his life to an order, the coming of which he never expects to see, implies that this future order, which justifies all his acts but which he will not enjoy, acts as a value for him. What is a value if not the call of something which does not yet exist?[14]

In order to account for these various requirements, a revolutionary philosophy ought to set aside the materialistic myth and endeavour to show: (1) That man is unjustifiable, that his existence is contingent, in that neither he nor any Providence has produced it; (2) That, as a result of this, any collective order established by men can be transcended towards other orders; (3) That the system of values current in a society reflects the structure of that society and tends to preserve it; (4) That it can thus always be transcended toward other systems which are not yet clearly perceived since the society of which they are the expression does not yet exist—but which are adumbrated and are, in a word, invented by the very effort of the members of society to transcend it.

The oppressed person lives out his original contingency, and revolutionary philosophy must reckon with this. But in living out his contingency he accepts the *de facto* existence of his oppressors and the absolute value of the ideologies they have produced. He becomes a revolutionary only through a movement of transcendence which challenges these rights and this ideology. The revolutionary philosopher has, above all, to explain the possibility of this movement of transcendence. It is obvious that its source is not to be found in the individual's purely natural and material existence, since the individual turns back on this existence to judge it from the viewpoint of the future.

This possibility of *rising above* a situation in order to get a perspective on it (a perspective which is not pure knowledge, but an indissoluble linking of understanding and action) is

[14] This ambiguity appears again in the Communist's judgments of his adversaries. For materialism ought actually to forbid his making judgments. A bourgeois is only the product of a rigorous necessity. But the climate of *l'Humanité* (the French Communist newspaper) is one of moral indignation.

precisely that which we call freedom. No materialism of any kind can ever explain it. A series of causes and effects may very well impel me to a gesture or to behaviour which itself will be an effect and which will modify the state of the world; it cannot make me look back at my situation in order to grasp it in its totality.

In short, it cannot account for revolutionary class consciousness. Dialectical materialism undoubtedly exists in order to explain and justify this transcendence toward the future. But it endeavours to ascribe freedom to things, not to man—which is absurd. A state of the world will never be able to produce class consciousness. And the Marxists are so well aware of this that they rely upon militants—that is, upon a conscious and concerted action—in order to activate the masses and awaken this consciousness within them.

That is all very well, but where do these same militants derive their understanding of the situation? Must they not have detached themselves at some time or other to get perspective? In order to avoid the revolutionary's being duped by his former masters, he should be shown that established values are simply given facts. But if they are given, and, consequently, capable of being transcended, this is not because they are values, but because they are established. And in order that there be no self-deception on his part, he must be given the means of understanding that the end he is pursuing—whether he call it antiphysis, classless society or the liberation of man—is also a value and that, if this value cannot be transcended, the reason is simply that it has not been realized.

Moreover, this is what Marx foresaw when he talked of something beyond Communism, and what Trotsky meant when he spoke of the permanent revolution. Revolutionary man claims to be a contingent being, unjustifiable but free, wholly plunged into a society which oppresses him, but capable of transcending that society through his efforts to change it. Idealism deceives him in that it binds him with rights and values that are already given; it conceals from him his power to blaze his own path. But materialism, by robbing him of his freedom, also deceives him. Revolutionary philosophy should be a philosophy of transcendence.

But the revolutionary himself mistrusts freedom—and that prior to any use of sophistry. And he is right. There have always been prophets to tell him he was free, and each time it was in order to fool him. Stoical freedom, Christian freedom, Bergsonian freedom, in hiding his chains from him, have only reinforced them. All of these can be reduced to a certain inner freedom that man could retain in any situation. This inner freedom is a pure idealist hoax; care is taken never to present it as the necessary condition of the *act*. It is really pure enjoyment of itself. If Epictetus, in chains, does not rebel, it is because he feels free, because he enjoys his freedom.

On that basis, one state is as good as another, the slave's situation is as good as the master's; why should anyone want to change it? This freedom is fundamentally reducible to a more or less clear affirmation of the autonomy of thought. But in conferring independence upon thought, this affirmation separates it from the situation—since truth is universal, one can think truth under any conditions. It also separates thought from action; since we are responsible only for intention, the act, in being realized, undergoes the pressure of the world's real forces which deform it and render it unrecognizable to its very author.

What remain for the slave are abstract thoughts and empty intentions, under the name of metaphysical freedom. And, meanwhile, his master's orders and the necessity of living have involved him in crude and concrete actions, and oblige him to think in concrete terms about matter and instruments. In fact, the liberating element for the oppressed person is work. In this sense it is work that is revolutionary to begin with. To be sure, it is *ordered* and has, at first, the appearance of the worker's enslavement. It is not likely that the worker would have chosen to do *this* work under *these* conditions and within *this* length of time for *these* wages, had it not been forced upon him.

The employer, more rigorous than the master of ancient times, goes so far as to determine in advance the worker's gestures and behaviour. He breaks down the worker's act into its component parts, takes certain of them away from him, and has them performed by other workers, reduces the worker's conscious and synthetic activity to a mere sum of constantly repeated gestures. Thus, by putting the worker's conduct on the same footing as property, the master tends to reduce the worker to the state of a mere thing.

Madame de Staël, in the account of her trip to Russia at the beginning of the nineteenth century, cites a striking example of this: "Each of the twenty musicians (in an orchestra of Russian serfs) played one single note each time it recurred. Each of these men bears the name of the note he is supposed to execute. People say, as they pass by, 'There's Mr. Narish-kine's "g," "e" or his "d".'" The individual is limited to a constant characteristic which defines him as atomic weight or melting temperature.

Modern Taylorism does the same thing. The worker be-comes the man of a single operation which he repeats a hundred times a day; he is a mere object, and to tell a shoe-stitcher or the Ford employee who places the needles on the speedometers that they retain, within the action in which they are engaged, an inner freedom of thought, would be childish or hateful. But at the same time, work offers the beginning of concrete liberation, even in extreme cases, because it is, first of all, the negation of the accidental and capricious order that is the master's. The victim at work no longer worries about pleasing the master, he escapes from the world of politeness, ceremony, psychology and the dance; he does not have to guess what goes on in the boss's head, he is no longer at the mercy of someone's humour. His work is im-posed upon him to begin with, of course, and its end product is finally stolen from him.

But within these two limits, his work bestows mastery over things upon him; the worker sees himself as a possibility of infinitely varying the form of a material object by acting upon it in conformance to certain universal rules. In other words, the determinism of matter gives him his first picture of his freedom. A worker is not a determinist in the way the scien-tist is; he does not make of determinism an explicitly formulated postulation. He lives it in his gestures, in the movement of the arm striking a rivet or pounding a crowbar. He is so thoroughly permeated with it that when the desired effect is not produced he tries to find out what hidden cause has prevented its realization, never conceiving of any waywardness or sudden and accidental break in the natural order. And since it is deep within his slavery, at the very moment at which the master's sweet pleasure transforms him into a thing that action, by bestowing upon him sovereignty over objects and a specialist's autonomy over which the master has no power liberates him, the idea of liberation is linked in his mind with that of determinism.

He does not learn of his freedom by a reflective movement back upon himself, but rather transcends his enslaved state by his action on phenomena which, through the very rigour of their connection, reflect the image of a concrete freedom, the power to modify these phenomena. And since the adumbration of his concrete freedom makes its appearance to him in the connecting-links of determinism, it is not surprising that he aims to replace the relationship of man to man, which seems to him that of a tyrannical freedom to a humiliated obedience, with that of man to thing and, finally—since the man who reigns over things is, in turn, and from another point of view a thing—by that of thing to thing.

Thus determinism, in so far as it is opposed to the psychology of civility, seems to him a kind of purifying thinking, a catharsis. And if he turns back to consider himself as a determined thing, he thereby liberates himself from his master's deadly freedom, for he sweeps them along into determinism's links, considering them, in turn, as things by explaining their commands in terms of their situation, instincts and history, that is, by plunging them into the universe. If all men are things, there are no more slaves, there are only slaves *de facto*.

Like Samson, who accepted burial under the ruins of the temple provided that the Philistines perished with him, the slave frees himself by doing away with his own and his master's freedom and by submerging himself with them in matter. The liberated society of which he conceives is, from

that point on, a reversal of the Kantian community of ends;
it is not based on the mutual recognition of freedoms. But
since the liberating relationship is the relationship between
man and things, that is what will form the basic structure of
this society.

It is only a question of destroying the oppressive relationship between men so that the slave's will and that of the
master, which exhaust themselves in struggling against one
another, can be turned back wholly upon things. The liberated society will be a harmonious enterprise of exploitation
of the world. Since it is produced by the absorption of the
privileged classes and is defined by work, that is by action
upon matter, and since it is in itself subject to deterministic
laws, the wheel comes full circle, the world is closed.

The revolutionary, in contradistinction to the rebel, actually
wants an *order*. And since the spiritual orders proposed to
him are always to one degree or another the sham images
of the society that oppresses him, he will choose material
order, that is the order of efficiency in which he figures both
as cause and effect. Here, too, materialism offers him its services. This myth offers the most precise image of a society
in which freedoms are alienated. Auguste Comte defined it as
the doctrine which tries to explain the upper in terms of the
lower. The words "upper" and "lower" are obviously not to
be understood here in their moral sense, but as designating
more or less complicated forms of organization.

Now, the worker is considered as an inferior by those
whom he nourishes and protects, and the oppressor class
originally considers itself as the superior class. Because its
internal structures are finer and more complex, it is this class
which produces the ideologies, culture and value systems.
The upper layers of society tend to explain the lower in
terms of the upper, whether by seeing in it a degradation of
the superior or by thinking that it exists *in order to* serve
the needs of the superior.

This kind of finalist explanation naturally attains the level
of a principle of interpretation of the universe. The explanation "from below," that is in terms of economic, technical
and, finally, biological conditioning is, in an inverse sense, the

one adopted by the oppressed individual because it makes of him the supporting element of the entire society. If the superior is only an emanation from the interior, then the "exquisite class" is merely an epiphenomenon. Should the oppressed refuse to cater to it, it will sicken and die; by itself it is nothing.

One has merely to widen this view, which is correct, and to make of it a general explanatory principle, and you have the beginning of materialism. And the materialist explanation of the universe, the explanation, that is, of the biological in terms of the physico-chemical and of thought by matter, becomes, in its turn, a justification of the revolutionary attitude; though an organized myth, the explanation makes what had been the victim's spontaneous impulse to rebellion against his oppressor into the universal mode of existence and of reality.

Here, too, materialism offers the revolutionary more than he asks for. For the revolutionary does not insist upon being a thing, but upon mastering things. It is true that in his work he has acquired a just appreciation of freedom. The freedom reflected for him by his action upon things is far removed from the Stoic's abstract freedom of thought. It becomes manifest within a particular situation into which the worker has been cast by the accident of his birth and through his master's whim or interest.

It makes its appearance within an undertaking which he has not originated of his own free will and which he will not terminate; it is not to be distinguished from his very commitment within this undertaking; but if, within his slavery, he becomes conscious of his freedom, it is because he gauges the efficacy of his concrete action. He does not have the pure idea of an autonomy which he does not enjoy, but he does know his power which is proportionate to his action. What he notices while engaged in this same action is that he transcends the present material state through a precise plan of arranging it in one fashion or another, and that, as this project is identical with the management of means directed toward ends, he really does succeed in arranging it as he had wished.

If he discovers the relation between cause and effect, it is not in submitting to it, but in the very act which transcends the material state (the adhesion of the coal to the walls of the mine, etc.) towards a certain end which illuminates and defines this state from within the future. Thus the relation of cause to effect is revealed in and through the efficacy of an act which is both plan and realization. It is, indeed, the tractability and, at the same time, the resistance of the universe which reflects for him the steadiness of causal series and the image of his freedom, but that is because his freedom is indistinguishable from the use of causal series toward an end which establishes this very freedom. Without the illumination bestowed upon it by this end the present situation could contain neither a causal relationship, nor the relationship of means to end, or rather, it would contain an indistinct and infinite number of means and ends, effects and causes, just as without the generating act of the mathematician who traces a figure in relating a series of chosen points according to a certain law, geometric space would contain an undifferentiated infinity of circles, ellipses, triangles and polygons.

Thus, in the realm of work, determinism does not reveal freedom in so far as it is an abstract natural law, but in so far as a human project carves out and illuminates a certain partial determinism within the infinite interaction of phenomena. And in this determinism, which proves itself simply through the efficacy of human action—as Archimedes' principle was already in use and understood by shipbuilders long before Archimedes had given it conceptual form—the relation of cause to effect is indistinguishable from that of means to end.

The organic unity of the worker's plan consists in the simultaneous emergence of an end which did not originally exist in the universe and which is manifested through the organization of means adopted to obtain it (for the end is no more than the synthetic unity of all the means manipulated for producing it) and the under layer which underlies these means and reveals itself, in turn, through their very organization. It is the relation of cause to effect; like Archimedes' principle, it constitutes both support and content for the shipbuilder's technique. In this sense, we may say that the atom was created by the atomic bomb, which was inconceivable except in the light of the Anglo-American plan for winning the war.

Thus freedom is to be discovered only in the act, and is one with the act; it forms the basis of the relations and inter-relations that constitute the act's internal structures. It never derives pleasure from itself, but reveals itself in and through its results. It is not an inner virtue which permits us to detach ourselves from very pressing situations, because, for man, there is no inside and no outside. But it is, on the contrary, the power to commit one's self in present action and to build a future; it generates a future which enables us to understand and to change the present.

Thus the worker really learns of his freedom through things; but precisely because he does learn of it through things, he is anything but a thing. And it is here that materialism deceives him and becomes, in spite of itself, an instrument in the hands of the oppressors. For if the worker discovers his freedom in his work, which is conceived as a primary relationship between man and material objects, in his relationship with his oppressor-master he thinks of himself as an object; it is the master who, in reducing him, through Taylorism or another process, to a mere sum of ever-identical operations, transforms him into a passive object, the mere support of constant properties.

Materialism, in decomposing man into behaviour patterns rigorously modelled upon Taylorist operations,[15] is playing into the master's hands. It is the master who sees the slave as a machine. By considering himself a mere natural product, as a "native," the slave sees himself through his master's eyes. He thinks of himself as an Other, and with the thoughts of the Other. The materialist revolutionary's conception harmonizes with that of his oppressors. And it may be objected that materialism ends by catching the master and transforming him into an object, like the slave.

But the master knows nothing of this and cares less; he lives within his ideologies, his rights, his culture. It is only to the slave's subjectivity that he appears an object. Instead of

[15] Behaviourism is the philosophy of Taylorism.

straining ourselves, by concealing his real freedom, to show him that the master is an object, it is, then, infinitely more valid and useful to let the slave discover his freedom to change the world, and, consequently, his own state, from his work. And if it be true that materialism, as explanation of the upper in terms of the lower, is a convenient image of the present social structures, it is then only all the more obvious that it is merely a myth in the Platonic sense of the word. For the revolutionary has no use for a symbolic expression of the present situation; he wants a kind of thinking that will enable him to forge the future. Now the materialist myth loses all meaning in a classless society in which neither uppers nor lowers will exist.

But, say the Marxists, if you teach man that he *is* free, you betray him; for he no longer needs to *become* free; can you conceive of a man free from birth who demands to be liberated? To this I reply that if man is not originally free, but determined once and for all, we cannot even conceive what his liberation might be. Some may say, "We will release human nature from its determining constraints." These people are fools.

What indeed can the nature of a man be, apart from that which he concretely is in his present existence? How can a Marxist believe in a *real* human nature, concealed, only, by oppressive circumstances? Other people claim to bring about the happiness of the species. But what is a happiness which is not *felt* and *experienced?* Happiness is, in its essence, subjectivity. How could it exist in the kingdom of objectivity? The only result one can really hope to attain in the hypothesis of universal determinism and from the point of view of objectivity is simply a more rational organization of society. But what value can an organization of this kind retain if it is not experienced as such by a free subjectivity and transcended toward new ends? No opposition really exists between these two necessities of action, namely that the agent be free and that the world in which he acts be determined. For these two things are not both necessary from the same point of view or in relation to the same realities.

Freedom is a structure of human action and appears only

in commitment; determinism is the law of the world. And the act only calls for partial linkages and local constants. Similarly, it is not true that a free man cannot hope to be liberated. For he is not free and bound in respect to the same things. His freedom is like the illumination of the situation into which he is cast. But other people's freedoms can render his situation unbearable, drive him to rebellion or to death.

If a slave's freedom is manifest in his work it is nonetheless true that this work is imposed, nullifying and destructive, that he is cheated of its products, that he is isolated by it, excluded from a society which exploits him and in which he does not share, applied as he is against matter by a *vis a tergo*. It is true that he is merely a link in a chain of which he knows neither the beginning nor the end; it is true that the master's look, his ideology and his orders tend to refuse him any existence other than the material one.

It is precisely in becoming revolutionaries, that is, in organizing with other members of their class to reject the tyranny of their masters, that slaves best manifest their freedom. Oppression leaves them no choice other than resignation or revolution. But in both cases they manifest their freedom to choose. And, finally, no matter what end is allotted to the revolutionary, he transcends it and sees in it only a stage. If he is looking for security or a better material organization of society, it is in order that they may serve as his point of departure.

This is how the Marxists themselves replied when reactionaries, speaking about a minor demand concerning wages, talked of the "sordid materialism of the masses." They gave one to understand that behind these material demands there was the affirmation of a humanism, that these workers were not only demanding a few more *sous,* but that their demand was a kind of concrete symbol of their demand to be men. Men; that is, freedoms in possession of their own destinies.[16] This remark holds true for the revolutionary's final purpose.

Class-consciousness demands a new humanism, above and beyond the rational organization of the community, it is an

[16] That is what Marx explains admirably in *Political Economy and Philosophy.*

alienated freedom which has taken freedom as its end. Socialism is merely the means which will allow for the realization
of the reign of freedom; a materialistic socialism is contradictory, therefore, because socialism establishes humanism as
its end, a humanism which materialism renders inconceivable.

One characteristic of idealism which the revolutionary particularly loathes is the tendency to represent changes in the
world as controlled by ideas, or better still, as changes in
ideas. Death, unemployment, strike-suppression, poverty and
hunger are not ideas. They are everyday realities that are
experienced in horror. They certainly have significances, but
they retain above all an underlayer of irrational opaqueness.

The First World War was not, as Chevalier said it was,
"Descartes against Kant"; it was the inexpiable deaths of
twelve million young men. The revolutionary, crushed beneath reality, refuses to let is sneak away. He knows that the
revolution will not be a mere consumption of ideas, but that
it will cost blood, sweat and human lives. He is in a position
to know that things are solid and sometimes insuperable
obstacles and that the best laid plan encounters resistances
which are often responsible for its failure. He knows that
action is not a felicitous combination of thoughts, but a whole
man's efforts against the obstinate impenetrability of the universe. He knows that when one has deciphered the meanings
in things that there remains an unassimilable residue, the
otherness, the irrationality, the opaqueness of the real, and
that it is this residue which in the end stifles and crushes.

Unlike the idealist whose slack thinking he denounces, he
wants to think hard. Or rather, against the adversity of objects he wishes to set up not the idea, but action which comes
down, finally, to effort, exhausting fatigue and sleeplessness.
Here again materialism seems to offer him the most satisfying
expression of his demand, since it affirms the predominance
of impenetrable matter over the idea. For materialism, all is
fact and conflict of forces, action. Thought itself becomes a
real phenomenon in a measurable world; it is produced by
matter and consumes energy. The famous predominance of
the object has to be conceived in terms of realism.

But is this interpretation so deeply satisfying? Does it not overstep its purpose and defraud the need which generated it? If it is true that nothing gives less of an impression of effort than the generation of ideas by other ideas, the effort fades away just as entirely as if we regard the universe as the balance of various forces. Nothing gives less of an impression of effort than a force applied to a physical point; it accomplishes the work of which it is capable—neither more nor less—and is transformed mechanically into kinetic or caloric energy.

Nowhere, and in no instance, does nature itself give us the impression of resistance overcome, of rebellion and submission, of lassitude. This applied force is always all that it is capable of being, and no more. And forces in opposition produce resultants according to the calm laws of mechanics. In order to account for reality as a resistance to be overcome by work, this resistance must be experienced by a subjectivity that seeks to subdue it. Nature conceived as pure objectivity is the opposite of the idea. But precisely because of this, it becomes transformed into idea; it is the pure idea of objectivity. The *real* vanishes.

For the real is that which is impermeable to subjectivity; it is the piece of sugar whose melting I wait for, as Bergson says, or, if you prefer, it is the subject's obligation to experience a similar waiting. It is the human design or scheme, it is my thirst which decides that it "takes a long time" to melt. When considered apart from a human situation, it melts neither slowly nor fast, but within a time which is dependent upon its nature, its thickness and the amount of water in which it is soaking.

It is human subjectivity which discovers the *adversity* of the real in and through the scheme it conceives to get beyond it toward the future. In order for a hill to be easy or hard to ascend, one must have planned to climb it to its summit. Both idealism and materialism cause the real to disappear in like manner, the one because it eliminates the object, the other because it eliminates subjectivity.

In order for reality to be revealed, it is necessary for a man to struggle against it. The revolutionary's realism, in a word, necessitates the existence of the world and of subjectivity;

better still, it calls for such a correlation of one with the other that neither a subjectivity outside the world nor a world which would not be illuminated by an effort on the part of a subjectivity can be conceived of.[17] The maximum of reality, the maximum of resistance, will be obtained if we suppose that man is, by definition, within-a-situation-in-the-world and that he comes to learn the stubbornness of reality in defining himself in relation to it.

Let us take note, moreover, of the fact that an over-narrow adhesion to universal determinism runs the risk of eliminating all of reality's *resistance*. I received the proof of this in a conversation with M. Garaudy and two of his friends. I asked them if the stakes were really down when Stalin signed the Russo-German pact and when the French communists decided to take part in the de Gaulle government; I asked if, in both cases, the people responsible had not *taken their chances* with the rather anguished feeling of their responsibilities. For it seems to me that freedom is principally characterized by the fact that you are never sure of winning with it and that the consequences of our acts are probable, only. But M. Garaudy interrupted me; for him the stakes are down in advance; there exists a science of history and the interlinking of facts is rigorous, and so we bet on a sure thing. He was carried so far away in his zeal that he ended by saying excitedly to me: "And what does Stalin's intelligence matter? I don't care a rap for it!" I might add that, under the severe glances of his friends, he blushed, lowered his eyes and added, with a rather devout look, "Besides, Stalin is very intelligent."

Thus, in contradiction to revolutionary realism which asserts that the least little result is attained with difficulty and amidst the greatest uncertainties, the materialist myth leads certain minds to a profound reassurance as to the outcome of their efforts. It is impossible, they think, for them to fail. History is a science, its consequences are already inscribed, we have only to decipher them. This attitude is quite patently a flight. The revolutionary has overthrown the myths of the

[17] It is, once again, Marx's point of view in 1844, that is until the unfortunate meeting with Engels.

bourgeoisie, and the working class has undertaken, through a thousand vicissitudes, victories and defeats, to forge its own destiny in freedom and in anguish.

But our Garaudys are afraid. What they seek in communism is not liberation, but a re-enforcement of discipline; there is nothing they fear so much as freedom; if they have renounced the *a priori* values of the class from which they come, it is in order to find *a priori* elements in scientific knowledge and paths already marked out in history. There are no risks and no anxiety; everything is sure and certain; the results are guaranteed. Reality immediately vanishes and history is merely an idea that develops.

M. Garaudy feels sheltered within this idea. Some communist intellectuals to whom I reported this conversation shrugged their shoulders. "Garaudy is a scientist," they told me with contempt, "he is a bourgeois Protestant who, for purposes of personal edification, has replaced the finger of God with historical materialism." I agree. I admit, also, that M. Garaudy did not seem to me to be a shining light, but after all, he writes a great deal and the communists do not disown him. And it is not by chance that most of the scientists have joined hands with the Communist Party and that this party, so hard on heresies, does not condemn them.

We must, at this point, repeat the following: the revolutionary, if he wishes to act, cannot regard historical events as the result of lawless contingencies; but he by no means demands that his path be cleared in advance; he wishes to clear it himself. Certain partial series, constancies and structural laws within determined social forms are what he needs in order to see ahead. If you give him more, everything fades away into ideas and history no longer has to be *made,* but rather to be *read,* day by day; the real becomes a dream.

We were called upon to choose between materialism and idealism, we were told that we would be unable to find a middle way between these two doctrines. Without preconceived ideas, we have allowed revolutionary demands to speak for themselves and we have seen that they trace, of themselves, the features of an odd sort of philosophy that dismisses idealism and materialism unsuited. The revolutionary act seemed to us, at first, the free act *par excellence*. Not free in an anarchist and individualist way at all; if that were true, the revolutionary, by the very nature of his situation, could only claim, with a greater or lesser degree of explicitness, the rights of the "exquisite class," that is, his integration with the upper social layers.

But as he demands, within the oppressed class and for the entire oppressed class, a more rational social status, his freedom resides in the act by which he demands the liberation of his whole class and, more generally, of all men. It springs from a recognition of other freedoms and it demands recognition on their part. Thus, from the beginning, it places itself on the level of solidarity. And the revolutionary act contains within itself the premises of a philosophy of freedom, or, rather, by its very existence it creates this philosophy.

But since, at the same time, the revolutionary discovers himself through and in his free designs, as an oppressed person within an oppressed class, his original position requires that we explain the nature of oppression. That means, once again, that men are free—for oppression of matter by matter cannot exist, but only the composition of forces—and that a certain relationship between freedoms can exist, so that one does not recognize the other and acts upon it from without to transform it into an *object*. And conversely, just as oppressed freedom wants to free itself by force, so the revolutionary attitude demands a theory of violence as an answer to oppression. Here too, materialistic terms are no more adequate to the explanation of violence than idealist ones are.

Idealism, which is a philosophy of digestion and assimilation, does not even conceive of the absolute and insurmountable pluralism of freedoms marshalled against one another; idealism is a sort of monism. But materialism is also monistic; there is no "conflict of opposites" within material unity. There are not really even any opposites; hot and cold are simply different degrees on the thermometric scale; you pass progressively from light to darkness; two equal forces in opposite directions cancel one another and simply produce a state of equilibrium. The idea of a conflict of opposites constitutes a projection of human relationships upon material relationships.

A revolutionary philosophy ought to account for the plurality of freedoms and show how each one can be an object for the other while being, at the same time, a freedom for itself. Only this double character of freedom and objectivity can explain the complex notions of oppression, conflict, failure and violence. For one never oppresses anything but a freedom, but one cannot oppress it if it lends itself in some way to this oppression, if, that is, it presents the appearance of a thing to the Other. The revolutionary movement and its plan—which is to make society pass through the violence of one state in which liberties are alienated to another state based on their mutual recognition—is to be understood in these terms.

Similarly, the revolutionary who *lives through* oppression bodily and in each of his gestures in no way wishes to underestimate the yoke imposed upon him nor to tolerate idealist criticism's dispelling this oppression in ideas. At the same time, he contests the rights of the privileged class and thereby destroys the general idea of rights. But it would be erroneous to believe, with the materialist, that he does this in order to replace them with the plain and simple fact. For facts can only generate facts, and not the representation of facts; the present generates another present, not the future.

Thus the revolutionary act demands that we transcend, in the unity of a synthesis, opposition—which can account for a society's disintegration, but not the *construction* of a new society—and idealism, which confers a legal existence upon facts. It calls for a new philosophy, with a different view of man's relations with the world. If the revolution should be possible, man ought to possess the contingent quality of the fact and be different, nevertheless, from the fact in his practical ability to transcend the present, to disengage himself from his situation.

This disengagement is in no way comparable to the negative movement through which the Stoic tries to take refuge in himself; it is by projecting himself ahead, in committing himself in ventures of one kind or another, that the revolutionary transcends the present; and since he is a man, doing a man's work, this power of disengagement must really be attributed to *all human activity*. The slightest human gesture can be understood in terms of the future; even the reactionary faces the future, since he is concerned with preparing a future that will be identical with the past.

The tactician's absolute realism demands that man be plunged into reality, menaced with concrete dangers, victim of a concrete oppression from which he will deliver himself through equally concrete acts. Blood, sweat, sorrow and death are not ideas; the rock that crushes and the bullet that kills are not ideas. But in order that objects may reveal what Bachelard rightly calls their "co-efficient of adversity," the light of a plan or illuminating scheme, be it only the very simple and crude one of living, is necessary.

It is not true, then, that man is outside Nature and the world, as the idealist has it, or that he is only up to his ankles in it, baulking like a bather having a dip while her head is in the clouds. He is completely in Nature's clutches, and at any moment Nature can crush him and annihilate him, body and soul. He is in her clutches from the very beginning: for him being born really means "coming into the world" in a situation not of his choice, with *this particular* body, *this* family, and *this* race, perhaps.

But if he happens to plan, as Marx expressly states, to "change the world," it means that he is, to begin with, a being for whom *the world* exists in its totality, as a piece of phosphorus or lead, which is a *part* of the world and ridden by forces to which it uncomprehendingly submits, will never be. This means that man transcends the world toward a future state from which he can contemplate it. It is in changing the world that we can come to know it. Neither the detached consciousness that would soar over the universe without being able to get a standpoint on it, nor the material object which reflects a condition without understanding it can ever "grasp" the totality of existence in a synthesis, even a purely conceptual one.